"Information through Innovation"

Working with Windows 3.1

Don Barker
Gonzaga University
School of Business Administration

Chia-Ling Barker
Greater Spokane Business Development Association

boyd & fraser publishing company

CREDITS:

Publisher: Tom Walker
Acquisitions Editor: James H. Edwards
Production Coordinator: Pat Stephan
Marketing Manager: Christopher Will
Interior Design and Composition: Custom Editorial Productions, Inc.
Cover Design: Ken Russo

© 1993 by boyd & fraser publishing company
A Divison of South-Western Publishing Company
Danvers, MA 01932

Manufactured in the United States of America

Names of all products mentioned herein are used for identification purposes only and may be trademarks and/or registered trademarks of their respective owners. South-Western Publishing Company and boyd & fraser publishing company disclaim any affiliation, association, or connection with, or sponsorship or endorsement by such owners.

Cover slide courtesy of Microsoft Corporation

Library of Congress Cataloging-in-Publication Data

Barker, Donald, 1953–
    Working with Windows 3.1/Don Barker, Chia-Ling Barker.
        p.   cm.
    Includes index.
    ISBN 0-87709-000-9
    1. Windows (Computer programs). 2. Microsoft Windows (Computer program) I. Barker, Chia-Ling. II.
Title

92-18456
CIP

56D65

PREFACE

Microsoft Windows has become the most popular way for business people to interact with their personal computers. As a result, students and professionals need to be familiar with Windows' capabilities in order to operate the majority of microcomputers in academic and corporate America.

Working with Windows 3.1 is designed to replace introductory courses on PC/MS-DOS with instruction on Microsoft Windows 3.1. Windows 3.1 is a graphical user interface that is much easier to learn and easier to use than the obscure and sometimes cryptic text-based environment of DOS. It also offers you a more powerful and productive means for working with your software applications.

This book teaches the fundamentals of using Microsoft Windows 3.1. Self-paced, hands-on tutorials help you quickly become proficient with the key features of the software. Step-by-step instructions provide a smooth and enjoyable learning experience.

Working with Windows 3.1 can be used by those with little or no computer experience. It is intended for use in a one-credit computer lab course or as a supplement to classes on software applications. Corporate trainers will find it ideal for seminars and self-paced study to educate business users. Finally, this book should benefit anyone who wants a comprehensive introduction to Microsoft Windows 3.1, the human-computer interface of the 1990s.

ABOUT MICROSOFT WINDOWS

Windows is a computer program that adds to and expands DOS. It gives users an easier way to work with a microcomputer system, by replacing the obscure, clumsy, and intimidating text-based environment of DOS with an intuitive, graceful, and friendly graphical user interface.

A graphical user interface or GUI (pronounced "gooey") lets a user communicate with a computer by pointing at easy-to-understand windows, menus, and icons (pictures) instead of typing in difficult-to-remember text commands. It is much easier (and more enjoyable) to work with a graphical user interface than a text-based one. A GUI lets you use a mouse to take direct control of the work on your monitor screen. You can thus swiftly finish a task that would require countless keystrokes on a keyboard.

Windows is an integrated environment where applications are consistent, accessible, and linkable. Whether you are working with a word processor, electronic spreadsheet, or database management system, you will know where to look for and how to use the same familiar menus and options. Integration allows you to cut and paste information from one application to another and even link different Windows applications together so that changes to one will automatically be reflected in the other.

Windows is also a memory manager that is designed to overcome the limitations inherent in DOS. It unleashes the power of your microcomputer so it can take advantage of its full potential. Windows enables the computer to run larger and more sophisticated programs, as well as multiple applications, simultaneously. For example, you may begin writing a report in a word processor, jump to a spreadsheet to calculate some numbers, switch to a database to add some records, and move back to the word processor without ever exiting or restarting an application.

With the introduction of version 3.1, Windows has become even more powerful and easier to use. This latest release is noticeably faster and more flexible than its predecessor, Windows 3.0. File handling capabilities have been vastly improved and a host of "scalable" fonts that can be used to produce truly dazzling printouts have been incorporated. Also, Windows now supports Object Linking and Embedding (OLE). OLE enables you to use different applications to create a single "seamless" document that is easily updated and modified. These features, along with many others, add up to a much richer and more enjoyable computing environment.

ABOUT THE BOOK

Although a number of reference books exist, *Working with Windows 3.1* is the first and, at present, the only textbook that teaches Windows 3.1. Unlike reference books, this text is a cumulative learning experience. The incremental development of a "real-world" project provides a consistent thread throughout the book, a thread that lets you learn the key features of Windows 3.1 in a natural and logical fashion.

Instead of being exposed to a laundry list of software commands, you'll be introduced to the cababilities of Windows in the context of a typical computing project. Thus, you'll not only discover how each command works, but also, more important, how they work together to perform critical tasks.

Chapter 1 introduces the concepts and background necessary for you to understand the role Windows plays in the world of microcomputing. In Chapter 2, the focus shifts to the basics of navigating in the Windows environment. Chapters 3 and 4 cover the primary components of Windows, Program Manager and File Manager. These applications enable you to control and organize the resources of a microcomputer system.

Chapters 5 and 6 present the most powerful Windows accessories: Write and Paintbrush. Write is an executive-level word processor, while Paintbrush is a full-featured drawing program. Chapters 5 and 6 reveal the most effective approaches for using these Windows applications.

Chapter 7 demonstrates the ease with which information can be transferred between programs with exercises that combine the text and graphics created earlier (with Write and Paintbrush) into a single impressive and professional-looking compound document. Chapter 8 takes you on a tour of Windows' sophisticated printing capabilities. Finally, Chapter 9 presents the many ways you can customize Windows to suit your own particular needs and tastes.

DISTINCTIVE FEATURES

Working with Windows 3.1 has a number of features that clearly distinguish it from other books on Microsoft Windows 3.1. The most important ones are listed below.

1. *Working with Windows 3.1* is designed to be worked through in front of a computer at your own pace. Step-by-step tutorials let you teach yourself the power and elegance of this popular graphical user interface.
2. A "real-world" project incrementally builds your awareness and mastery of Windows 3.1. It provides the ideal medium for learning and remembering the capabilities of Windows in the context of an actual application.
3. Self-paced hands-on lab exercises take advantage of Windows' intuitive nature to let you rapidly and "painlessly" become a productive computer user.

4. Over 200 illustrations minimize frustration, with ample points of reference for comparing your work with the book. These visual reinforcements offer constant reassurance that you are progressing correctly.

5. Each lesson has been extensively tested and refined to ensure clarity and reliability

6. Windows makes it possible to work with multiple applications and to conveniently transfer information between them. Special emphasis is placed on these capabilities because they can vastly increase the quality of your work as well as your productivity.

7. Three types of "signposts" alert you to potential opportunities, dangers, and points of interest. For easy recognition, they are set off by boxes and titled Hints, Hazards, and Notes.

8. You can work through this text with little or no previous computer experience. All the necessary fundamentals for using a microcomputer are skillfully presented at the appropriate times.

9. Every chapter begins with an overview of the material to be presented and ends with a *Coming Attractions...* section to prepare you for upcoming topics.

10. Learning objectives clearly spell out what you should be able to accomplish after completing each chapter.

11. Review exercises provide reinforcement of the information introduced in the chapter tutorials. These practice problems offer a convenient way to assess your progress.

12. Each chapter concludes with a set of review questions to test comprehension of important concepts. Key terms are also defined at the end of every chapter for quick and easy reference.

SCOPE

Working with Windows 3.1 features easy-to-follow and thorough tutorials to teach you the concepts, features, and procedures necessary to be an efficient and effective Windows user. However, for reasons of safety and book length, we have avoided in-depth coverage of those elements that could potentially cripple, or even completely disable, the Windows environment.

For the most part, this requires a less detailed account of the PIF Editor, Windows Setup, and Control Panel utilities. These programs let you install and configure an array of hardware and software options. Since we assume Windows has been correctly installed, it seems unwise to run the risk of accidentally changing these critical settings by having you experiment with them. When modifications of this nature are required, it's best to refer to the documentation that accompanies Windows 3.1.

Windows comes with a wide array of accessory software. Most of these programs are simple in nature and can be successfully used with only a brief visit to the Windows Help facility. Thus, we opted to concentrate on the two most sophisticated Windows accessories: Write and Paintbrush. This narrower focus allows us to dedicate the space necessary to present the key features and, perhaps more important, the procedures for achieving optimal results with these two powerful programs.

ABOUT THE AUTHORS

Don Barker is a co-author of four popular textbooks by boyd & fraser: *Working with Windows 3, Working with WordPerfect for Windows, Working with Lotus 1-2-3 for Windows,* and *Using Harvard Graphics for Business Presentations.* His credits also include *Developing Business Expert Systems with LEVEL5* and *Lotus 1-2-3, dBASE III PLUS, and WordPerfect: Exercises and Applications,* both published by Merrill Publishing. Don is a contributing editor for the computer magazine *PCAI: Intelligent Solutions for Desktop Computers.* His other publications include an impressive list of both academic and trade articles that deal with the innovative uses of computer technology.

As an Assistant Professor of Information Systems in the School of Business Administration at Gonzaga University, Don is able to develop and test his textbook tutorials thoroughly before publication, ensuring a reliable and effective learning experience for the student. He holds a Master's degree in Business Administration from Eastern Washington University and has worked as a business development specialist and computer consultant.

Chia-Ling Barker is the co-author of *Working with Windows 3* and *Lotus 1-2-3, dBASE III PLUS, and WordPerfect: Exercises and Applications.* She has published a myriad of articles dealing with the creative use of business software. She also develops and teaches a variety of software application seminars for individuals and corporations.

Chia-Ling is a loan officer for the Greater Spokane Business Development Association. She has worked as business manager for a television station, financial analyst for an international conglomerate, and controller for a manufacturer. With her extensive business experience, she is intimately familiar with the needs and concerns of corporate computer users. Chia-Ling holds a Master's degree in Business Administration from Eastern Washington University.

ACKNOWLEDGMENTS

We wish to thank Dan Cooper for his invaluable contributions. His insights, suggestions, and assistance provided an important foundation for this book. Bob Toshack was instrumental in verifying the accuracy and soundness of the tutorials in this text. The Instructor's Manual also profited from his input. We also wish to thank Robert Larson, Jody Tschritter, and Dave Stewart for their contributions.

Finally, without the whole-hearted encouragement of the Dean, faculty, staff, and students of the School of Business Administration at Gonzaga University, this book would never have seen the light of day.

Don Barker
Chia-Ling Barker
July 1992

CONTENTS

CHAPTER 1

Introduction

● *Objectives*

Upon completing this chapter, you'll be able to describe:

1. **The function and components of a microcomputer system.**
2. **The purpose of Microsoft Windows 3.1.**
3. **Why you should use Windows.**
4. **What you need to work with Windows 3.1.**

OVERVIEW

We'll begin this chapter by looking at the purpose and components of a microcomputer system. This information will provide you with the background you will need to understand the function and benefits of Microsoft Windows 3.1. You'll learn about the graphical environment of Windows 3.1 and the role it plays in the wider world of microcomputing. Along the way, we'll attempt to give you some compelling reasons for wanting to use Windows 3.1, including:

- a much easier way to communicate with your computer.
- a more convenient way to move information.
- an increased amount of computing power.

The chapter closes with a list of the requirements for running Windows 3.1 under each of its two possible operating modes (standard and enhanced).

WHAT IS A MICROCOMPUTER?

A **microcomputer** is an amazing device. It typically fits on a surface no larger than a desktop but packs enough power to perform an almost

1

endless variety of tasks. You can use it to reconcile a checkbook, write a letter, keep track of inventory, design a bridge, publish a magazine, and much more. Because most microcomputers are used by only one person, they are often called **personal computers**.

To operate a microcomputer or personal computer system, you need to be familiar with its major components and how they work together to process information. A microcomputer system is composed of **hardware**, the physical parts, and **software**, the instructions or programs that direct the hardware. Both are required to make the system work.

Hardware and software combine to perform three distinct activities: input, processing, and output. **Input** consists of entering **data**, such as numbers and text, into the computer. **Processing** is the activity whereby raw data is manipulated or transformed to produce **information**, a more organized and, hopefully, meaningful form of the original data. **Output** is the act of displaying the processed data or information.

For example, when you compose a letter on a microcomputer system, you type in text, edit it, and print out a copy. Software instructions tell the hardware how to input the characters you type, how to process your edits, and how to output the results as a printed document.

Let's now take a closer look at the hardware components responsible for performing the functions of input, processing, and ouput.

Hardware

Figure 1-1 illustrates the standard hardware configuration of a microcomputer system. The components shown there fall into three categories: input devices, processing units, and output devices. **Input devices** enable you to enter new data or retrieve stored data for use by the system. The **system unit** contains the microprocessor and memory necessary to convert data into information. The system unit and disk drives are typically housed together in the same box or main unit. The disk drives store and retrieve data for use in processing. The disk drives serve both input and output functions. Information, data, and programs are stored in **files** on disks used by the disk drives. The keyboard, monitor, and printer are attached to this main unit via cables. Finally, **output devices** are responsible for presenting or storing the results.

Figure 1–1. The hardware components of a standard microcomputer system.

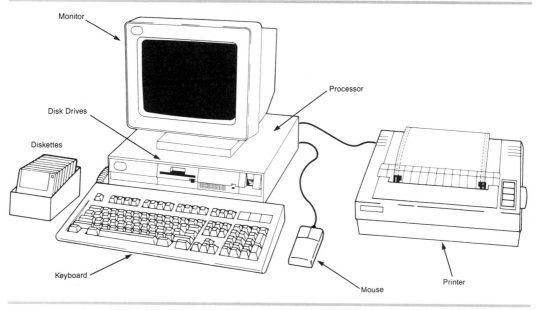

Input Devices

A computer keyboard is the most common piece of input equipment. It looks and operates much like a typewriter keyboard (see Figure 1–2).

Figure 1–2. A computer keyboard from an IBM AT.

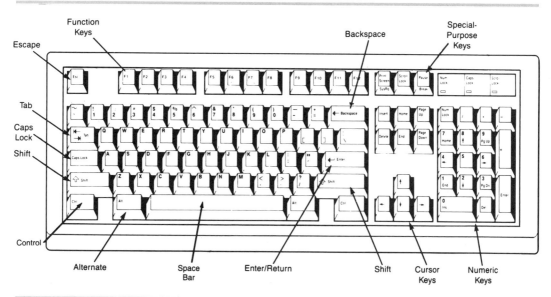

Besides the usual letters, numbers, and punctuation marks, a computer keyboard has additional keys for interacting with the computer.

KEY	**ACTION**
Alt (Alternate)	Used in combination with other keys to issue software-dependent commands.
←↑↓→ (Arrows)	Move the cursor in the direction of the pointing arrow (e.g., up, down, left, and right). The cursor is a little flashing line that shows your present location on the display screen.
Backspace	Erases characters to the left of the cursor (see Delete).
Break	Terminates or stops some programs.
Caps Lock	Causes letters to appear in uppercase until pressed again.
Ctrl (Control)	Used in combination with other keys to issue software-dependent commands.
Del (Delete)	Erases characters to the right of the cursor (see Backspace).
Enter	Tells the computer to process what has been typed. In creating documents, it works much like the carriage return on a typewriter—pressing it causes the cursor to start a new line.
Esc (Escape)	Typically cancels a previous command or moves you one step back in a program. However, the action performed can vary, depending on the program you use.
F1–F12 (Function)	Select frequently used operations in a program. The function keys are located across the top of the keyboard (in older keyboards, they are positioned to the far left).
Ins (Insert)	Enters new characters at the cursor location. It causes existing entries to shift over.
Numeric Keypad	Provides quick entry of numeric data or cursor movement (see Num Lock). This array of keys is located on the right side of the keyboard and is laid out like a calculator.
Num Lock (Number Lock)	Switches the function of the numeric keypad between number entry and cursor movement.

Pause	Temporarily suspends the operation of the current program.
Print Screen	Used in conjunction with the Shift key to print a copy of your screen. However, in Windows applications, the screen copy is sent to another program (Clipboard) instead of directly to the printer.
Return	See Enter key.
Scroll Lock	Enables the up and down arrow keys to scroll the entire screen up or down instead of just the cursor.
Shift	When held down, produces uppercase letters or the symbols shown on the top part of the key. Just as on a typewriter, there are two Shift keys located on either side of the keyboard.
Tab	Moves cursor a predefined number of spaces to the right. Holding down the Shift key and pressing Tab causes the cursor to move a preset number of spaces to the left.

◇ HAZARD

Simultaneously pressing the Ctrl, Alt, and Del keys in Windows 3.1 brings up a screen offering three options. You can choose to (1) return to the desktop just as you left it, (2) exit from the current application but return to Windows, or (3) completely reset your computer (just as if you turned it off and on again). The last two options will cause you to lose all your unsaved work! They should only be used in an emergency situation (e.g., where an application has locked up).

Although the keyboard is the primary tool for entering data, the **mouse, a pointing device**, is gaining acceptance rapidly. This trend is occurring for several reasons. First, a mouse allows you to do things that would be difficult, if not impossible, with a keyboard (e.g., drawing a picture). Second, pointing appears to be a more "intuitive" or "natural" way of communicating with a computer. Finally, a lot of software requires a mouse for optimal performance (e.g., Windows 3.1).

A mouse works by controlling a pointer on your display screen. You slide the mouse over a flat surface, such as your desktop, in the direction you want the screen pointer to move. The buttons on the mouse are used to select from screen options or to signal a command. (Chapter 2 will cover the details of using a mouse.)

System Unit

The system unit houses the "motherboard" as illustrated in **Figure 1-3**. The two most important components on the motherboard are the microprocessor and the temporary memory. Together, they determine the capacity and power of your microcomputer. The permanent storage devices, or disk drives, are also located in the system unit.

Figure 1-3.
A typical system or "motherboard" of an AT-class microcomputer.

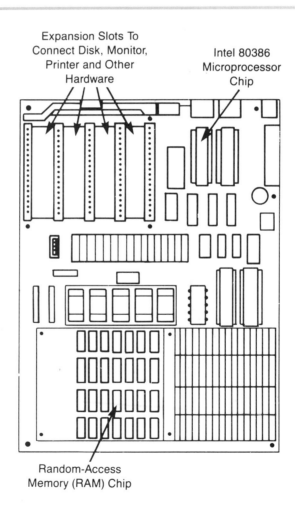

Expansion Slots To Connect Disk, Monitor, Printer and Other Hardware

Intel 80386 Microprocessor Chip

Random-Access Memory (RAM) Chip

The **microprocessor,** or **central processing unit (CPU),** performs all the actual computing. It uses thousands of miniature electronic "switches" to execute program instructions and to process data. In a microcomputer, all these "switches" (transistors) are packed into a single microprocessor chip no bigger than a matchbook!

IBM and IBM-compatible personal computers use microprocessor chips from the Intel Corporation. These include the 8088, 8086, 80286, 80386sx, 80386, and 80486. The Intel 8088 chip was used in the original IBM PC (Personal Computer) introduced in 1981. By today's standards, it is quite slow and antiquated. For example, the IBM PS/2 model 90 is built around the Intel 80486 and, as a result, is roughly 30 times faster than an IBM PC.

—**NOTE**_____

It's important to understand the differences between these chips because Windows 3.1 adapts itself to the type of microprocessor and the amount of memory available. As you move down in processor power and memory, Windows 3.1 loses features and capabilities. (In fact, 8088 and 8086 processors are unable to run Windows 3.1.) We'll cover these changes later in the section titled *What You Need to Use Windows 3.1.*

Table 1-1 compares the various Intel chips. Notice that three key factors assess performance: clock speed, word size, and bus size. **Clock speed** controls the rate at which data is processed. It's measured in megahertz, or millions of cycles per second. For instance, a clock speed of 4.7 megahertz (Mhz) translates to 4.7 million cycles per second. The higher the clock speed, the faster data will be processed.

Table 1-1. Comparison table for Intel microprocessors used in IBM and IBM-compatible microcomputers.

Chip	Clock Speed (MHz)	Word Size (bits)	Bus Size (bits)
8088	4.77	16	8
8086	4.77	16	16
80286	8, 10, 12	32	16
80386sx	16, 20	32	32
80386	20, 25, 33	32	32
80486	33, 50	32	32

Word size is the amount of data that a microprocessor can work with at one time. Word size is measured in bits. A bit is simply a 0 (zero) or 1 (the basic alphabet of all computers). A larger word size means more data is processed at a time. **Bus size** refers to the dimensions of the input/output path that connects the microprocessor to its external devices, such as the keyboard or monitor. It determines how much data is transmitted and received at a time. A large bus size increases processing speed because the microprocessor doesn't wait as long to send or receive data.

Data and instructions are stored in temporary or **random access memory (RAM)** during processing by the microprocessor. RAM is temporary because the information stored there disappears when the power is turned off.

Memory is measured in bytes. A **byte** uses 8 bits to store a single character (e.g., A, B, C, 1, 2, 3, etc.). Because microcomputers can address thousands, millions, and even billions of bytes of memory, the notations **kilobytes (Kb)**, **megabytes (Mb)**, or **gigabytes (Gb)** are often used.

1 Kb	1,024 bytes (about a thousand characters)
1 Mb	1,048,576 bytes (about a million characters)
1 Gb	1,073,741,824 bytes (about a billion characters)

Microprocessors vary in the amount of RAM they are capable of using (see Figure 1–4). The Intel 8088 addresses a maximum of only 640 Kb; the 80286 can access 16 Mb; and the 80386 (or 80486) can address a whopping 4 Gb! Memory below 640 Kb is called **conventional** while the memory above 640 Kb is called **extended**. These terms grew out of the need to describe memory that extended beyond the original or conventional memory of the 8088 processor.

When it has access to more addressable memory, a processor can run larger and more sophisticated programs. This extra memory can also be used to run multiple programs simultaneously. Unfortunately, these benefits were not realized until quite recently. The reason stems from a software, not a hardware, limitation. Later in this chapter, you'll learn why this problem exists and how Windows has solved it.

A **disk drive** provides the means to store permanently both data and programs. It is designed to read into RAM information stored in a file on a magnetic disk or write information from RAM to a file on a disk. There are two basic types of disk drives: floppy disk drives and fixed or hard disk drives.

Figure 1–4.
Conventional and extended memory available to Windows from the Intel 80286, 80386, and 80486 microprocessors.

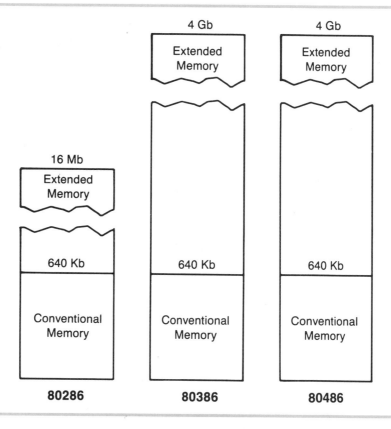

A **floppy disk drive** uses **floppy disks** (or diskettes) to store information in files. Floppy disks are lightweight, square, thin, and flexible (see Figure 1–5). They are enclosed in plastic jackets to protect their magnetic surfaces from damage.

Floppy disk drives are designed to handle one of two disk sizes: 5¼″ or 3½″. Both sizes come in low and high density formats. **High density disks** use tightly compacted magnetic material to retain additional information. They require a floppy drive especially built to take advantage of their dense surfaces. However, it is still possible to use **low density disks** with a high density drive.

◯ **HAZARD**_____

Make sure you know the type of floppy drive and disks you are using. Special precautions must be taken when mixing low and high density formats or data loss may occur! The section *Formatting Disks* in Chapter 4 covers this topic in depth.

Figure 1–5.
3½″ and 5¼″
disks are the
two most
widely used
types of
floppy disks.

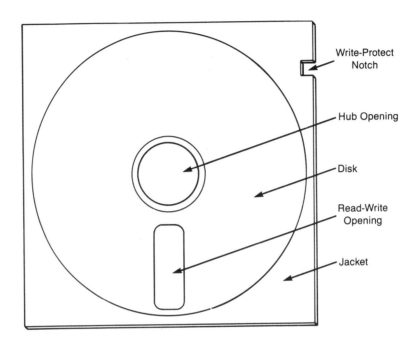

Write-Protect Notch

Hub Opening

Disk

Read-Write Opening

Jacket

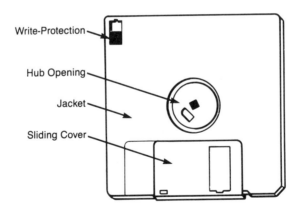

Write-Protection

Hub Opening

Jacket

Sliding Cover

A low density 5¼″ floppy disk stores a maximum of 360 Kb, while the high density version holds up to 1.2 Mb. The low density 3½″ disk stores 720 Kb and the high density version 1.44 Mb.

Floppy disk drives are mounted in the front panel of the computer so you can easily insert and remove diskettes. Computer systems may include either one or two floppy disk drives in addition to a hard drive. (Figure 1–1 shows a system with a single floppy disk drive.) In a system with two floppy disk drives, the drives are mounted one above the other or side by side. If your computer has two floppy drives, the top (or left) one is typically referred to as **drive A**, while the other is called **drive B**.

Floppy disks are a convenient but fragile medium for saving a permanent record of your work. But if you observe the precautions listed below, they can also be a reliable medium.

- Be sure to handle the disk so that you avoid touching the surface exposed by the oval opening. The oils from your skin can damage the disk.
- Keep your disks as close to room temperature as possible. Excessive heat or cold can damage or even destroy them. (Leaving them in a car or near a heater is asking for trouble.)
- Be sure not to bend a disk, especially when you insert it or remove it from a disk drive. Also, check to make sure the label is facing up when you insert a disk.
- Do not write on a disk with a pencil or ballpoint pen. Lead dust and pressure can damage the disk's sensitive surface. Try to fill out labels before you place them on disks. If you have to write on a label that is already on a disk, use a felt-tip pen to label the disk gently.
- Always store your disks in their protective paper or plastic sleeves to prevent damage from dust.
- Avoid placing your disks on or near objects that emit magnetic fields (e.g., stereo speakers, televisions, and videocassette recorders). These devices can corrupt or erase the data on your disks.

A **hard disk drive** uses one or more rigid, nonremovable disks for storing information. Since these disks or platters are permanently sealed inside a drive assembly, they turn much faster than a floppy disk can. This, along with a denser surface, enables a platter to retain substantially more information in a much greater number of files than a comparably sized floppy disk. It also speeds up the data storage and retrieval processes.

The storage capacities of hard disks range from 10 Mb into the hundreds of megabytes. The most common sizes are 20, 30, 40, and 80 Mb. As the size of programs has grown, so has the need for hard disks. Today, it's simply impractical or downright impossible to run most software without a hard disk. Typically, all the programs and data for a microcomputer are stored in files on the hard disk, leaving the floppy drives for copying and backing up information.

Output Devices

A **monitor** makes it possible for you to interact with your microcomputer. It uses a screen (much like a television's) to display messages. When you type characters on your keyboard, they appear on the monitor. This provides a convenient way for you to verify and keep track of what you enter into the computer. The computer is also able to display its own messages using the monitor screen. This visual give-and-take creates a level of interaction and intimacy that, with the exception of speech, would otherwise be impossible to maintain.

In addition to text, a computer monitor can display graphics, such as charts and pictures. It uses **pixels** (short for picture elements) to display both text and graphics. The higher the number of pixels, the greater the **resolution** or clarity of the image.

A monitor may be either monochrome or color. A *monochrome* monitor uses a single color to display text, usually green, amber, or white on a black background. Graphic images are produced by using different shades of the single color. Monochrome monitors have the highest resolution, making them an excellent choice for working long periods with text-based programs. However, when it comes to displaying the subtleties and highlights of a detailed graphic, they are severely limited.

A *color* monitor displays more than one color. The actual number depends upon the quality of both the monitor and the display adapter card. A **display adapter card** connects the monitor to the system unit. The three major types of color monitor and adapter card combinations are CGA, EGA, and VGA.

- **CGA (color graphics adapter)** offers the least in terms of color selection and resolution (it's also the oldest). It displays a total of only 16 colors and can display no more than four colors on the screen at one time.
- **EGA (enhanced graphics adapter)** resolution and color selection are vastly superior to CGA, with the ability to display 16 out of 64 colors.
- **VGA (video graphics array)** resolution and color selection are superior to EGA, supporting 256 colors from a palette of thousands. (An extension of the VGA standard, *Super VGA*, provides even higher resolution and wider color assortment.)

The **printer**, like the monitor, is an output device for interacting with your microcomputer. But instead of displaying video images, the printer produces a **hardcopy** or paper **printout** of information. This enables you to keep a permanent record of your work and conveniently share it with others.

Some printers produce both text and graphics, while others print only text. Printers also vary in the quality of text they are capable of producing. The four most popular categories of printers are described below (see Figure 1–6).

- A **dot-matrix** printer uses a set of pins that strike an inked ribbon to print a series of dots. Although these dots can be arranged to form both text and graphics, they produce only draft-quality characters. This is because the dots are round and far enough apart so that they form characters with tiny spaces in them. These characters lack the solid or detailed appearance of letter-quality text (i.e., typewriter quality). On the positive side, dot-matrix printers are fairly fast (roughly half a page a minute) and inexpensive.

- A **daisy-wheel** printer uses raised characters mounted on a spinning wheel to strike an inked ribbon. Even though a daisy-wheel is no more expensive than a dot-matrix printer, it produces letter-quality print. Unfortunately, daisy-wheels are unable to print graphics. The trade-off, graphics for high-quality text, makes sense if you are on a tight budget, you are most concerned about document appearance, and you do not need to print graphics. Still, daisy-wheel printers are very slow (averaging less than one page every five minutes) and noisy.

- An **ink-jet** printer sprays ink to form both letter-quality text and graphics. It's fast (typically four pages a minute), silent, and only slightly more expensive than a dot-matrix or daisy-wheel printer. However, some ink-jet printers require a specially treated paper.

- A **laser** printer uses a process similar to photocopying to produce near-typeset quality and high clarity graphics. It is extremely fast (averaging eight pages a minute) and very quiet. But laser printers also tend to be the most expensive printer option.

Software

Software is the set of instructions, or programs, that tell the hardware what activities to perform. The two most common categories of software are application packages and operating systems.

Figure 1–6. Dot-matrix, daisy-wheel, ink-jet, and laser printers are the four most common types of printers used with microcomputers.

Dot-Matrix Printer

Daisy-Wheel Printer

Ink-Jet Printer

Laser Printer

Application Packages

Application packages are computer programs designed to perform specific activities or tasks. There are three major categories of application software.

- **Word processors** (e.g., WordPerfect 5.1 for Windows) help you to create, edit, format, and print such documents as business memos, research papers, articles, and even books.
- **Electronic spreadsheets** (e.g., Lotus 1-2-3 for Windows) use the familiar column and row format of a worksheet to manipulate numbers and text. They enable you to create financial models and reports that automatically update calculations when existing values are changed.

● **Database management systems (DBMS)** (e.g., Paradox for Windows) make it easy to store, search, and sort vast amounts of information.

Although these groups account for a majority of the applications, many smaller categories exist. Other examples include communication programs to receive and transmit data over telephone lines, graphics programs to create all kinds of pictures and charts, and accounting software to track and report business transactions.

Operating Systems

An **operating system** is the set of programs that controls the basic operations of your microcomputer system. Much as a police officer directs traffic, it supervises the activities of input, processing, and output. The operating system handles such tasks as interpreting what you enter from the keyboard, moving information in and out of computer memory, and routing messages to your monitor or printer.

The operating system for IBM and IBM-compatible personal computers is **DOS**, which stands for *disk operating system*. This acronym is a bit misleading because DOS is responsible for managing the entire computer system, not just the disk drives. Through DOS, you tell the computer to run software applications such as word processors, electronic spreadsheets, and database management systems. In addition, DOS coordinates the communications between the application and the computer hardware (see Figure 1-7).

Figure 1-7. DOS makes it possible for application software to function with the hardware of a microcomputer

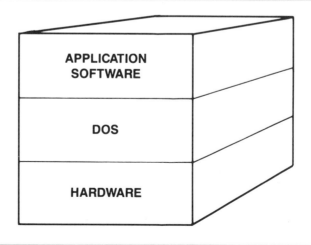

DOS acts much like an interpreter in the United Nations. It translates the requests from a software application (one ambassador) into the language of the hardware (another ambassador). This is why all applications require DOS in order to function. DOS must always be loaded into RAM before any other software.

Although DOS operates behind the scenes to perform many of the activities necessary for running your applications, you still need to master a formidable group of cryptic and terse commands to work in DOS. Even after you have mastered these commands, you must use them on a regular basis or they'll soon fade from your memory.

WHAT IS MICROSOFT WINDOWS 3.1?

Microsoft Windows 3.1 is a computer program that adds to and expands DOS (see Figure 1–8). It gives you an easier way to work with your microcomputer system by replacing the obscure, clumsy, and intimidating text-based environment of DOS with an intuitive, graceful, and friendly graphical user interface (GUI).

Windows is an integrated environment where applications are consistent, accessible, and linkable. Whether you're working with a

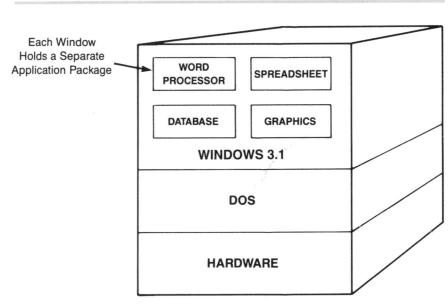

Figure 1–8. Microsoft Windows 3.1 adds to and expands DOS. It lets you interact with both your applications and computer hardware through the GUI.

word processor, electronic spreadsheet, or database management system, you'll know where to look for and how to use familiar menus and options. Integration allows you to transfer information from one application to another. You can even link different Windows applications together so that any changes in one will automatically be reflected in the other.

Windows is a memory manager designed to overcome the limitations inherent in DOS. Windows unleashes the power of your microcomputer so that the computer can reach its full potential. Windows enables you to run larger and more sophisticated programs, as well as run multiple applications simultaneously.

Thus, Windows is a graphical user interface, an integrated environment, and a memory manager. In the following sections, you'll learn more about each of these facilities. We'll also introduce you to the wide variety of accessory programs included with Windows 3.1.

Graphical User Interface

A **graphical user interface** or **GUI** (pronounced ''gooey'') lets you communicate with your computer by pointing at easy-to-understand menus and icons (pictures) instead of typing difficult-to-remember text commands. Since pointing is one of the primary forms of communication, a mouse is the preferred input device.

It is much easier (and more enjoyable) to work with a graphical user interface than a text-based one. In a GUI, you use a mouse to take direct control of the work on your screen. This allows you to finish swiftly a task that would normally require countless keystrokes with a keyboard.

A graphical environment also enables you to view text and graphics just as they'll appear on a printout. This capability is called **WYSIWYG** (What-You-See-Is-What-You-Get) and is extremely useful in producing professional-quality documents. WYSIWYG lets you rapidly and accurately create a document that is guaranteed to look the same in print form as it did on your monitor screen.

Microsoft Windows 3.1 is a full-featured GUI that treats your monitor screen like a **desktop**. The surface of this imaginary desk displays all your work in rectangular boxes called **windows**. Each software application has its own window (see Figure 1–9). You can view several applications at once and easily move between them. For example, you can write a report in a word processor, jump to a spreadsheet to calculate some numbers, switch to a database to add some records,

Figure 1-9. The desktop in Microsoft Windows 3.1 with a word processor, an electronic spreadsheet, and a database showing in separate windows.

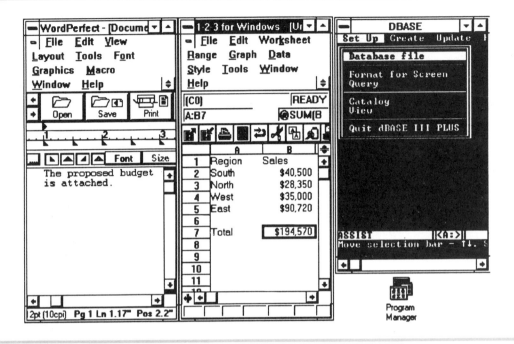

and move back to the word processor without ever exiting or restarting an application. Windows lets you add, remove, and arrange applications as if they were items on a real desk. If your desktop gets too crowded, you can always shrink the **application windows** down to **application icons**. You gain space on your desktop without actually exiting the programs. You can restore the minimized applications to their full window size when you need to.

Integrated Environment

Windows provides an integrated environment where applications look and act approximately the same way. This reduces the time it takes you to learn new applications because they are similar to the ones you already know. An integrated environment also allows you to transfer data easily between programs. In addition, you can create "compound" documents that allow separate applications to work together in a transparent and seamless way.

Ease of Learning

Application software specifically created for Windows, such as Lotus 1-2-3 for Windows, WordPerfect for Windows, and Paradox for Windows, all share a consistent and predictable user interface. In all these applications, you'll find familiar drop-down menus, dialog boxes, and icons. You can expect these features to look, feel, and act the same in every application.

After you've learned your first Windows application, you'll essentially be able to use other applications with only a minimum of training. This is because all windows applications share a common graphical environment in which they must conform to the same user interface guidelines.

Another benefit of integration is that when a better spreadsheet, word processor, or other Windows application comes along, you can adopt it without investing heavily in retraining.

In the past, to use integrated packages in DOS, you had to commit to a single set of programs that were predetermined and "welded together" by the software developer. If you didn't like one of the programs—say, the word processor—you either put up with it or threw out the entire package. Windows gives you the freedom to pick and choose your applications and still maintain an integrated environment.

Sharing Data between Applications

As you become experienced in working with multiple applications, you'll come to appreciate the ease with which Windows lets you share information between them. You simply cut or copy the information you want from one application and paste it into another application. **Clipboard** is the utility program that acts as a temporary storage area for the information you are transferring between applications.

For example, let's say you want to create an illustrated memo to welcome and guide new employees around on their first day with your company. First, you use a word processor to type the memo (see Figure 1-10a). Next, you use a graphics application to draw a floor plan (see Figure 1-10b). Finally, you combine the floor plan with your memo by copying the drawing into Clipboard and pasting it into the word processing document (see Figure 1-10c).

Clipboard provides a fast and convenient way to get all the information required to complete a project in one place at one time. It can even be used to move data between applications not specifically designed for Windows. The ability to work with both Windows and

Figure 1–10. Transferring data between applications.

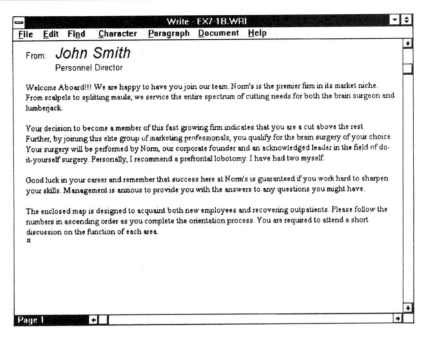

(a) Document created with a word processor.

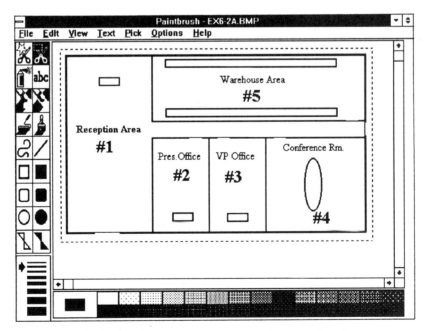

(b) Drawing of a floor plan made with a graphics application.

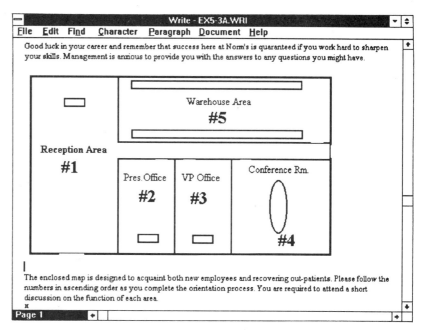

(c) Document with the floor plan drawing pasted into the text.

non-Windows (DOS) programs makes Clipboard an especially flexible and powerful tool for increasing your productivity.

Object Linking and Embedding (OLE)

Object Linking and Embedding or **OLE** lets you create a single document with data (objects) "embedded" from and "linked" to different applications. This compound document offers direct access to other applications for fast and easy editing of data (objects). OLE can also provide connections that automatically update the objects in a document when changes are made to them by other programs.

Here's how OLE could simplify the integration of text and graphics in the illustrated memo of Figure 1-10c, assuming that both the word processor and the graphics application support OLE. Suppose you want to edit the floor plan pasted (embedded) in the word processing document. A simple mouse action causes the graphics program to appear and display the floor plan (see Figure 1-11a). Any modification to the floor plan you make using the graphics program (e.g., adding a

Figure 1–11.
Object Link-
ing and
Embedding
(OLE).

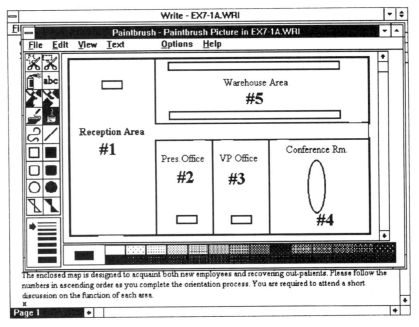

(a) Graphics program with the floor plan from the word processing
document.

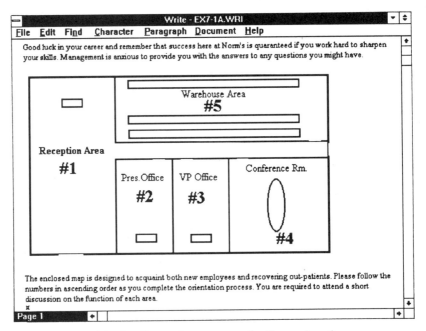

(b) Document with the floor plan automatically updated.

third "shelf" to the "Warehouse Area.") is automatically reflected in the word processing document (see Figure 1–11b).

OLE opens up some very exciting opportunities for developing your own customized documents. It can be used to combine data from several programs to form a compound document tailored to your specific needs. It might be a document designed to produce a report with information drawn from a spreadsheet, database management system, and graphics application. Whatever the problem or need, OLE presents an almost endless number of possibilities to create innovative and customized solutions.

Memory Manager

The operating system for IBM and IBM-compatible computers (DOS) was originally written to work with the Intel 8088 microprocessor. As you may recall, the 8088 can only address a maximum of 640 Kb of RAM. Over the past decade, newer and more powerful microprocessors have been introduced (refer back to Figure 1–4). However, to ensure compatibility with software developed for the 8088, each new version of DOS has retained its original 640 Kb memory limit. So, even though the later processors are physically capable of accessing millions more bytes of RAM, the restrictions inherent in DOS prevent users from tapping this dormant capacity.

Again, Windows 3.1 comes to the rescue by unleashing the hidden power of your microcomputer while still maintaining compatibility with DOS applications. Windows 3.1 extends the memory-handling capability of DOS so that your microcomputer can access more of the available RAM. Gone are the days of the 640 Kb memory barrier.

Larger and More Sophisticated Applications

Easy-to-use graphics programs typically require a great deal more memory than text-based applications. Until the advent of Windows 3.1, software developers were severely limited in terms of the quality and features they could build into graphics-based programs for IBM and IBM-compatible personal computers. Now, unhampered by previous memory restrictions, developers are producing larger and more sophisticated applications that are both easier to use and more powerful.

Multitasking

Windows' superior memory management enables you to run multiple software applications simultaneously. Windows allows you to open as many applications as your memory capacity permits. Windows' advanced multitasking facilities allow it to allocate processing power to more than one application at a time. For example, you can use your word processor to write a letter in one window while a spreadsheet performs calculations in another.

Access to extended memory is particularly important for multitasking. It makes additional RAM, beyond the conventional 640 Kb, accessible for running multiple applications. Since microprocessors vary in the amount of RAM they can address, they are the key to determining the multitasking capability of a microcomputer.

Windows' Operating Modes

Recognizing this fact, Microsoft designed Windows 3.1 to adapt itself automatically to the type of processor present and the amount of memory available in a microcomputer system. It does this by choosing one of two operating modes: standard or enhanced. Each mode is specifically tailored to provide the maximum performance given the available hardware.

- In the **standard mode,** Windows 3.1 can access the entire 16 Mb of extended memory available to 80286-based machines. Multitasking is possible for Windows applications (the speed and number depend on the amount of RAM actually installed). You can run DOS programs too; however, when you are working with a non-Windows application, processing of all Windows programs is suspended. The reverse is also true: While you are in a Windows application, processing of DOS programs will halt.

- The **enhanced mode** provides Windows 3.1 with access to the full 4 Gb of RAM available to the Intel 80386 or 80486 processor. Windows 3.1 is able to perform multitasking with both Windows and non-Windows (DOS) applications in the enhanced mode. It uses the "protected mode" of the 80386 or 80486 chip to divide extended memory into 640 Kb segments that look, to a DOS application, just like the conventional memory in an 8088-based microcomputer. Thus, more than one DOS application can run at the same time. You can work with a DOS or Windows application while several other DOS or Windows programs run in the background (the number again depends on the size of memory).

In addition, the enhanced mode makes use of the virtual memory capacity of the 80386 or 80486. With virtual memory, the processor uses a combination of RAM and hard disk storage to create the illusion of more RAM than actually exists. Virtual memory lets you run more or larger programs than would otherwise be possible.

As you can see, these two operational modes enable Windows 3.1 to add multitasking capabilities as processing power and memory increase. It's also worth noting that higher capacity hardware dramatically improves Windows' speed and responsiveness.

Windows' Accessories

Windows 3.1 also comes with a set of accessory programs designed to assist you in a variety of tasks. The three main accessories are Write, Paintbrush, and Terminal. *Write* is a fairly full-featured word processor, *Paintbrush* is a sophisticated drawing program, and *Terminal* is a communications package for sending and receiving data (via a modem) over a telephone line.

Other smaller accessory programs include a Clock, appointment Calendar, Cardfile, Calculator, Notepad, Macro Recorder, Object Packager, and Character Map. Some of these accessories are intended to help you manage your daily activities (Clock, Calendar, Cardfile, and Notepad); others are designed to optimize the performance and flexibility of Windows (Macro Recorder, Object Packager, and Character Map).

WHAT YOU NEED TO USE WINDOWS 3.1

There are some basic or general hardware and software requirements for using Windows 3.1 in either of its two operational modes. In addition, each operating mode has its own specific requirements. These needs, along with several recommendations, are listed below.

General System Requirements

At minimum, Windows 3.1 requires an 80286-based IBM or IBM-compatible microcomputer with at least 1 Mb of RAM, DOS 3.1 or later, a hard disk drive with 8–10 Mb free, a floppy disk drive, and a graphics monitor and adapter card. You'll want a color monitor (preferably VGA) to take advantage of Windows' spectacular displays. You'll need one of the printers supported by Windows 3.1 (see the *User's Guide*) to complete the exercises in this text. Finally, *we also require a mouse for these exercises*, although you can use Windows in a somewhat limited way with a keyboard.

Specific System Requirements

The level of hardware required for running Windows 3.1 escalates as you move up from the standard operating mode to the enhanced. The following list details the demands for operating under each mode.

- To operate in the *standard mode*, you'll need an 80286-based computer with 1 Mb of RAM (640 Kb of conventional memory and 384 Kb extended memory). You'll want to have 2 Mb of memory or more when multitasking large Windows applications.
- The *enhanced mode* is Windows' most demanding mode of operations. It requires an 80386-based computer with 2 Mb or more RAM (we recommend at least 4 Mb).

Remember, these system requirements are minimums, and the more memory and processor power you have available, the faster and more responsive Windows 3.1 becomes. This also holds true for the application packages you run under Windows.

COMING ATTRACTIONS . . .

We began this chapter by briefly touring the hardware and software components that constitute a microcomputer system. You learned about the various types of hardware: input devices, system unit, and output devices. Of course, hardware is useless without the instructions provided by software. The two major categories of software, application packages and operating systems, were discussed.

Our attention then turned to the role Windows 3.1 plays in microcomputing and why you should be interested in using it. You saw that Windows 3.1 provides a graphical user interface, an integrated environment, and advanced memory management. These facilities make Windows easy to learn, easy to use, and a very powerful and flexible way to communicate with your microcomputer system. We concluded with a look at the requirements for running Windows under each of its operational modes: standard and enhanced.

In the next chapter, we'll give you a chance to apply the concepts and ideas you've encountered here. This knowledge will come in handy as you begin to use Microsoft Windows 3.1 to interact with your computer. Understanding the fundamentals of a graphical user interface, and the hardware behind it, will prove invaluable for navigating through this new realm.

Chapters 3 and 4 present the major components of Windows: Program Manager and File Manager. You'll discover how to use these applications to manage and organize your programs and files efficiently and effectively. These early chapters will prepare you for the grander adventures that await you later on.

KEY TERMS

Application icons   A graphical representation (picture) of a running application that has been minimized. Application icons are visible on the desktop (Windows background).

Application packages   Computer programs designed to perform specific activities or tasks. Common application package categories are word processors, electronic spreadsheets, and database management systems.

Application windows   A rectangular screen area that contains a software application. Application windows can be opened and closed, resized, and moved. You can have several windows open at a time on the desktop.

Bus size   Determines the amount of data that can be sent to or received from the system unit and its external devices such as the keyboard, monitor, and disk drives. The larger the bus size, the faster the data can be transferred.

Byte   A memory or storage unit equal to one character. A byte is the unit of measure used by the computer to measure quantities of data or information.

CGA (color graphics adapter)   Video standard that supports just 16 colors with only 4 colors visible on the screen at a time. Resolution is poor. This is the least desirable of the color video standards.

Clipboard   The utility program used for temporary storage of information being transferred from one application to another.

Conventional memory   The first 640 Kb of random access memory.

Daisy-wheel   A type of printer that uses raised characters mounted on a spinning wheel to strike an inked ribbon. Daisy-wheels produce higher quality textual output but are slower than dot-matrix printers.

Data   The raw material of information. Facts such as text or numbers suitable for processing by the computer system.

Database management systems (DBMS)   Software that provides a means of creating files to hold pertinent data, maintaining and modifying those files, and then retrieving useful and ordered information from the files.

Desktop   The background screen for Windows. The Windows desktop is similar to the surface of the desk you use at work or home. Many of the same tasks you perform on your real desk can be performed on the Windows desktop.

Disk drives   Mechanical devices used to store information on magnetic media. Disk drives store information in much the same way that audio cassette recorders are able to store (record) and retrieve (play back) audio signals. Disk drives are usually referred to as either "hard drives" or "floppy drives." Hard drives (internal drives) are sealed units capable of storing large amounts of information, usually 20 Mb or more. Floppy drives feature removable diskettes that typically store either 360 Kb, 720 Kb, 1.2 Mb, or 1.44 Mb of information.

Display adapter card   Transforms the signals from the system unit into useful visual information for display on the monitor. This controller card is attached to the microprocessor via a motherboard slot and also is attached to the monitor via a cable.

DOS   See Operating System.

Dot-matrix   A type of printer that uses a bundle of pins to strike an inked ribbon. Characters are formed by the series of round dots created by an individual pin's impact on the ribbon against the paper.

Drive A, B, and C   Disk drive designation letters (names) that the computer can use for reference. Typically, drive A and drive B refer to the floppy drives found on microcomputer systems. Many microcomputers have only one floppy drive, which is always referred to as drive A. Drive C is the name given to the hard drive (internal drive) found on most systems.

EGA (enhanced graphics adapter)   Color video standard that displays 16 colors at a time from a palette of 64 colors. EGA resolution is much higher than CGA resolution.

Electronic spreadsheets   Software that enables you to create financial models and reports that automatically update calculations when existing values are changed.

Enhanced mode   Windows operating mode that requires an 80386 (or higher) microprocessor and at least 2 Mb of memory. This mode permits Windows to use its virtual memory capabilities. Virtual memory allows Windows to allocate free space on the computer's hard disk drive as additional processing memory. Windows 3.1 achieves its highest level of performance and full range of capabilities when functioning in this mode.

Extended memory   Computer memory beyond the first 640 Kb of random access memory.

File   A storage area for programs, data, and information. Files are stored on the computer's disk drives.

Floppy disk drive   Floppy drives feature removable diskettes that typically store either 360 Kb, 720 Kb, 1.2 Mb, or 1.44 Mb of information.

Floppy disks   Plastic disks encased in a protective sleeve. Floppy disks have a magnetic coating, similar to the coating on audio cassette tape, that can store information which the floppy disk drive is able to manipulate and organize.

Gigabyte (Gb)   Equal to 1,073,741,824 bytes and approximately equal to 1 billion characters.

Graphical user interface (GUI)   A means of communicating with your computer by simply pointing at easy-to-understand menus and pictures (icons). The Apple Macintosh line of computers pioneered this type of interface. Windows 3.1 is a full-featured GUI that strives to improve on the Macintosh standard.

Hard disk drive   Sealed internal drive units capable of storing large amounts of data and information, usually 20 Mb or more.

Hardware   The devices that physically enter, process, store and retrieve, and deliver data and information. All computer systems contain three types of hardware components: microprocessor, input devices, and output devices. Hardware refers to the electronic, magnetic, and mechanical components of the computer system.

Information   Meaningful and useful facts that are extracted from data fed to the computer. The end result of the decision-making or data-processing function. The quality of the information is limited to the quality of the data used to create the processed information.

Ink-jet   A type of printer that sprays ink through a template to form both letter-quality text and graphics. Ink-jet printers are fast but require costly ink cartridges and may also require specially coated paper.

Input   The process of entering data into the data processing system.

Input devices   Equipment used to move data into the system unit. Common input devices include keyboards, pointing devices such as a mouse, and disk drives.

Integrated environment   A computing environment that enforces a more uniform look and feel on all the software that functions within it. Integration improves the ease of learning for new integrated software applications because all software must comply with the standards inherent in the environment.

Kilobyte (Kb)   Equal to 1,024 bytes and approximately equal to 1,000 characters.

Laser   A type of printer that uses a photocopy process to produce near typeset quality output. Laser printers are fast but are the most expensive type of printers.

Low and high density disk formats   Format density determines the amount of data that can be stored on the floppy disk. It is important to know the format density of the disk drive on the computer you are using.

Megabyte (Mb)   Equal to 1,048,576 bytes and approximately equal to 1 million characters.

Memory management   The function performed by Windows 3.1 that lets software applications function at the peak efficiency capacity of the computer's hardware.

Microcomputer or **personal computer**   A type of small computer, consisting of a microprocessor and input/output devices.

Microprocessor or **central processing unit (CPU)**   The brain of the computer. It is an integrated circuit that performs a variety of operations on the data in accordance with a set of instructions provided by the software.

Microsoft Windows 3.1   A computer program that adds to and expands DOS. Windows provides an easier means of communicating with the microcomputer. Windows lets the computer user become master of the task at hand rather than slave to the obscurity of software commands and procedures.

Monitor   A video display that the computer uses as an output device. It allows for interaction between the user and computer by displaying data and processed information.

Mouse   A pointing device. Moving the mouse on a flat surface controls a pointer on the screen.

Multitasking   A function of Windows' superior memory management that enables multiple applications to operate at the same time.

Object Linking and Embedding (OLE)   A feature of Windows' integrated environment that enables you to create compound documents which work together in a "seamless" manner. OLE lets you "embed" and "link" data (objects) from multiple applications in a single document.

This compound document offers direct access to these applications. When two applications are linked, a modification to the data in one application is automatically reflected in the other.

Operating system   The set of programs responsible for controlling the basic operations of the microcomputer system. IBM-compatible computer systems use the disk operating system (DOS) produced by Microsoft (the producers of Windows 3.1).

Output   The act of displaying, either on the computer monitor or in printed form, the processed data (information).

Output devices   Devices that move data out of the processing unit, thus making it available for use by the computer user. Common output devices include the computer monitor, printers or plotters, and disk drives.

Pixels   An acronym for picture elements. A pixel represents one point on the screen surface of the monitor. A monitor uses a grid system to define its pixels. A monitor with 640 × 480 resolution has 640 vertical columns and 480 horizontal rows. The number of pixels is equal to the product of these two numbers (307,200 pixels with 640 × 480 resolution). The higher the resolution, the greater the number of pixels, and the clearer the image will appear.

Pointing devices   Alternative input devices used to enter data or navigate through software (such as Windows 3.1). Pointing devices provide greater freedom of cursor movement. Types include the mouse, stylus, trackballs, and electronic sketchpads.

Printer   An output device that converts information stored in the computer into printed output.

Printout or **hardcopy**   The printed output from a printer.

Processing   The manipulation or transformation of data into information by the computer. This is a problem-solving process that uses the inputted or stored data in combination with the hardware and software to produce the desired output.

Random access memory (RAM)   Temporary memory used by the microprocessor to hold instructions and data prior to or just after processing. The data is maintained in memory just as long as power is supplied to the circuits. When the computer is turned off, the contents of the memory are lost.

Resolution   The clarity of displayed or printed output. The resolution of a computer monitor is measured by the number of pixels on the screen; the higher the number, the greater the clarity. Resolution from a printer is measured in dots per inch (DPI); again, the higher the number, the greater the clarity.

Software or **programs**   A series of instructions that directs the information-processing operations performed by the hardware. The two broad software categories are application software and system software.

Standard mode   The normal operating mode for Windows 3.1. This mode provides access to extended memory (memory above the 640 Kb limit of conventional memory) and also enables multiple applications to run at the same time.

System unit or **primary system**   The microprocessor and temporary memory necessary to convert data into information. Some common operations performed by the system unit include manipulating, classifying, sorting, summarizing, and calculating.

VGA (video graphics array)   Video standard that is the current industry standard. VGA supports 256 colors with a palette of thousands of colors. Resolution is clear and sharp.

Window   A rectangular portion of the screen that contains an application or document. A window can be opened and closed, resized, and moved. You may have several open at one time. You may also shrink (minimize) a window to an icon or enlarge (maximize) it to fill the entire desktop.

Windows' operating modes   Windows can analyze the computer's hardware and then switch itself to different modes of operation that best suit the microcomputer's hardware configuration.

Word processors   Software designed to help you create written documents such as memos, research papers, articles, and books.

Word size   The size of the data blocks processed at one time by the system unit. Word size is measured in bits. A bit is either a 0 or 1. Zero corresponds with Off and 1 with On. The larger the word size, the faster the data can be processed.

WYSIWYG   An acronym for What-You-See-Is-What-You-Get. This capability allows you to view a document on your monitor in the form it will appear when printed.

REVIEW QUESTIONS

True or False Questions

1. **T   F**   Microcomputers are often referred to as personal computers.

2. **T   F**   Hardware refers to the physical components of a computer system such as the keyboard, microprocessor, monitor, and printer.

3. **T   F**   Software refers to floppy disks, cables, and paper because these items are soft or flexible.

4. **T   F**   All computer systems have the following three items: input devices, a system unit or primary system, and output devices.

5. **T   F**   Information is the raw material of the data-processing function.

6. **T   F**   A mouse is an output device.

7. **T   F**   Windows 3.1 utilizes a graphical user interface.

8. **T   F**   Random access memory loses its contents if the power is shut off.

9. **T   F**   Floppy diskettes are impervious to temperature, excessive handling, and dust.

10. **T   F**   Windows 3.1 lets users run larger, more sophisticated applications than could be run without Windows 3.1.

Multiple Choice Questions

1. Which of the three Windows' operating modes enables Windows to function at its full capacity?

    a. Super mode
    b. Standard mode
    c. Enhanced mode

2. Which microprocessor chip is the most powerful?

    a. 80286
    b. 8088
    c. 80386
    d. 8086

3. Which of the following units of measure represents the largest amount?

    a. Gigabyte
    b. Kilobyte
    c. Megabyte
    d. Byte

4. Which of the following is an example of an output device?

    a. Keyboard
    b. Mouse
    c. Microprocessor
    d. Monitor

5. Which of the following characteristics is NOT true of hard disk drives?

    a. Removable diskettes
    b. High storage capacity
    c. Referred to as drive C
    d. Also called a fixed or internal drive

6. Which of the following video display standards produces the highest degree of resolution?

    a. VGA
    b. CGA
    c. EGA

7. Which of the following is NOT a type of printer?

    a. Laser
    b. Dot-matrix
    c. Spinning-wheel
    d. Ink-jet

8. Which of the following is NOT an example of application software?

    a. Word processors
    b. Disk operating system
    c. Electronic spreadsheets
    d. Database management software

9. What is the maximum amount of random access memory that Windows 3.1 in enhanced mode can utilize?

   a. 2 Mb
   b. 640 Kb

   c. 16 Mb
   d. 4 Gb

10. Which of the following Windows accessories can be used to receive data from another computer?

   a. Write
   b. Terminal

   c. Paintbrush
   d. Clipboard

Getting Started

Upon completing this chapter, you'll be able to:

1. **Start and exit Windows.**
2. **Use the mouse to select menus, commands, and icons.**
3. **Start and exit an application.**
4. **Control the size and placement of a window.**
5. **Obtain help on any subject in Windows.**

OVERVIEW

The tutorial labs in this chapter are designed to give you the fundamental concepts and skills necessary to work with Windows 3.1. Windows uses a collection of windows, menus, and icons to assist you in managing your applications and system resources. To be an effective Windows user, you'll need to become familiar with the way each of these items functions.

LAB 2–1   GETTING AROUND IN WINDOWS

This lab introduces you to Windows' graphical environment by showing you how to use menus, group windows, and icons to start an application. As you perform these operations, your adeptness with the mouse will gradually improve. You'll end the lab by practicing the steps for safely exiting both an application and the Windows environment.

Starting Windows

Your computer system may be set up to start Windows automatically when it is switched on. If this is not the case, you'll need to follow these steps.

1. At the DOS prompt, type: WIN
2. Now press the Enter key.

The first time Windows is started, it displays a screen like the one shown in Figure 2-1. The Windows desktop will contain Program Manager with the Main group open inside it. **Program Manager** is the central staging area for all the work you'll do in Windows. It enables you to organize and launch your applications. (We'll explore the capabilities of Program Manager in Chapter 3.)

The Main group displays the icons for File Manager, Control Panel, Print Manager, Clipboard Viewer, MS-DOS Prompt, Windows Setup, PIF Editor, and Read Me. These programs help you manage your computer system and Windows environment and will occupy much of our attention in subsequent chapters. Other groups of applications are represented by the icons shown at the bottom of Program Manager.

Don't worry if your desktop doesn't exactly match Figure 2-1. One of Windows' best qualities is its ability to be customized. Previous sessions with Windows may have left different items on the desktop. The number of group icons may also vary depending on the applications currently installed on your machine. Regardless of these differences, the same basic elements are always present, and you'll soon discover how to manipulate them to your own tastes.

Figure 2-1. The opening screen of Windows 3.1.

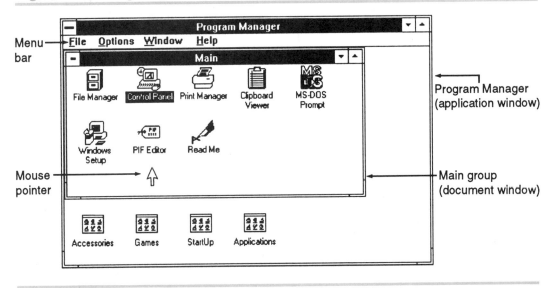

Recognizing Window Types

(handwritten: ① Group ② Application ③ Document)

There are two basic kinds of windows: application and document.
Application windows hold programs that are currently running. For
example, Program Manager is running in an application window. A
document window is a framed work area inside an application window. The Main group window in Figure 2–1 is a document window
belonging to Program Manager. An application, like Program Manager,
can have multiple document windows. Document windows are easy to
spot because, unlike application windows, they have no visible menu
options.

Using the Pointer

Find the arrow-shaped pointer ($\mathbb{R}$) on your screen. This mouse
pointer is your means of communicating with Windows. It will change
shape to indicate its current capabilities. For instance, when you size a
window, it assumes the shape of a double arrow ($\Longleftrightarrow$). The single
arrow shape allows you to choose a command, activate a program, or
move a window. (See **Pointer** in the *Key Terms* section at the end of
this chapter for a complete list of pointer shapes and their meanings.)

Your mouse controls the movement of the pointer. For instance, if
you slide the mouse to the right, the pointer moves to the right. Like-
wise, maneuvering it to the left moves the pointer left. If you run out
of room, just pick the mouse up and set it down where there is more
room. Lifting the mouse has no effect on the pointer.

___ NOTE _____

The tutorial exercises in this book are designed to be completed
using a mouse. For those desperate or fanatical enough, the keyboard equivalents can be found in Windows 3.1's documentation.
However, we strongly urge that you use a mouse because much of
the grace and elegance of Windows 3.1 is lost without it.

_____

It's time to gain some experience in navigating around your imaginary desktop. The instructions below will take you on a brief tour.

1. Slide your mouse forward until the pointer rests at the top of the
   screen.
2. Move the pointer to the upper right corner.

3. Pull the mouse down and to the left so that the pointer moves diagonally from the upper right corner to the lower left corner of your desktop.

4. Repeat step 3, except this time start in the upper left corner and move to the lower right.

5. Now practice moving the pointer around until you feel comfortable with the mouse.

Learning to move the pointer is only half the story. To select items on the screen, you'll also have to become familiar with the use of the left mouse button. It can be used in one of three ways: clicking, double-clicking, or dragging. **Clicking** is a single press and release, **double-clicking** is two rapid presses, and **dragging** consists of depressing the button while moving the mouse. These mouse actions can be combined with the keys on your keyboard to perform special functions such as selecting more than one item.

You can use these motions to select menus and commands to perform other interesting operations. In the next section, you'll get a chance to put these mouse actions to work.

*[handwritten margin note: * Click/Drag TRiple-Click Drag/Drop]*

_____**NOTE**_____

If Program Manager has been reduced to an icon in the lower portion of your screen, position your pointer on it and double-click. This will restore Program Manager to a window.

_____

Working with Menus

A **command** is a word or phrase that instructs Windows to carry out a specific activity. Commands that are designed to achieve some collective purpose are grouped into a **menu** for convenient access. In Windows, the **menu bar**, located at the top of an application window, lists the menus available for the current application (see Figure 2–1). These menus will vary somewhat from application to application. For example, the menu bar for Program Manager includes the menus File, Options, Window, and Help. (We'll talk in more detail about each of these in Chapter 3, *Managing Programs*.)

To select a menu from the menu bar, position your pointer over the name and click. Clicking on a name in the menu bar will cause a box that contains a list of commands to drop down. To cancel the selection of a menu, simply click on the name again or click anywhere outside the drop-down menu.

To see how these procedures work, follow these steps.

1. Move the mouse so the tip of the pointer rests on the Window option in the menu bar.
2. Click the left mouse button once to trigger the drop-down menu. (If the menu doesn't appear, move the pointer so that more of the tip rests on the word "Window," and click again.)
3. Move the pointer outside the menu box.
4. Click to cancel the menu.
5. Repeat steps 1 and 2 to reopen the Window menu.

Figure 2-2.

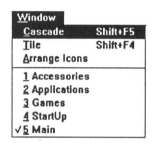

Figure 2-2 displays the Window menu. **Drop-down menus** like this one observe several conventions. First, horizontal lines are used to group related options. Second, commands are dimmed when they are unavailable. Third, checkmarks are used with toggle commands to signal they're switched on. Fourth, dots after a name tell you that additional information is needed to carry out the command (e.g., *Open...*). *ELIPSIS- OPENS DIALOG BOX*

The numbered commands below the horizontal line in this menu are used to open group windows.

Group windows organize applications by category so you can quickly locate the program you wish to run. At present, the Main group is toggled on. Let's switch to the Accessories group so you can start the Clock program. To select a command from a drop-down menu, simply click on it.

6. Position the pointer on the command *Accessories*.
7. Then click once.

● **HINT**_____

A faster one-step method for selecting a command is to position the pointer on the menu name, hold the left mouse button down, drag the pointer to the desired option, and release. When you release, the command is executed.

Understanding Icons

Your desktop should now resemble the one pictured in Figure 2–3. The Accessories group window has replaced the Main group window. This window displays the icons that represent the accessory programs installed on your system. If you look closely at each icon, you'll see that it is actually made up of two parts: a graphic (picture) and a label.

Figure 2–3.
The Windows desktop with Windows' Accessories group displayed.

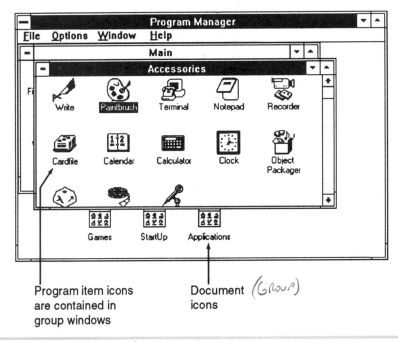

Program item icons are contained in group windows

Document (Group) icons

Icons can depict program items, documents, or applications. **Program item icons** appear only in group windows and are used to start applications.

Document icons represent documents that can be expanded into document windows. Notice that document icons all look the same (see Figure 2–3). Only their titles serve to distinguish them.

Application icons, introduced in the last chapter, represent programs running in the background. They can be expanded into application windows. We'll show you how to expand icons into windows and collapse them back again in Lab 2–2, *Controlling a Window*.

You can move an icon by placing your pointer on it, holding down the left mouse button, dragging it to a new location, and then releasing it. In Chapter 3, *Managing Programs*, we'll use this technique to add program item icons to a new group window. In Chapter 4, *Managing Files*, it'll provide us with a fast and easy method to copy and move files.

Starting an Application

To start an application from Program Manager, just double-click on the program item icon representing the application. The pointer will change into an hourglass to indicate you must wait while Windows launches the application.

1. Position the pointer on the program item icon titled Clock.
2. Now double-click.

Using Clock

Doubling-clicking on the Clock icon will cause Clock to appear on your desktop, as shown in Figure 2–4. Clock can display time in one of two ways: digital or analog. The first time Clock is started, it will display in digital. In the digital mode, Clock also displays the current date. To change the clock face, click on the Settings menu and pick either the *Analog* or *Digital* command.

Figure 2–4.

1. Click on the Settings options in the menu bar.
2. Click on the *Analog* command (if Analog is already toggled on, pick *Digital* instead).

If you accidentally click on the Program Manager or Accessories group windows, Clock will disappear! Don't panic, it's still on your desktop—it's hidden behind Program Manager. We'll talk about switching between application windows in the next chapter, but for now just press and hold down the Alt key and then push the Esc key once to switch back to the Clock window.

● **HINT**

You can use the moving and sizing techniques demonstrated in Lab 2–2 to reposition and reduce Clock so you see it while working with other applications.

Quitting an Application

Figure 2–5.

Control-menu box

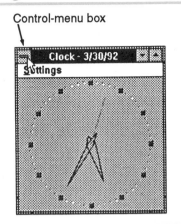

Most Windows applications have a File menu with an *Exit* option. You should make a habit of using it because the *Exit* command checks to see if you have saved your work. If not, it will give you the option to do so. However, since Clock has no File menu, you can safely close it by double-clicking on the control-menu box (the tiny box with the dash line) in the upper left corner of its application window.

1. Position your pointer on the control-menu box shown in Figure 2–5.
2. Now double-click. (If you fail to click rapidly enough, a drop-down menu will appear. Ignore it and double-click on the control-menu box again.)

Ending a Windows Session

Always quit Windows from Program Manager. This will guarantee you an opportunity to save any work you neglected to store on disk earlier. By default, Windows will also save the changes you have made to its environment (e.g., showing the Accessories work group open). You can tell Windows to "forget" these alterations by turning off the *Save Settings on Exit* command from the Options menu. You should always make sure this setting is disabled before ending a Windows session. Switching this option off causes Windows to retain its original look and feel for the next user.

1. Click on Options in the menu bar of Program Manager.
2. If the *Save Settings on Exit* command has a check mark in front of it, click the command once to remove the mark and toggle the option off.
3. If the *Save Settings on Exit* command doesn't display a check mark, it is presently turned off. To close the Options menu, click outside the menu's borders.

To end a Windows session, choose the *Exit Windows...* command from the File menu in Program Manager.

4. Click on File in the menu bar of Program Manager.
5. Click the command *Exit Windows...*

The **dialog box** shown in Figure 2-6 will appear. Windows uses dialog boxes to request and provide additional information. In this case, Windows is making sure you really want to quit. Clicking on the *OK* button in the dialog box will end the Windows session and return you to the DOS prompt. Selecting the *Cancel* button will nullify the *Exit Windows...* command and return you to Program Manager.

Figure 2-6.
The Exit
Windows
dialog box.

6. Click on the *OK* button to end the session.

When the DOS prompt appears, you can safely shut down your computer system.

⊘ **HAZARD**_____

Never turn off your computer before exiting Windows. This will cause the changes you've made to Windows, plus any other work not yet saved, to be lost.

LAB 2-2   CONTROLLING A WINDOW

In this lab, you'll be formally introduced to the elements of a window. You'll learn to use these elements to collapse, expand, restore, move, size, and close a window. These techniques will assist you in controlling and organizing your desktop.

Recognizing the Elements of a Window

Although we've casually peeked through a window or two, it's now time to take a closer look inside. As you have seen, a window is a boxed area where applications run, documents display, and other activities occur. Figure 2-7 illustrates the common parts of a window. Some of these parts may be familiar, while others, no doubt, are new to you. Take a moment to study the following descriptions.

Figure 2–7. The common parts of a window.

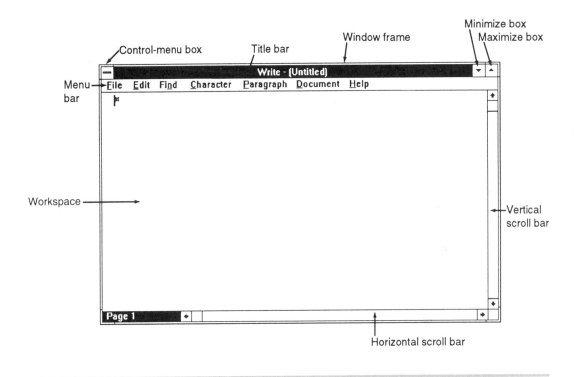

- The **frame** is the border around the outside of a window.
- **Scroll bars,** located along the right and bottom of a window, allow you to view parts of a document too large to fit in a window.
- The **control-menu box,** in the upper left corner of a window, closes a window. (It also provides keyboard users with a menu for moving, sizing, minimizing, maximizing, closing, and switching between windows.)
- The **title bar** displays the name of the application or document. It is positioned at the top of a window. When more than one window is open on the desktop, the title bar of the active window (the one you're working with) will have a different color or intensity from the others.
- The **menu bar** lists the menus available for a particular window. You'll find it just below the title bar. Most menu bars contain a File menu, Edit menu, and Help menu.

● The **maximize box**, in the upper right corner of a window, expands a window to its maximum size. Windows applications enlarge to cover the entire desktop, while document windows can only grow to the borders of an application. After a window is expanded, the maximize box becomes a restore box. You can use it to return the window to its previous dimensions.
● The **minimize box**, just left of the maximize box, reduces a window to an icon.
● The **workspace**, in the center area of a window, is where most of the work on an application is carried out.

These window elements provide you with a great deal of control over your desktop environment. They let you organize and arrange the way things are displayed. The following exercises will give you an opportunity to practice manipulating them.

Scrolling the Contents of a Window

When a window is too small for all of its contents to display, a scroll bar appears so you can move the concealed portions into view (see Figure 2–8). To scroll a document, you drag the scroll box along the scroll bar to a position that corresponds approximately with the location you want to view (e.g., top, middle, or bottom of a document). In order to demonstrate how a scroll bar works, we'll need to skip ahead a bit and call up a Help window. (The Windows Help facility will be fully explained in the next Lab.)

1. Start Windows.
2. If Program Manager has been reduced to an icon, double-click on it.
3. Click on Help in Program Manager's menu bar.
4. Click on the *How to Use Help* command in the Help menu.

A window will materialize looking much like the one pictured in Figure 2–8.

5. Point at the down arrow on the vertical scroll bar and click once.

   Notice the text scrolls up one line.

6. To scroll up one more line, click on the same down arrow again.

Figure 2–8.
A Help
window with
an annotated
scroll bar.

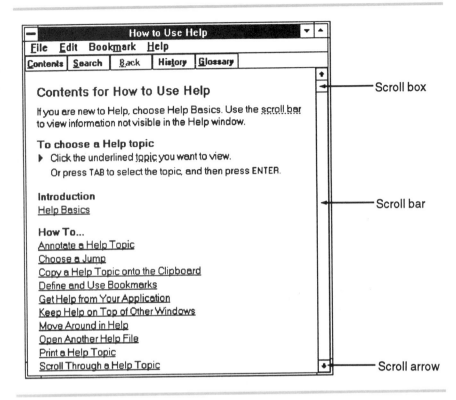

7. Point at the same scroll arrow, but this time press and hold down the mouse button until the scroll box reaches the bottom of the vertical scroll bar.

You should now be looking at the bottom of the document. To see the top of the document, you can click on the up arrow until the scroll box reaches the top of the bar. However, the fastest means to reach the top or bottom of a document is to drag the scroll box in that direction.

8. Point at the scroll box, press and hold down the left mouse button, slide the scroll box to the top of the bar, and release the button.

The top of the document is again visible. When working with long documents, the scroll bar can be used to move one page at a time.

9. Position the pointer below the scroll box on the scroll bar and click once.

Note the document scrolls down a page.

10. To move the text a page upward, point at the scroll bar somewhere above the scroll box and click once.
11. To exit Help, click on File in Help's menu bar. From the File menu, select the *Exit* command.

You can use the same actions to scroll across a wide document using a horizontal scroll bar. The table below summarizes the scroll bar actions.

TO SCROLL	ACTION
One line at a time	Click one of the scroll arrows.
Multiple lines	Point at one of the scroll arrows and press and hold down the left mouse button.
One page at a time	Click on one side or the other of the scroll box.
To any place	Drag the scroll box in the direction you want to view.

Collapsing a Window to an Icon

Just like the surface of a real desk, your Windows desktop can become cluttered. As you open more windows, the available space on the desktop diminishes. Fortunately, Windows provides a convenient way to shrink applications and documents without closing them. If you click on the minimize box of a window, the window will be reduced to an icon. As icons, applications continue to run in the background without consuming as much space on your desktop. Documents reduced to icons also remain in memory and are available for immediate use.

To gain experience in minimizing windows, follow these steps.

1. Choose the *Accessories* group from the Window menu in Program Manager and then start the program Clock (if necessary, refer back to Lab 2–1 for instructions).
2. Move the pointer so it's over the minimize box (▼) in the upper right corner of the Clock window.
3. Click once to reduce the application to an icon.
4. To shrink Program Manager to an icon, click on its minimize box.

Your screen will resemble the one portrayed in Figure 2–9. Both Clock and Program Manager now reside as icons in the lower left

Figure 2-9.
An almost
empty
desktop with
Clock and
Program
Manager
reduced to
icons.

corner of your screen. In their reduced state, they take up little room
on the desktop.

Expanding an Icon to a Window

To expand an icon into a window, simply double-click on it. If you
click too slowly, the control-menu will pop up. Then, to complete the
expansion process you must either double-click on the icon again or
select the Restore command from the control-menu.

1. Point at the Program Manager icon in the lower left corner of your
   desktop.
2. Double-click to expand the icon to a window.
3. Double-click on the Clock icon.

   Program Manager and Clock will enlarge to their original size and
place on the desktop.

⊘ HAZARD

If you accidentally double-click on the Clock icon in the Accessories group window, you'll start a second clock running. To remove
it, double-click on its control-menu box.

Expanding a Window

When you are working with a single application or a program such as Paintbrush, you'll want it to display as much detail as possible. A Windows application can be enlarged so that it occupies your whole desktop. A document window can be expanded to fill the entire workspace of an application. You enlarge a window by clicking on its maximize box.

1. Place your pointer over the maximize box (▲) in the upper right corner of the Program Manager window.
2. Click once to enlarge the window.

The Program Manager window will expand to occupy all of your desktop, and the Clock application will disappear (see Figure 2-10). However, Clock remains on your desktop, hidden behind the full-screen Program Manager. In Chapter 3, we'll show you how to find and bring a concealed window into the foreground.

Figure 2-10. Program Manager enlarged to fill the entire desktop.

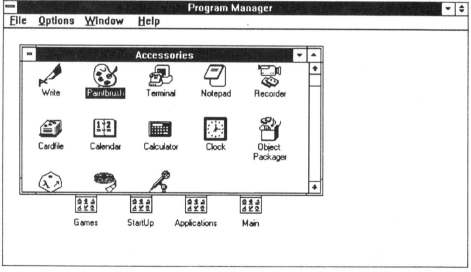

Restoring a Window to Its Previous Size

When you expand a window to cover the whole screen, the maximize box becomes a restore box. Clicking on the restore box will cause a window to return to its previous size and location.

1. Move the pointer so that it rests on the restore box (the one with a double arrow in the upper right corner).
2. Click once, and Program Manager assumes its former size and location.

Moving a Window

When you want to view more than one application at a time, you'll need to rearrange your desktop. Windows makes this an easy task by allowing you to move both application and document windows. An application window can be repositioned anywhere on your desktop, while the movement of a document window is restricted to the borders of its application.

To move a window, you can click on the title bar, drag it to a new location, and release. As you drag it, an outline will appear to help you determine the space it will occupy when released. Let's see if we can move the Program Manager window so both it and the Clock application are visible.

1. Position the pointer on the title bar of Program Manager.
2. Press and hold down the left mouse button. Drag the window around until you expose as much of the Clock window as possible. Be sure you end up with all of Program Manager in view.
3. Release the left mouse button to place the window in the new position.

Your desktop should loosely resemble the one shown in Figure 2-11. Clock and Program Manager may be arranged differently, but notice there is simply insufficient room to display both of the applications.

Sizing a Window

Resizing a window provides another way to make more room on your desktop. You can resize a window by using your mouse to grab a side or corner and drag it. The first step in this process (and the most tricky) is to place the pointer so it exactly straddles a side or corner of a window. You'll know the pointer is in the correct position when it changes shape.

If you are adjusting the sides, the pointer will assume the shape of a horizontal double-headed arrow. When you are moving the top or bottom borders, the pointer will appear as a vertical double-headed arrow. Positioning the pointer on the corner of a window lets you change its height and width simultaneously.

Figure 2–11. The desktop after repositioning Program Manager.

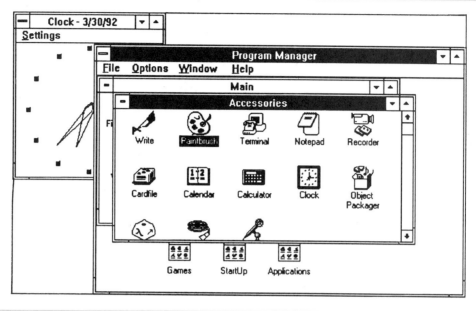

Let's see how this works by sizing Clock so it and Program Manager will both fit on your desktop.

1. Click on the title bar of the Clock to make it the active window.

    The Clock will come to the foreground.

2. Position the pointer in the lower right corner of the Clock window. (You'll know the pointer is in the right location when it changes to a slanted double arrow.)

3. Now press and hold down the left mouse button. Move the mouse so the Clock window shrinks in size.

4. When the window is roughly 2 inches by 2 inches, release the mouse button.

5. Move the Clock window to the lower right corner of the desktop (or to a place where it doesn't overlap the Program Manager window).

Compare your screen to the one pictured in Figure 2–12. Both Program Manager and Clock should be in clear view. Moving and sizing windows offer you a powerful combination for customizing your desktop. As you learn to use more applications, you'll need these procedures to manage your work.

Figure 2–12.
The desktop
with Clock
and Program
Manager in
plain view.

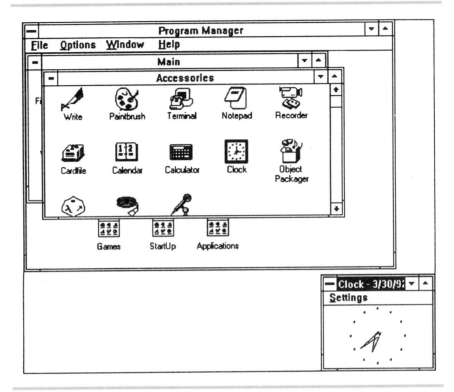

Closing a Window

Double-clicking on the control-menu box of a window will close it. However, in the case of an application window, it is always better to quit by selecting the *Exit* command from the File menu. Closing an application clears it from your desktop, but the program may continue to occupy space in memory. Worse yet, some applications close without saving your work!

Closing is a fast and convenient way to clear away windows when you're sure there is nothing to be lost. Document windows like the application groups in Program Manager can be safely closed by double-clicking on their control-menu boxes. When they are closed, they simply become icons at the bottom of Program Manager. Accessories such as Clock can also be closed. Since Clock uses no files, the potential for losing data is nonexistent.

1. To close the Accessories group, double-click on its control-menu box.

2. Close the Clock application in the same manner.

3. Check to make sure the *Save Settings on Exit* command in the Options menu is toggled off. Then end your Windows sessions by selecting *Exit Windows...* from the File menu in Program Manager and clicking the *OK* button when the confirming dialog box appears.

⊘ HAZARD

When you are working with a non-Windows (DOS) application, never close its window. Instead, exit the application the way you normally would in DOS; otherwise, you may damage any open files.

LAB 2-3   GETTING HELP

Getting help when you encounter a problem can save you both frustration and time. In this lab, you'll learn to use Windows' **Help** facility to locate the information you need to solve problems and explore new options. You'll experiment with the Contents, Back, History, Glossary, and Search features of Help.

Starting Help

You can receive assistance from Windows, and most Windows applications, in three different ways:

Help menu   Choose Help from the menu bar of an application and use the Help options to locate information on the desired topic.

F1   Press the F1 function key to display the Help Contents available for the current application and select the appropriate topic.

Help button If available, click the *Help* button on a dialog box for related information.

NOTE

Some applications will provide help with a selected command, open dialog box, or visible message when the F1 function key is pressed.

Suppose you are in Program Manager and want to know more about the procedure for quitting Program Manager. You can use the Help facility to find this information. Let's try it.

1. Start Windows.
2. Click on Help in the Program Manager's menu bar.

Figure 2-13.

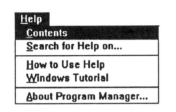

The drop-down menu, portrayed in Figure 2-13, displays the categories of Help available for Program Manager. These items are typical of what you'll find in the Help menus of most Windows applications. Below is a brief explanation of what each of these commands does when selected.

- **Contents** displays a list of the Help topics available for the current (active) application.
- **Search for Help on...** brings up the search facility in Help (we'll talk about this feature shortly).
- **How to Use Help** provides instructions for using the facilities available in Help.
- **Windows Tutorial** invokes a brief hands-on introduction to the Windows environment.
- **About [Application]** shows the copyright, version, and name of the current program. When this command is invoked from certain applications (e.g., Program Manager or File Manager), it also reveals the mode of operations Windows is currently running under (standard or enhanced) and the memory available.

Checking the Contents

To see an alphabetized index of the topics available for the current application, just click on the *Contents* command in the Help menu.

1. With the Help menu displayed, point at the *Contents* command.
2. Click once to produce the window pictured in Figure 2-14.

The Help Contents lists the Help topics available for Program Manager by category. We can use it to locate information on quitting Program Manager.

3. If necessary, scroll to the topic *Quit Windows*. Once it is visible, place your mouse pointer on it.

Figure 2–14.
The first
Help window
for Program
Manager.

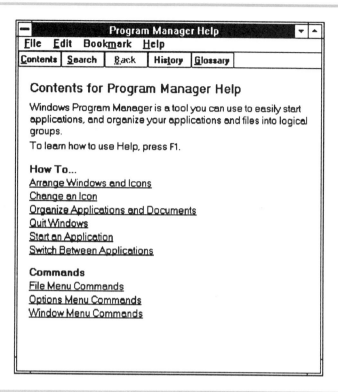

Notice that the mouse pointer changes to the shape of a hand. This indicates that additional information is available.

4. Cick once to display the topic.

Your screen should match Figure 2–15. Take a moment to read about the procedure for exiting Windows.

● **HINT**

On occasion, you might want to move and resize a Help window so you can refer to it while working with an application. Help windows can also be maximized for easier reading.

Until now we've ignored the function buttons across the top of the Help window. These buttons enable you to find topics quickly. For instance, the *Contents* button sends you to the list of topics available for

Figure 2–15.
Help
procedure for
Quitting
Windows.

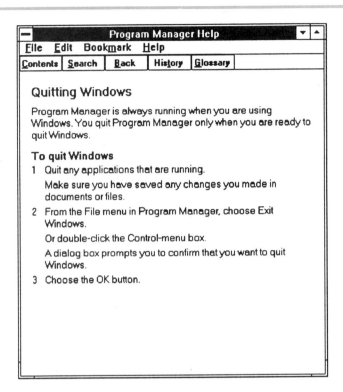

the current application. In our case, this happens to be the window
where we began our journey.

5. Point at the *Contents* button.
6. Click once to bring up the original Help Contents window.

Back

Clicking on the **Back** button sends you to the previous Help window.
If you continue to click on this button, you will eventually retrace your
steps through all the topics you've seen.

1. Position the pointer on the *Back* button.
2. Click once to go to the previous topic, *Quitting Windows*.
3. Click again to see the Contents list you used for selecting the topic
   Quit Windows.

The *Back* function button is now dimmed, signaling that it's no longer
available. You have arrived at the entry point into the Help system.

___NOTE_____

The **Next** button (▶▶) and the **Previous** (◀◀) button appear when additional related topics are available for viewing. You can use these arrow buttons to move through the topics. When you reach the last topic the *Next* button will dim, indicating it's no longer active. The *Previous* button takes you to the previous topic in a series. It will dim when you reach the first topic in the chain.

History

Figure 2–16.

The **History** button lets you select any topic you have visited in the current Windows session. When you click the *History* button, a History dialog box will appear with a list of the topics you have previously viewed (see Figure 2–16). To see one again, just double-click on it.

1. Click on the *History* button in the menu bar of the Help window.
2. When the History dialog box appears, double-click on the topic *Quitting Windows*.

The Help window changes to display the *Quitting Windows* topic. As you can see, the *History* button provides a very convenient way to return to an earlier topic.

Glossary

Figure 2–17.

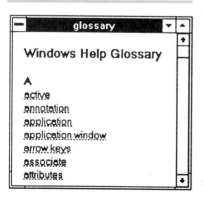

The **Glossary** button opens a glossary window with a list of definitions of terms specific to Windows. For an explanation of any item, simply use the scroll bar to locate the term, and then click on it.

1. Click on the *Glossary* button in the menu bar of the Help window.

The glossary window shown in Figure 2–17 will appear. It displays an alphabetical list of the key terms used in Windows.

2. To view the definition for the term "menu bar," use the scroll bar to find it and then click on it.

A message window will materialize with a glossary definition for the chosen item, as shown in Figure 2–18. When you finish reading a glossary definition, click anywhere on your desktop to make the message window vanish.

Figure 2–18.
Glossary
menu
description
box.

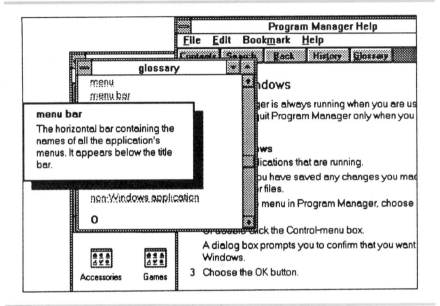

3. Click on the message window to clear it away.
4. Double-click on the control-menu box of the glossary window to close it.

___NOTE_____

Some Help screens contain words or phrases displayed in green and underlined with dots. This type of highlighting signifies they are key terms. As in the glossary window, you can view a glossary definition by simply clicking on the key term.

Search

The **Search** button is the fastest way to locate a particular topic. You use it by selecting or typing a key word or phrase and letting Help find the information for you.

1. Click on the *Search* button.

Help displays the dialog box shown in Figure 2-19. You can either type a phrase in the text box or select one from the list box just below. Let's use the search facility to see how rapidly we can locate the *Quitting Windows* topic.

Figure 2-19.
The Search
dialog box
locates topics
that match
the key term
you enter or
select.

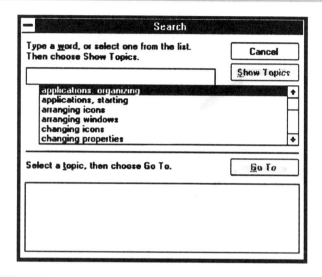

2. In the text box, type: Quitting Windows

Notice that Help has already located the topic before you can finish typing the words "Quitting Windows." It is highlighted in the list box just below where you were typing. To see a list of related topics, select the *Show Topics* button.

3. Click on the *Show Topics* button in the Search dialog box.

A list of topics that closely relate to or match the key word or phrase is displayed at the bottom of the Search dialog box. In this case, only one topic was found, as illustrated in Figure 2-20. The first topic in this list box is always highlighted. When multiple topics are present, you can choose another by simply clicking on it.

To view the highlighted topic, click the *Go To* button. To cancel the whole search procedure any time, click the Close button.

4. Select the *Go To* button.

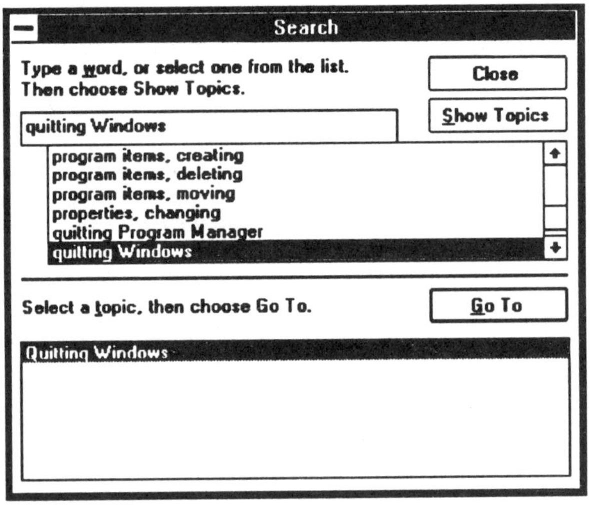

Figure 2–20.
A list box
displays the
topic(s) found
that relate to
your key
word or
phrase.

The *Search...* command displays the same information that took numerous steps to locate with the *Contents* command. It should be obvious from this example that, if you know the word or phrase you want help on, *Search...* is a far more efficient way to find information than checking indices.

___NOTE___

Search... is not case-sensitive. This means that the key words or phrases you enter can either be in lowercase or uppercase. Also, it's unnecessary to type the entire word. Windows will search for topics that come as close as possible to matching a partial term.

Printing Help

You can get a printout of any topic in Help. First, find the item you want to print, then select the *Print Topic* command from the File menu in Help. As the topic is being printed, a dialog box will appear displaying a *Cancel* button. You can stop printing by clicking the *Cancel* button.

1. Make sure your printer is turned on and ready to print.
2. To print a copy of the current topic, select the *Print Topic* command from the File menu in Help.

3. When the topic is finished printing, quit Help by selecting the *Exit* command from the File menu.
4. Exit Windows from Program Manager after verifying that the *Save Settings on Exit* command in the Options menu is toggled off.

NOTE

The menu bar in the Help window contains two other items not mentioned above: Edit and Bookmark. The *Copy...* command in the Edit menu lets you place a topic in Clipboard for printing or pasting to another application. The *Annotate...* command in Edit makes it possible to add your own comments to a particular topic. The *Define...* command in the Bookmark menu allows you to mark the topics you use often for quick reference. For more information on using these commands, press the F1 function key while in the Help window and choose the *Help commands* option.

COMING ATTRACTIONS . . .

Congratulations. You've mastered the primary concepts and skills necessary for using Windows. To recap quickly, you began by working with the menus and icons that start and stop an application, proceeded from there to organize and manipulate the items on your desktop, and ended by using Help to find information on a variety of topics.

In Chapters 3 and 4, you'll expand your Windows expertise by becoming proficient at managing both programs and files.

KEY TERMS

About [Application]   Help menu option that shows the copyright, version, and name of the current application. When this command is selected from certain applications (e.g., Program Manager or File Manager), it also reveals the mode of operations Windows is currently running under (standard or enhanced) and the memory available.

Annotate...   Edit menu command that lets you add your own comments to a topic.

Application icon   A graphical representation (picture) of a running application that has been minimized. Application icons are visible on the desktop (Windows background).

Application window   A rectangular screen area that contains a software application. Application windows can be opened and closed, resized, and moved. You can have several windows open at a time on the desktop.

Back   Help button that lets you return to the previous Help window.

Clicking   A term referring to a single press of the left mouse button.

Command   A word or phrase that instructs Windows to carry out some specific activity.

Contents   Help button that displays the index of topics available for the current application.

Control-menu box   Double-clicking on this window element (a small box located in the upper left corner of a window) closes the window.

Copy...   Edit menu command that lets you copy a topic to Clipboard for printing or pasting to another application.

Define...   Bookmark menu command that marks a topic for quick reference.

Dialog boxes   Rectangular boxes that appear anytime a command with an ellipsis (...) is executed. Dialog boxes request and/or provide information.

Document icons   Graphic symbols that represent documents which can be expanded into document windows. Document icons all look the same; only their titles serve to distinguish them.

Document windows   Variety of window found inside an application window. Multiple document windows permit you to work with more than one project at a time.

Double-clicking   Two rapid presses and releases of the left mouse button.

Dragging   A procedure for relocating an object on the Windows desktop. It involves pointing at the item, pressing and holding the left mouse button, sliding the mouse in the direction you want it to move, and releasing the button when the item is positioned in the new location.

Drop-down menus   A submenu that appears when an option is selected from the menu bar.

Frame   The border surrounding all windows.

Glossary   Help button that produces a list of definitions for terms used in the current application.

Help   A menu bar option, appearing in many application windows, that provides on-line assistance for users.

History   Help button that shows a list of previous topics so you can easily return to an earlier information display.

How to Use Help   Help option that presents brief instructions on the Windows Help facility.

Maximize box   Clicking on this window element (a small box with an up arrow in the upper right corner of a window) expands the window to fill the entire desktop.

Menu   A means of grouping together commands designed to achieve some collective purpose.

Menu bar   Bar located at the top of an application window that lists the options available for the current application.

Minimize box   Clicking on this window element, the box just left of the maximize box, will reduce a window to an icon.

Next   Help arrow button that allows you to move forward through a series of related topics.

Pointer   A small graphic image that floats on the screen and moves correspondingly with the motions of your mouse. The pointer will assume a different shape to indicate its present capabilities. Figure 2-21 illustrates the various pointer shapes and associated functions.

Previous   Help arrow button that allows you to move back through a series of related topics.

Print Topic   File menu command in the Help window that lets you print the current topic.

Program item icons   Icons that start applications and appear only in the group windows of Program Manager.

Program Manager   The central staging area for launching and managing applications from Windows.

Scroll bars   Window elements, along the right and bottom of a window, that let you view parts of a document too large to fit in the window.

Search   Help button that is the fastest method for finding a particular Help topic.

Search for Help on...   Help option that activates the search facility for locating key terms and commands.

Title bar   Window element, at the top of a window, that displays the name of the application or document. When there is more than one window on the desktop, the title bar of the active window (the one you're working with) changes color or intensity.

WIN   The command entered at the DOS prompt to activate the Windows environment.

Windows Tutorial   Help option that activates a brief step-by-step introduction to the Windows environment.

Workspace   The area in the center of a window where most of the work on an application is carried out.

Figure 2-21. Pointer shapes.

Shape	Name	Purpose
⇨	Arrow	Moves a window and activates an application.
 ⧗	Hour-glass	Indicates that Windows is occupied with a task requiring its full attention. You must wait until the cursor changes shape before continuing.
 ⬌⬍	Sizing	Adjusts the size of a window by dragging a corner or a side.
⊘	Prevent	Indicates you're attempting to perform a nonallowable action.
 👆	Hand	Jumps between Help topics.
I	I-Beam	Lets you type text.
 +	Cross-hair	Lets you work with graphic images (you'll see this shape later in Paintbrush).

EXERCISES

The practice exercises in this and the ensuing chapters will provide a review of the concepts and techniques covered in the lab tutorials. Each exercise will conclude with a printout that you can verify with your instructor. Always make sure you have a printout at the end of each exercise.

2-1. The instructions below will furnish you with the opportunity to review the material presented in Lab 2-1. You'll also learn how to use another Windows accessory program—Notepad.

Graded Exercise

    a. Start Windows if it is not already active.
    b. Click on Window in the menu bar of Program Manager.
    c. Choose the Accessories group by clicking on the *Accessories* option in the drop-down Window menu.
    d. Load Clock by double-clicking on the Clock icon in the Accessories group window.
    e. Minimize Clock by clicking on its minimize box.
    f. Load Notepad by double-clicking on the Notepad icon in the Accessories group window.

Notepad is a very simple text editor (word processor). You are going to use Notepad to enter some text and then print a copy of it.

g. Type the following text, substituting your name and the current
date where indicated. Press the Enter key at the end of each line to
move the cursor down to the next line.

Windows 3.1 Tutorial
Chapter 2
Exercise 2-1
[Your name]
[Today's date]

Compare your screen to the one shown in Figure 2–22. Then make sure your
printer is on-line and ready to print.

Figure 2–22.
Notepad with
text displayed
in its work-
space.

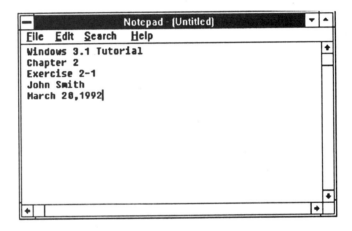

h. To print your text, click on the *Print* command in the File menu of
Notepad.
i. Quit Notepad by clicking on the *Exit* command from the File menu.
Click the *No* button when Notepad asks if you want to save the
document.
j. Restore the Clock window by double-clicking on its icon.
k. Quit Clock by double-clicking on the control-menu box in the
upper left corner of its window.
l. You may now quit Windows after verifying that the *Save Settings on
Exit* command in the Options menu of Program Manager is
switched off.

2–2. In this exercise, you'll review the concepts and procedures covered in Lab 2–2. We'll focus on the techniques for manipulating windows and icons. At the end of the session, you'll print a Help topic.

> **a.** If necessary, launch Windows.
> **b.** Choose the Accessories option from the Window menu in Program Manager.
> **c.** Start Clock by double-clicking on its icon in the Accessories group window.
> **d.** To resize the Clock window, place your pointer on the right border of the window. When the cursor assumes the shape of the sizing pointer, press and hold the left mouse button.
> **e.** Drag the frame of the window all the way to the right edge of your desktop and release the button.

Note that this action makes the window wider but not taller.

> **f.** Next, place the pointer in the upper left corner of the Clock window. The pointer will change to the shape of the sizing pointer angled at approximately a 45° angle. Drag the frame to the right and down. When the frame is approximately one-half the width and height of the original Clock window, release the mouse button.
> **g.** Minimize Clock by clicking on its minimize box.

The Clock window will shrink to an icon in the lower portion of the screen.

> **h.** Load Notepad by double-clicking its icon in the Accessories group window.

Notepad is a simple word or text processor for creating short documents such as memos and notes. However, for our present purposes, you'll be using it to practice your window manipulation skills.

> **i.** Move the pointer to the title bar of the Notepad window and drag it to the bottom of the screen.
> **j.** Then move the window back to the top of the screen using the same technique.
> **k.** Minimize Notepad and Program Manager.

All your application windows should now be minimized (see Figure 2–23). We can now practice arranging the icons on your desktop.

Figure 2–23.
The Windows
desktop with
Clock, Note-
pad, and
Program
Manager
reduced to
icons.

Figure 2–23.
The Windows
desktop with
Clock, Note-
pad, and
Program
Manager
reduced to
icons.

l. To organize your desktop so it matches Figure 2–24, drag the Program Manager icon to the upper left corner of the screen, drag the Clock icon to the center, and drag Notepad to the lower right.

m. Now, move the icons for Program Manager, Clock, and Notepad to the bottom of the desktop, as pictured in Figure 2–23.

n. Open the Program Manager window by double-clicking on its icon. Next, access the Help menu by clicking on it in the menu bar of Program Manager. Then select the *Contents* command from the Help menu.

o. Click on the topic *Start an Application* displayed in green.

p. When the topic appears, click on the topic *Starting an Application from a Group.*

q. After the information on the selected topic materializes, take a moment to review it. Maximize the window for easier viewing of the entire topic.

r. Make sure your printer is ready and then choose the *Print Topic* command from the File menu to print a copy of the current topic. Restore the Help window to its original size.

s. Quit the Help, Clock, and Notepad applications. To exit a mini-mized application, first expand the application icon by double-

Figure 2-24.
The icons for
Program
Manager,
Clock, and
Notepad
arranged in
the upper
left, center,
and lower
right of the
Windows
desktop.

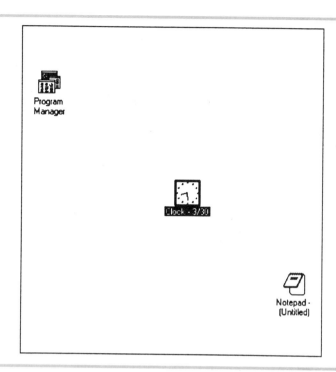

clicking on it and then select the *Exit* command from the File menu. (In the case of the Clock application, you'll need to double-click on its control-menu box to close it.)

t. Minimize the Accessories group window and activate the Main group by selecting it from the Window menu in Program Manager.

u. You may end your Windows session after verifying that the *Save Settings on Exit* command in the Options menu of Program Manager is switched off.

2-3. The following directions review the concepts and procedures demonstrated in Lab 2-3. You'll practice using the most interesting features in the Windows Help facility.

Graded Exercise

a. If it is not already active, start Windows.

b. Select the *Contents* command from the Help menu in Program Manager.

c. Maximize the Help window.

d. Click on the topic *Organizing Applications and Documents*.

e. When the next Help screen appears, select the topic *Arranging Windows and Icons*.

f. Since the phrase "title bar" is displayed in green, you can view additional information about this term by pointing at it and pressing the left mouse button. Click again when you finish reading the explanation.

g. Click on the *Back* button to return to the original list of topics in the Program Manager Help Contents.

h. Click on the *Search* button to display the Search dialog box and enter the following term in the text box: starting applications

i. Click the *Show Topics* button to display the results of the search.

j. Click on the *Starting an Application* option in the bottom list box and select the *Go To* button.

k. When the topic appears, use the *Print Topic* command from the File menu to produce a hardcopy of it.

l. Close the Help window and exit Windows after verifying that the *Save Settings on Exit* command in the Options menu of Program Manager is switched off.

REVIEW QUESTIONS

True or False Questions

1. **T   F**   Using the *Search* feature of Help is slower and less efficient than the *Next* and *Previous* buttons.

2. **T   F**   Contents is a list of the Help topics available for the current application.

3. **T   F**   Icons cannot be moved across the Windows desktop.

4. **T   F**   To start Windows, simply type GO WINDOWS at the DOS prompt.

5. **T   F**   Windows can be used without a mouse, but it's very difficult.

6. **T   F**   Double-clicking means to click both the right and left mouse buttons simultaneously.

7. **T   F**   Double-clicking the control-menu box of a window closes the window.

8. **T   F**   Scroll bars are used to make the active window larger or smaller.

9. **T   F**   Maximizing a window expands the window to fill the entire desktop (screen).

10. **T   F**   Clicking the *Back* button in the Help window sends you to the previous Help window.

Multiple Choice Questions

1. Which of these Help features is a brief tutorial of how to use Windows' Help facility?

   a. Contents
   b. How to Use Help
   c. Commands

   d. Procedures
   e. None of the above

2. Which of the following are examples of a basic window type?

   a. Text window
   b. Document window
   c. Application window

   d. b and c
   e. a and c

3. The basic skills of mouse navigation include all but one of these techniques.

   a. Clicking
   b. Double-clicking

   c. Triple-clicking
   d. Dragging

4. Which pointer shape indicates that you can enter text?

   a. Hand pointer
   b. Hourglass pointer

   c. Arrow pointer
   d. I-beam pointer

   2 — which indicate wait, processing ?-b

5. Which window command shrinks an application window to an icon?

   a. Maximize
   b. Restore
   c. Neutralize

   d. Iconize
   e. None of the above

6. Which icon type represents a program running in the background?

   a. Program item icons
   b. Applications icons

   c. Document icons
   d. Graphic icons

7. Which is NOT a characteristic of the Search option?

   a. Accessed from the Help window
   b. Faster than History
   c. Efficient

   d. b and c
   e. None of the above

8. In order to move a window, you place the mouse pointer on which part of it?

   a. Scroll bar
   b. Title bar
   c. Menu bar

   d. Movement guidance bar
   e. None of the above

9. Which of the following is used to request and provide additional information?

   a. Help boxes
   b. Control boxes

   c. Dialog boxes
   d. Exit boxes

10. Which window element displays the name of the application?

    a. Title bar   d. Frame

    b. Menu bar   e. None of the above

    c. Workspace

CHAPTER 3

Managing Programs

● *Objectives*

When you complete this chapter, you'll be able to:

1. **Switch among different application windows.**
2. **Organize application windows and application icons.**
3. **Exit applications safely.**
4. **Use and recognize group windows and program icons.**
5. **Customize Program Manager by adding program icons and group windows.**
6. **Copy and move program icons.**
7. **Organize program icons and group windows.**
8. **Delete program icons and group windows.**

OVERVIEW

In this chapter, we'll discuss Task List and Program Manager. With Task List, you can rapidly switch between applications and automatically organize their appearance on your desktop. Program Manager, perhaps the most important component of Microsoft Windows 3.1, provides the passageway to all your applications. It allows you to find and launch the right application quickly and easily. You'll learn to recognize and customize the elements that make up the graphical environment of Program Manager.

LAB 3–1   USING TASK LIST

Task List enables you to switch among applications, safely exit from running programs, and organize the windows and icons on your desktop. This lab shows you how to select the window you want to work in, display windows in a variety of patterns that give you unique perspectives, tidy up your desktop by neatly arranging icons, and clear unnecessary applications from your desktop.

Switching among Application Windows

When you have multiple windows open on your desktop, the one you're currently working with is called the **active** window. As you saw in the last chapter, the active window appears in the foreground, partially or completely covering the inactive windows in the background. You can easily recognize the active window because its title bar is a different color or intensity from the inactive windows.

The simplest way of switching to an inactive window is to click on it. However, if the application you wish to work in is entirely obscured by other windows, you'll need another way of activating it. Task List provides the means for switching among open applications, whether they are visible or not. Unlike Program Manager and File Manager, Task List is not a separate application—it is always available.

You can double-click anywhere on the desktop to display Task List. When the entire desktop is taken up by application windows, you can call Task List by selecting the *Switch To...* command from the control-menu in any window. Let's practice switching between applications by first clicking on them and then using Task List.

CTRL+ESC

1. Start Windows.
2. Select the Accessories group window from Program Manager and launch the Clock application.
3. If necessary, move Clock so that part of it lies outside the borders of Program Manager.
4. Click on Program Manager to make it the active window.
5. To make Clock the active window, click on it.
6. Move the Clock window so that all of it lies within the borders of Program Manager (see Figure 3–1).
7. Click on Program Manager to make it the active window.

Clock has disappeared behind Program Manager. Since you can't click on what you can't see, you'll need to summon Task List to switch to the Clock window and bring it into the foreground again.

8. Point at an empty portion of your desktop and double-click.

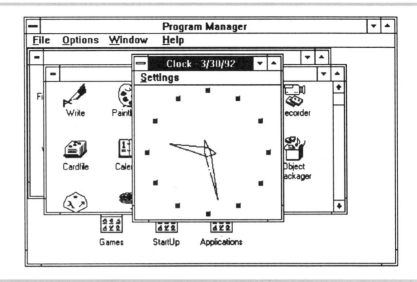

Figure 3–1.
The Clock
positioned
within the
borders of the
Program
Manager
window.

Figure 3–2 shows the Task List dialog box. Task List uses it to display the applications presently open on your desktop. The active application is listed at the top, with other applications ordered by how recently they were activated. The six buttons in the lower portion of the dialog box give you these options:

- **Switch To** the highlighted application.
- **End Task** safely exits the highlighted application.
- **Cancel** quits Task List. (You can also exit Task List by clicking on any window or icon.)
- **Cascade** organizes the applications on your desktop into an overlapping stack so that the title bar of each remains visible.

Figure 3–2.
The Task List
dialog box.

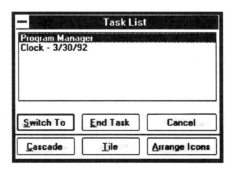

- **Tile** organizes applications in smaller sized windows so that each is given an equal space on your desktop.
- **Arrange Icons** organizes icons evenly across the bottom of your desktop.

There are two ways to switch to another application from Task List. One method involves clicking on the application (which highlights it) and then selecting the *Switch To* button. The other way is simply to double-click on the application.

  9. Select the Clock application from Task List.
10. Choose the *Switch To* button.

Clock is again in the foreground as the active window. Task List makes it possible to activate easily any open application. But what if the desktop is entirely covered and you can't call Task List by double-clicking?

Figure 3–3.

11. Click on the maximize box of Program Manager so that it covers your whole desktop. (Clock will again disappear.)
12. To summon Task List, point at the control-menu box in the upper left of the Program Manager window and click once.

The control menu drops down, as pictured in Figure 3–3. The first six commands in this menu are for use with a keyboard. They duplicate the mouse actions you learned in Chapter 2. However, the last command, *Switch To...*, will cause Task List to materialize even when the entire desktop is obscured.

___NOTE_____

Another method of calling Task List is to hold down the Ctrl key and press the Esc key. This is especially useful for switching between DOS applications that require the full-screen mode for operation.

_____

13. Click on the *Switch To...* command in the control-menu to call Task List.
14. Double-click on Clock in the dialog box.

Once again, Clock becomes active and visible. Whether you are working with two applications, like Clock and Program Manager, or ten, you use the same techniques to activate a window. You either point and click, if any part of the desired application is visible, or you call Task List and switch to it when the window is totally concealed.

Arranging Application Windows and Application Icons

You can organize your desktop by manually sizing and moving windows; however, Task List will automatically do this for you. The *Tile, Cascade,* and *Arrange Icons* buttons arrange both windows and icons in preset patterns for easy viewing.

Choosing the *Tile* button sorts your application windows so they occupy an equal area of the desktop.

1. Return Program Manager to its original size by clicking the restore box in the upper right corner of your screen. Clock will disappear when Program Manager becomes the active window.
2. Now double-click on the icon for Paintbrush.
3. Move the Paintbrush window so that the Accessories group window is exposed. If necessary, you can move part of Paintbrush beyond the borders of the desktop. (Although some of its contents may disappear from view, they remain intact.)
4. Double-click on the icon for Write.

You now have four application windows open on your desktop: Program Manager, Clock, Paintbrush, and Write. At this point, you cannot view all the windows at once.

5. Summon Task List. The four applications should be listed in the order shown in Figure 3-4.
6. Click on the *Tile* button.

Your screen is now evenly portioned among the applications (see Figure 3-5), so you can view all four of them simultaneously. To select a particular application to work on, simply click on it. If you need more work space, choose the maximize box and the application will fill the entire desktop.

Another way to gain more work area is to display your application in a cascade style. Selecting *Cascade* causes the application windows on your desktop to display diagonally with their title bars showing.

Figure 3–4.
Task List lets
you arrange
application
windows in
either a tile or
cascade
layout.

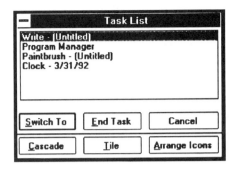

Figure 3–5. The *Tile* button, in Task List, partitions the surface of the desktop
equally among applications.

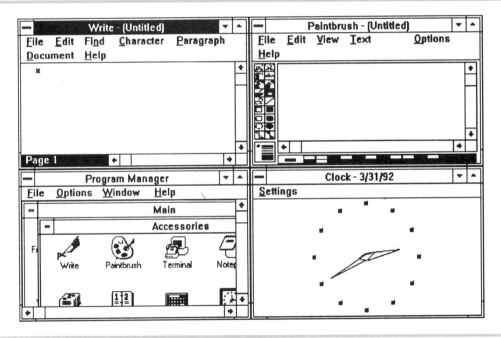

7. To bring up Task List, select the control-menu from any application and click on the command *Switch To...*
8. Click on the *Cascade* button.

Your desktop should look like Figure 3–6, although the application windows may be arranged differently. The order of windows depends upon the sequence in which they were most recently activated.

Figure 3-6. The *Cascade* button, in Task List, layers the application windows so that each title bar is visible.

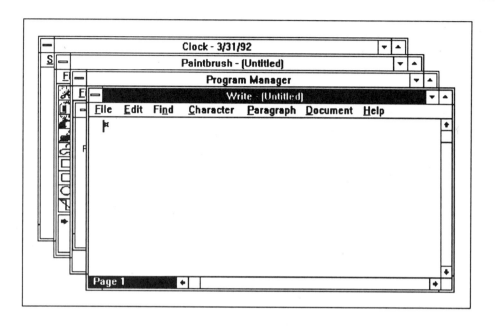

If you are running several applications as icons and have moved them for convenience, you can tidy up your desktop with the *Arrange Icons* button. Clicking it rearranges all application icons evenly across the bottom of your desktop. To see how this works, follow these steps.

 9. Click on the Program Manager's minimize box.
10. Next, use the same action to collapse Write to an icon.
11. Reduce Clock to an icon.
12. Point at the Program Manager's icon, hold down the mouse button, and move the icon to the position shown in Figure 3-7.
13. Relocate both the Write and Clock icons to match Figure 3-7.
14. Call Task List and select the *Arrange Icons* button.

The application icons on your desktop should now be evenly spaced across the bottom, as shown in Figure 3-8. Sometimes the space between icons is insufficient to prevent their titles from overlapping. We'll show you how to correct this problem in Chapter 9.

Figure 3–7. You can drag application icons to any location on the desktop.

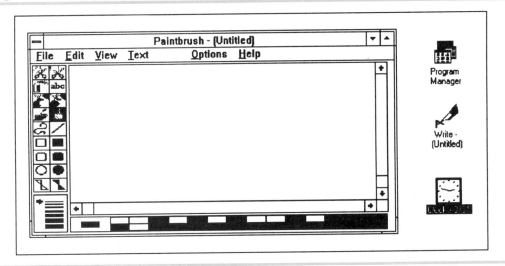

Figure 3–8.
The *Arrange Icons* button, in Task List, repositions your application icons at the bottom of the desktop.

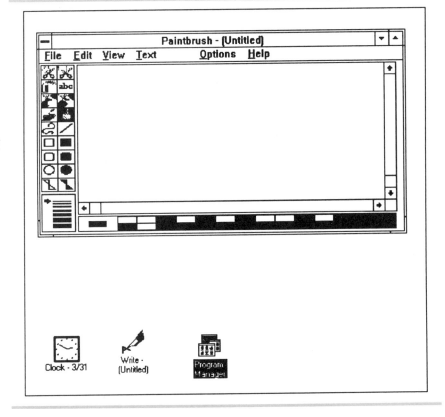

Exiting Applications

Task List will also let you exit applications on your desktop without losing the changes you've made. To quit an application, call Task List, highlight the program, and choose the *End Task* button. The next window on the list moves to the top and becomes active.

1. Summon Task List and use *End Task* to exit Clock.
2. Call Task List again and this time quit the Write application.
3. Exit Paintbrush from Task List.
4. Finally, exit Program Manager from Task List after making sure the *Save Settings on Exit* command in the Options menu of Program Manager is switched off.

LAB 3–2   USING PROGRAM MANAGER

Program Manager is the central staging area for starting and organizing all your application packages. When you begin a Windows session, it appears automatically and continues to run throughout your session. When you quit Program Manager, you quit Windows.

Lab 3–2 demonstrates how to add, move, arrange, and delete program icons and group windows. We'll put all of these capabilities to work in creating a Desktop Publishing group tailored for producing graphically oriented documents.

Using Group Windows and Program Icons

Program Manager uses a series of interior (group) windows to arrange applications into meaningful categories so you can quickly and easily find and launch a program, as illustrated in Figure 3–9. To start an application, you simply select the correct group window and double-click on its program item icon. To choose a group window, you click on its title bar, double-click on its group icon (located at the bottom of Program Manager), or pick it from the Window menu (in the menu bar).

Recognizing Group Windows and Program Icons

Program Manager will display five standard group windows, each with its own program item icons, as shown in Figure 3–10.

Figure 3–9.
Program
Manager with
its Main
group
window
displayed and
the other
groups
represented
by icons
across the
bottom of the
desktop.

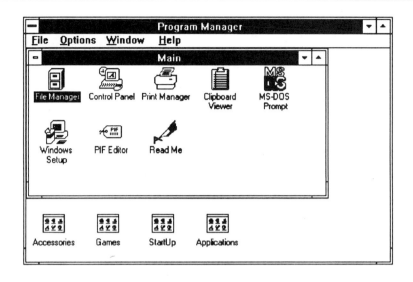

Figure 3–9.
Program
Manager with
its Main
group
window
displayed and
the other
groups
represented
by icons
across the
bottom of the
desktop.

Figure 3–10.
Program
Manager has
five prede-
fined group
windows.

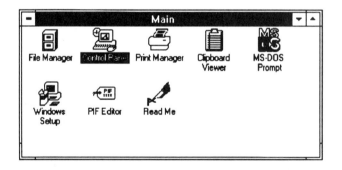

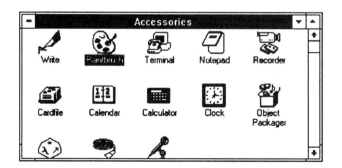

Figure 3–10.
Continued.

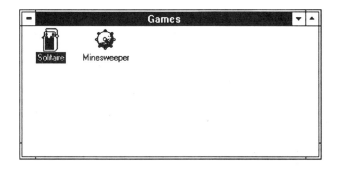

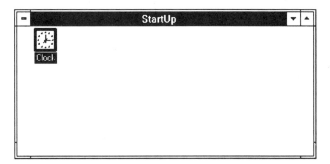

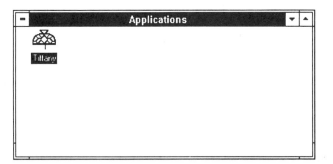

● The **Main group** consists of the File Manager, Control Panel, Print Manager, Clipboard Viewer, MS-DOS Prompt, Windows Setup, PIF Editor, and Read Me.

● The **Accessories group** includes Write, Paintbrush, Terminal, Notepad, Recorder, Cardfile, Calendar, Calculator, Clock, Object Packager, Character Map, Media Player, and Sound Recorder.

● The **Games group** displays two games, Solitaire and Minesweeper.

- The **Startup group** holds programs that you want to start automatically when Windows is launched. For example, placing Clock in this work group will cause it to start each time you launch Windows.
- The **Applications group** contains programs found on your hard disk during the installation process.

The Main group applications are used to manage the Windows environment and your system resources. Each of these programs is briefly described below.

File Manager

- **File Manager** helps you organize the files stored on disk. With it, you can easily find, move, copy, delete, rename, and print disk files.

Control Panel

- **Control Panel** lets you customize the way Windows is configured by altering its startup or default settings. You can change such things as the color scheme, the spacing between the items on your desktop, and even the printer and monitor you are using.

Print Manager

- **Print Manager** allows you to continue working even while you are printing a file. When you tell a Windows application to print, it sends the file to Print Manager instead of to the printer. Print Manager handles the printing task, thus freeing your application for use. From Print Manager, you can also control the order in which files are printed or halt printing of any file.

Clipboard
Viewer

- **Clipboard Viewer** lets you see the temporary storage area for transferring information within or between applications.

MS-DOS
Prompt

- **MS-DOS Prompt** takes you to the bleak world of DOS. Typing "exit" returns you to the haven of Windows.

Windows
Setup

- **Windows Setup** assists you in adding new applications and changing hardware configurations.

PIF Editor

- **PIF Editor** is used to edit Program Information Files, which Windows employs to operate certain non-Windows applications. This program is intended for use by advanced Windows users.

Read Me

- **Read Me** provides information about using Windows.

The Accessories group includes applications for word processing, drawing, and communications along with several less complex, but useful, programs. These applications are described below.

Write

- **Write** is an easy-to-use but limited word processor. It is suitable for day-to-day correspondence such as letters, memos, and short reports. However, it suffers from the lack of either a spell-checker or thesaurus.

Paintbrush

- **Paintbrush** is a full-featured drawing program for creating simple or elaborate color graphics.

Terminal

- **Terminal** allows you to connect your computer to other computers and exchange information via a modem and standard telephone lines.

Notepad

- **Notepad** is a text editor. Text editors are simple word processors and should only be used for short documents such as notes and memos.

Recorder

- **Recorder** registers a sequence of keystrokes and mouse actions to be played back at a later time. This accessory is intended for experienced Windows users.

Cardfile

- **Cardfile** is a self-sorting group of electronic index cards. You can use it to keep track of important information such as names, addresses, and phone numbers.

Calendar

- **Calendar** combines the two most commonly used time-management tools: a month-at-a-glance calendar and a daily appointment book. Calendar has a perpetual calendar and an appointment alarm.

Calculator

- **Calculator** includes a standard calculator as well as a scientific calculator. The standard calculator allows you to do simple calculations and store them in memory. The scientific calculator allows you to do advanced scientific and statistical calculations.

Clock

- **Clock** displays time in either digital or analog format.

Object Packager

- **Object Packager** embeds information from applications that don't support Object Linking and Embedding (OLE) in OLE-compatible applications. (See Chapter 7 for an explanation of Object Linking and Embedding.)

Character Map

- **Character Map** displays a table of the available characters for a font. You can use it to copy and paste special characters into your Windows applications.

Media Player

Sound
Recorder

- **Media Player** accesses CD-ROM disks for playback of multimedia presentations.
- **Sound Recorder** works with a sound device (e.g., a sound board) to record music or other sounds for play-back in a multimedia presentation.

The Games group gives you the opportunity to have fun while you sharpen your skills with the mouse.

Solitaire

Minesweeper

- **Solitaire** is a single-player card game. The computer acts as dealer and scorekeeper.
- **Minesweeper** is a strategy game with the objective of clearing a field containing hidden mines.

The program icons appearing in the Applications group will vary depending upon the programs currently installed on your system. Additional work groups may be present, such as WordPerfect, Lotus Applications, or Paradox for Windows. These work groups will feature program icons specific to their applications. However, they are accessed in the same manner as the applications in the standard group windows.

In the following sections, you'll learn to add to, copy, move, arrange, and delete these program icons. Besides changing the contents of a group window, you'll get a chance to create a new group, use it, and then remove it.

Adding Program Icons

When Windows is installed, it automatically creates four group windows (Main, Accessories, Games, and Startup) and adds the appropriate program item icons to each window. During installation, you are also given the opportunity to select other programs to be added. However, once installed, you must use Control Panel or Program Manager to add more applications. In Chapter 9, we'll discuss the operations of Control Panel. For the moment, we'll concentrate on Program Manager and its more flexible approach to adding applications.

We are going to add a second Write icon to the Accessories group window. The first step in adding a program item icon is to choose the group window you want it placed in.

1. Start Windows.

2. To select the Accessories group window, either double-click its icon at the bottom of Program Manager or pick it from the Window menu.

The next step is to open the File menu in Program Manager and click the *New...* command.

3. Click on File in the menu bar.
4. Choose the *New...* command.

The New Program Object dialog box will appear, as portrayed in Figure 3–11. This dialog box lets you add a new Program Group window or Program Item icon. Since *Program Item* is already selected by default, you need only click the *OK* button. Selecting the *Cancel* button will abort the operation and return you to Program Manager. Clicking the *Help* button will summon assistance on how to use this dialog box.

Figure 3–11.
The New
Program
Object dialog
box.

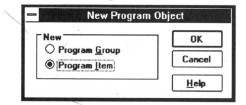

5. Click on *OK*.

Clicking *OK* in the New Program Object dialog box causes the Program Item Properties dialog box to open, as shown in Figure 3–12. You enter the label for the new icon in the *Description* text box, then type the name of the file that starts the application in the *Command Line* text box. The last two text boxes are optional. The *Working Directory* text box lets you enter a subdirectory for storing the new application's data files, while the *Shortcut Key* text box makes it possible to start the program with keystrokes.

6. In the *Description* text box, type: Write-2

If you are unaware or unsure of the file name that launches the application, click on the *Browse...* button in the Program Item Properties dialog box.

Figure 3–12.
The Program
Item Proper-
ties dialog
box lets you
create a new
program item
icon.

7. Choose the *Browse...* button.

This action will cause the Browse dialog box to appear with a list of available program files, as pictured in Figure 3–13. To view a different directory, select it from the *Directories* list box. (A directory is simply a group of files stored under the same name. We'll talk more about directories in Chapter 4, *Managing Files.*) To view a different disk drive, click on the arrow in the *Drives* drop-down list box and select the drive you want.

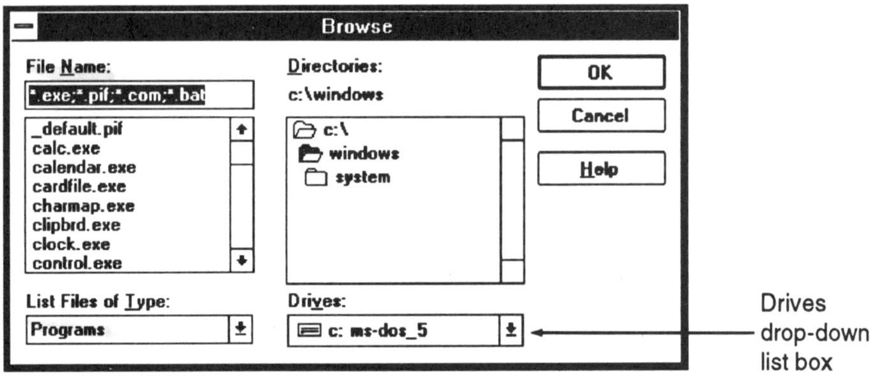

Figure 3–13.
The Browse
dialog box
displays a list
of available
programs.

Since the file name we are searching for is in the current directory, you can simply highlight it and then click the *OK* button.

8. Scroll down to the write.exe file at the bottom of the list and click it.
9. Click the *OK* button.

After clicking the *OK* button, you are returned to the Program Item Properties dialog box. Notice the *Command Line* text box has been filled in for you. At this point, you can select the *OK* button to add the application to the Accessories group. Program Manager will display it with the icon provided by the developers of the program.

10. Click the *OK* button in the Program Item Properties dialog box to add Write-2 to the Accessories group window.

At this point, your Accessories group should match the one shown in Figure 3–14.

Figure 3–14.
The Accessories window shows a second Write icon.

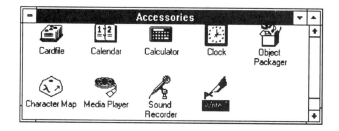

___NOTE___

DOS applications do not have icons. So Program Manager assigns a default DOS icon. However, by clicking the *Change Icon...* button in the Program Item Properties dialog box, you can change the default DOS icon to a generic icon. The Select Icon dialog box allows you to choose from a list of generic icons for such applications as word processors, spreadsheets, and databases.

Adding Group Windows

Adding a group window is simpler than adding a program item. You begin the same way, by opening the File menu in Program Manager and picking the *New...* command. But this time, when the New Program Object dialog box appears, you select the *Program Group* instead of the *Program Item* option. This causes the Program Group Properties dialog box to be displayed, as illustrated in Figure 3–15. The *Description* text box lets you name the group window. You can ignore the *Group File* text box because Program Manager automatically names the group file for you.

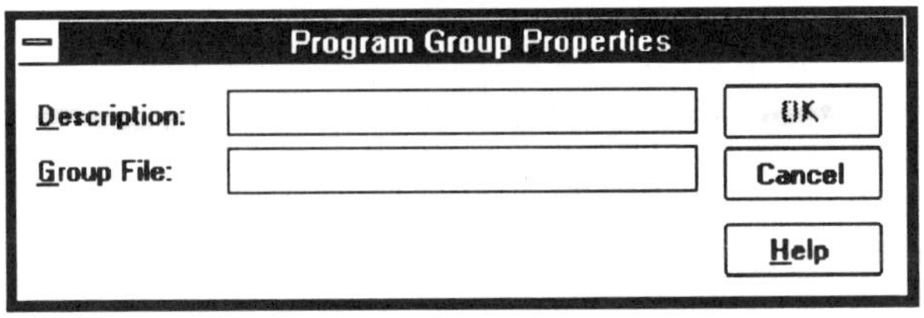

Figure 3–15.
The Program
Group
Properties
dialog box.

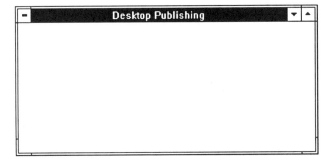

1. Open the File menu in Program Manager and choose the *New...*
   command.
2. Click on the *Program Group* option in the New Program Object
   dialog box and then select *OK*.
3. In the *Description* text box of the Program Group Properties dialog
   box, type: **Desktop Publishing** Leave the Group File text box
   blank.
4. Click the *OK* button, and the new group window pictured in Figure
   3-16 appears.

Figure 3–16.
The group
window
"Desktop
Publishing"
currently
contains no
program item
icons.

Copying Program Icons

You **copy** an icon from one group window to another by holding down
the Ctrl key, dragging the icon to the other window, positioning it, and
releasing. To facilitate this process, it's best first to reposition the group
windows you're copying from and to. They should be placed next to
each other but not overlapping. This ensures that both windows will
remain visible while you're copying between them.

The techniques for moving and resizing group windows are the
same as for application windows. However, group windows must

remain within Program Manager's workspace. If part of a group window is moved beyond the borders of Program Manager, a scroll bar(s) appears so you can bring it back into view.

Now that you have created the Desktop Publishing group window, all you need to do is to place the icons for Paintbrush and Write in it. To transfer program item icons between group windows, you can either copy or move them. When you copy an icon from one group to another, both groups end up with the same icon. Since we want to place the Paintbrush icon in our new group, and at the same time retain it for the Accessories group, we'll copy it.

1. Reduce the Main group window to an icon.
2. Use the move and size procedures you learned in the previous chapter to reposition the Accessories window and the Desktop Publishing window so that they closely resemble Figure 3-17.

Figure 3-17.
Placing group windows next to each other, but not overlapping, makes copying icons between them easier and faster.

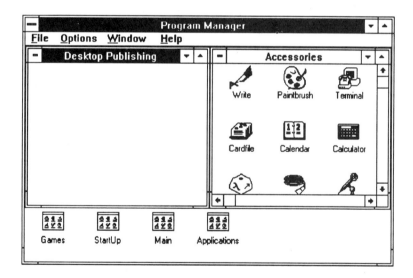

3. Scroll the Accessories window to expose the Paintbrush icon, point at it, press and hold down the Ctrl key, and hold down the left mouse button.
4. Drag the copy of Paintbrush to the Desktop Publishing group window, place the icon approximately in the position shown in Figure 3-18, release the Ctrl key, and then release the mouse button.

Figure 3–18.
The Desktop
Publishing
group after
the program
icons for
Paintbrush
and Write-2
have been
transferred
from the
Accessories
group.

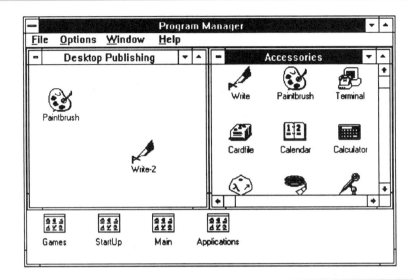

Moving Program Icons

To **move** an icon between group windows, you drag it from one window to the other, position the icon, and release it. The mouse pointer will change to a little round circle with a line through it when it is outside a group window. This shape signals that you can't release the icon there.

With the Paintbrush icon already in the Desktop Publishing window, you need only add the Write program to complete the new work group. Since you created a second icon for this application, Write-2, you can simply move it from the Accessories group to the Desktop Publishing group.

1. Locate the Write-2 icon in the Accessories window.
2. Point at it, hold the mouse button, and drag the icon to the Desktop Publishing window.
3. Position it as shown in Figure 3–18 and then release the mouse button.

Arranging Program Icons

When you copy or move program icons, your group windows can become disorganized and untidy. Moving, resizing, and arranging group windows can also cause problems with the way program icons display. You can manually drag the icons into a more organized format or let Program Manager do it for you. The *Arrange Icons* command, in the Windows menu, automatically organizes all the program icons in the currently active window. It rearranges them to take advantage of the window's present size and shape.

Let's use Program Manager to rearrange the icons in our new group window.

1. If the Desktop Publishing window isn't active, click on it.
2. From the Windows menu, select the *Arrange Icons* command and watch the Paintbrush and Write-2 icons form a straight line, as illustrated in Figure 3–19.

Figure 3–19. The Desktop Publishing group window after the *Arrange Icons* command has been issued.

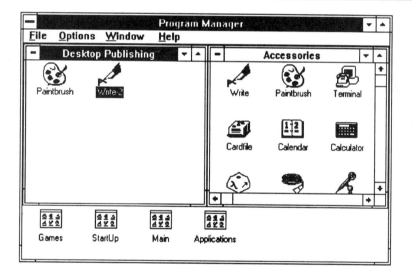

___NOTE_____

If you don't want to hassle with activating group windows and issuing *Arrange Icons* commands each time a group window becomes disordered, you can use the *Auto Arrange* option. *Auto Arrange* is toggled on from the Options menu in Program Manager. When it's on, a check mark will appear in front of it. Now, whenever group windows are moved, sized, or arranged, the program icons will be organized to fit the new layout. Toggling the *Auto Arrange* switch again turns off the option.

Arranging Group Windows

As you open and move group windows, they have a tendency to cover or completely obscure each other. Program Manager provides two commands for automatically rearranging group windows: *Cascade* and *Tile*. *Cascade* resizes and layers your group windows into a stack with titles showing. *Tile* portions the workspace in Program Manager evenly among the open group windows. Both the *Cascade* and the *Tile* commands are located in the Windows menu of the Program Manager.

When you first start Windows, Program Manager cascades all open group windows. The active group window is always in front of the stack. Clicking the title bar of a group window farther back in the stack immediately moves it to the front and makes it the active window. To reorder the stack, you'll need to issue the *Cascade* command.

Let's use the *Cascade* command to clean up the working space in Program Manager.

1. Open the Windows menu in Program Manager.
2. Click the *Cascade* command.

After clicking on *Cascade*, your screen should look like Figure 3-20 with the Desktop Publishing group in front. Also observe that the group icons across the bottom of Program Manager were rearranged to take better advantage of the available space.

Figure 3-20.
The *Cascade* command layers the group windows so their title bars are visible.

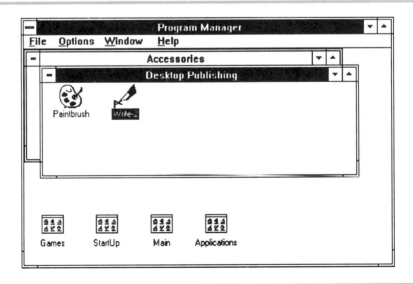

When you are working with more than five group windows, use *Tile* to arrange them instead of *Cascade*. Cascading will cause the windows to overlap and conceal their contents. Tiling guarantees an even division of the available workspace among groups. In a tiled layout, the active window is always located in the upper left corner of the workspace. Activating a different group window has no effect on the position of the window, unlike in a layered stack where the active window comes to the forefront.

3. Open the Main group window.
4. Issue the *Tile* command from the Windows menu in Program Manager.

Figure 3–21 displays the Main group, Desktop Publishing group, and Accessories group from left to right, respectively.

Figure 3–21. The *Tile* command allots each group window an equal portion of the available workspace in Program Manager.

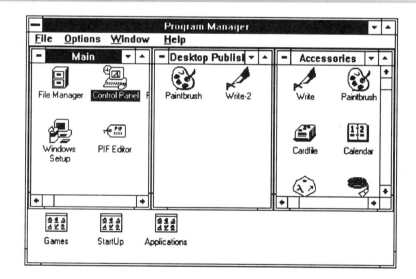

Deleting Program Icons

The time will come when you no longer have use for a particular application or even an entire group of applications. Windows makes it easy to remove program icons and group windows from Program Manager. However, it should be made abundantly clear that deleting an icon or group has no effect on the files stored on your disk. It only erases the **graphical link** between Windows and the program files on your disk.

DEL Key

To delete a program item icon from a group window, click on the icon, choose the *Delete...* command from the File menu in Program Manager, and *Yes* when asked to verify the deletion.

1. Click on the icon for Write-2.
2. Select the *Delete...* command from the File menu in Program Manager.
3. When the Delete dialog box appears (see Figure 3–22), click the *Yes* button to confirm the removal of the Write-2 program icon.

Figure 3–22.
The Delete
dialog box.

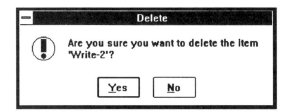

Deleting Group Windows

There are two ways to delete a group window. You can take the time to delete or move all the program icons from the group, make it the active window, select *Delete...* from the File menu, and verify the deletion order. A second, and quicker, method is to reduce the window to an icon, click on it, select *Delete...* from the File menu, and respond *Yes* to confirm the deletion. This technique removes both the group window and its program icons at the same time.

1. Collapse the Desktop Publishing window into an icon by clicking on its minimize box.
2. Click once on the Desktop Publishing icon. (If the control-menu pops up, ignore it.)
3. Issue the *Delete...* command from the File menu.
4. When the Delete dialog box appears, check to make sure the Desktop Publishing group is chosen for deletion. (If not, cancel the operation.)
5. Click the *Yes* button to confirm the removal of the work group.
6. To review this procedure, use Windows' Help facility to locate and print the topic *Deleting Groups*.

7. As always, exit Windows only after making sure the *Save Settings on Exit* command in the Options menu of Program Manager is switched off.

COMING ATTRACTIONS . . .

You're now able to switch among multiple applications, organize them on your desktop, and clear them away. You've also learned to customize the way programs are represented in Program Manager. By adding, arranging, and removing group windows and program icons, you can tailor Windows to suit your personal requirements.

In Chapter 4, you'll discover how Windows makes managing disk files as easy, and fun, as managing programs.

KEY TERMS

Accessories group   Work group window that includes Write, Paintbrush, Terminal, Notepad, Recorder, Cardfile, Calendar, Calculator, Clock, and Object Packager.

Active   When you have multiple windows open on your desktop, the one you're currently working with is called the active window. The active window is easily recognized because its title bar has a different color or intensity from the other windows.

Applications group   Group that contains programs found on your hard disk during the installation of Microsoft Windows 3.1.

Arrange Icons   Window menu command that organizes icons evenly across the bottom of your desktop.

Calculator   A Windows accessory program that provides the functions of a standard calculator as well as a scientific calculator. The standard calculator allows you to do simple calculations and store them in memory. The scientific calculator lets you do advanced scientific and statistical calculations.

Calendar   The Windows Calendar combines the two most commonly used time-management tools: a month-at-a-glance calendar and a daily appointment book. Calendar has a perpetual calendar and an appointment alarm.

Cancel   Task List command that quits the Task List. (You can also exit Task List by clicking on any window or icon.)

Cardfile   A Windows accessory program that offers the capabilities of an index card file for keeping track of information such as names, addresses, and phone numbers.

Cascade   The Task List command that organizes the applications on your desktop into an overlapping stack so that the title bar of each remains visible.

Character Map   A Windows accessory program that displays a table of the available characters for a font. You can use it to copy and paste special characters into your Windows applications.

Clipboard Viewer   A Windows utility that lets you see the temporary storage area for transferring information within and between applications.

Clock   A Windows accessory program that displays time in either digital or analog format.

Control Panel   The Windows utility, accessed from the Main group window, that offers options for customizing Windows. You can change such things as the color scheme, the spacing between the items on your desktop, and even the printer and monitor you are using.

Copy   You copy an icon from one group window to another by holding down the Ctrl key, dragging the icon to the other window, positioning it, and releasing.

Delete   The Program Manager File menu command that lets you delete Program item icons and group windows. The files and programs are not deleted, just the windows and icons assigned to represent them with Windows.

End Task   The Task List command that safely exits the active or highlighted application.

File Manager   The Windows utility, launched from the Main group window, that helps you organize the files stored on disk. With it, you can easily find, move, copy, delete, rename, and print disk files.

Games group   Work group window that displays two games, Solitaire and Minesweeper.

Graphical link   The method that Windows uses to attach icons and groups to the underlying files on the disk.

Main group   Work group that consists of File Manager, Control Panel, Print Manager, Clipboard, MS-DOS Prompt, Windows Setup, PIF Editor, and Read Me.

Media Player   A Windows accessory program that accesses CD-ROM disks for play-back of multimedia presentations.

Minesweeper   A strategy game with the objective of clearing a field containing hidden mines. You are provided with two devices for accomplishing the stated goal, a mine detector and your (imaginary) foot.

Move   To move an icon between group windows, you drag it from one window to the other, position the icon, and release it.

MS-DOS Prompt   The Main group option that takes you to the bleak world of DOS. Typing exit returns you to the haven of Windows.

Notepad   A Windows accessory program for creating and editing short documents such as notes and memos.

Object Packager   Windows accessory program that lets you create icons to represent information from other applications.

Paintbrush   Windows accessory program that lets you create colorful and detailed drawings.

PIF Editor   Windows program that is used to edit Program Information Files, which Windows employs to operate certain non-Windows applications. It is intended for use by advanced Windows users.

Print Manager   Windows utility that automatically handles the printing of all Windows files and, therefore, lets you continue working even while you are printing.

Program Manager   The Windows utility that is the central staging platform for starting and organizing all your application packages. When you begin a Windows session, Program Manager appears automatically and continues to run throughout the session.

Read Me   A program item in the Main work group that launches Write and loads a document with information on using Windows.

Recorder   Windows utility that lets you record a sequence of keystrokes to be played back at a later time. It is intended for use by experienced Windows users.

Solitaire   A single-player card game. The computer acts as dealer and scorekeeper.

Sound Recorder   Windows accessory program that works with a sound device (e.g., a sound board) to record music or other sounds for playback in a multimedia presentation.

Startup group   Work group window that automatically starts applications when Windows is launched.

Switch To   The Task List command that switches the active window to the highlighted application.

Task List   The Windows utility that enables you to switch among applications, safely exit from running programs, and organize the windows and icons on your desktop.

Terminal   The Windows accessory program that allows you to connect your computer to other computers and exchange information via a modem and a standard telephone line.

Tile   The Task List command that divides your desktop evenly among the application windows currently open.

Windows Setup   The Windows utility, accessed from the Main group option window, that lets you add new applications and change hardware configurations.

Write   The Windows accessory program that provides an executive-level word processor for creating, editing, formatting, and printing documents. It does not contain a spell-checker or thesaurus.

EXERCISES

3-1. This exercise furnishes you the opportunity to review the concepts and techniques demonstrated in Lab 3-1.

a. Start Windows if it is not already active.
b. Select the Accessories group.
c. Load and minimize Clock, Notepad, and Calculator.
d. Summon Task List.
e. Switch to Clock and maximize it.
f. Call Task List and make Notepad the active window. Do not minimize Clock first! Enter the following text in Notepad:

Windows 3.1 Tutorial
Chapter 3
Exercise 3-1
[Your Name]
[Today's Date]

g. Call Task List and make Calculator the active window. Do not minimize Notepad first!
h. Use the *Tile* button from the Task List to organize the windows you now have active.

Compare your screen to the one pictured in Figure 3-23.

i. Make Notepad the active window. Do not resize the window. Leave it tiled. On the line directly below the date, type the names of the six buttons found in the Task List dialog box. Use the Backspace or Delete keys to correct any typographical errors.
j. Check to be sure your printer is ready and on-line. Print your work by selecting the *Print* command from Notepad's File menu.
k. Exit Notepad without saving your document.
l. Use Task List to exit from Clock and Calculator.
m. Exit Windows after making certain the *Save Settings on Exit* command in the Options menu of Program Manager is toggled off.

3-2. The instructions below will review the material in Lab 3-2. You'll create two new group windows and fill them with program item icons.

a. If necessary, start Windows.
b. Select the Accessories group window by double-clicking on its icon.

// MAIN Group

Figure 3-23. Several application windows in a tiled format.

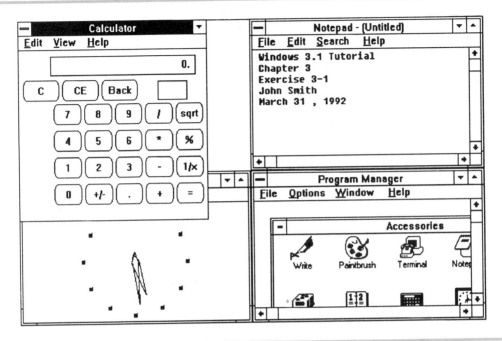

c. Maximize the Program Manager window.
d. Create a new group window by selecting the *New...* command from the Program Manager File menu. Select the *Program Group* option.
e. To name the new group window, click the *Description* text box, and type: Exercise 3-2a
f. Click *OK* to establish the group window.
g. Repeat the last three steps to create a group window called Exercise 3-2b.
h. Select *Tile* from the Program Manager Window menu.

Your screen should now be similar to the one shown in Figure 3-24.

i. Copy the icons for the applications Write, Paintbrush, Terminal, and Notepad to the Exercise 3-2b group window.
j. Now move Write and Notepad from the Exercise 3-2b group window to the Exercise 3-2a group window. Organize the program item icons in both of the new group windows with the *Arrange Icons* command.

Figure 3–24. The Main, Accessories, and the two new empty group windows.

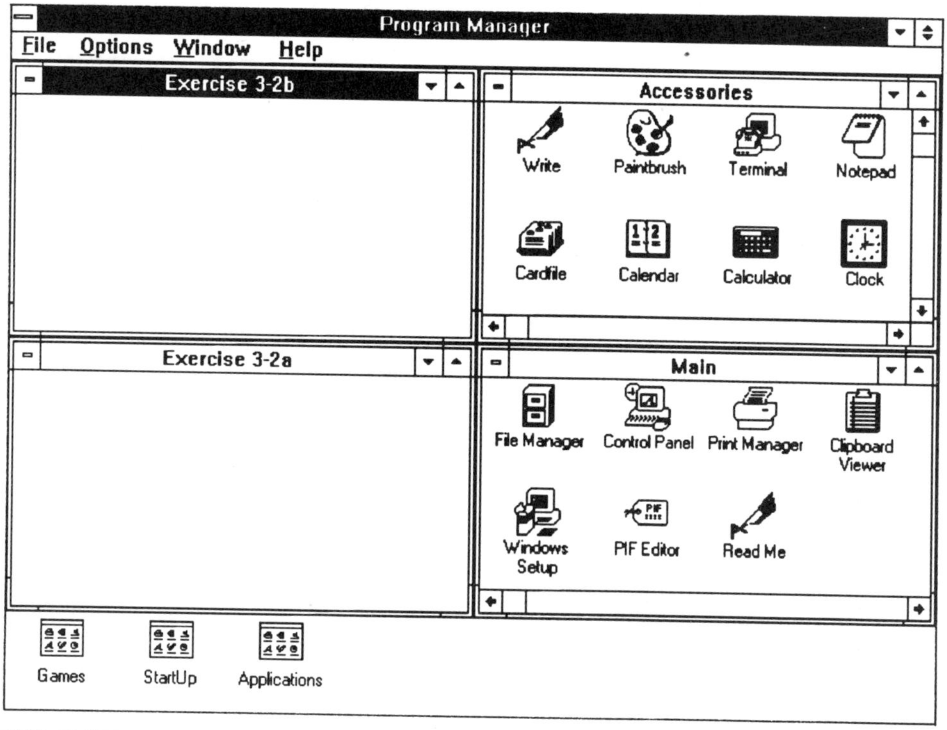

Check your desktop against the one portrayed in Figure 3–25.

k. Use Windows' Help facility to locate and print the topic *Changing Icons*.

l. Delete the two group windows you created.

m. Exit Windows after making sure the *Save Settings on Exit* command in the Options menu of Program Manager is toggled off.

• PRINT SCREEN

• PASTE TO WRITE DOC

• PRINT WRITE DOC. (W/ NAME)

REVIEW QUESTIONS

True or False Questions

1. **T F** You can activate Task List by holding down the Ctrl key and pressing the Esc key.

2. **T F** You copy an icon from one group window to another by holding down the Ctrl key, dragging the icon to the other window, positioning it, and releasing the mouse button.

Figure 3–25. The two new group windows now display several program icons.

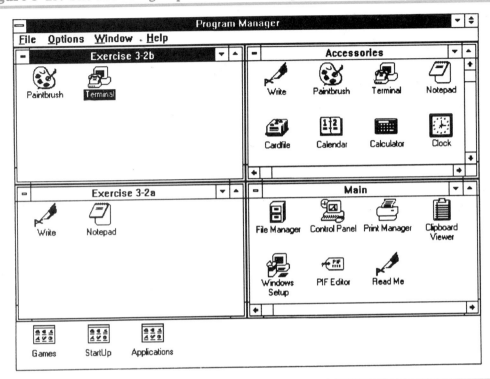

3. **T F** Notepad is a full-featured drawing program for creating simple or elaborate color graphics.

4. **T F** The *Cascade* button divides the available desktop space among the open applications windows.

5. **T F** You move an icon by dragging it from one window to another while holding down the Ctrl key.

6. **T F** The simplest way of switching to an inactive window is to click on it.

7. **T F** When working with more than five windows, you should use the *Tile* option to organize them.

8. **T F** Additional group windows can be added by choosing the *New...* command from the Program Manager File menu and completing the New dialog box.

9. **T F** When you delete a program item icon, you also delete the application it represents.

10. **T F** The command *Arrange Icons* will cause the icons on the desktop to be reorganized in alphabetical order.

Multiple Choice Questions

1. The central or core application of the Windows environment is which of the following?

   a. Control Panel
   b. File Manager
   c. Program Manager
   d. Main group
   e. None of the above

2. In which group would you find the Cardfile application?

   a. Main group
   b. Accessories group
   c. Games group
   d. Windows Applications group
   e. a or c

3. Which of the Windows applications assists you in adding new applications and changing hardware configurations?

   a. Clipboard
   b. File Manager
   c. Control Panel
   d. PIF Editor
   e. None of the above

4. The fastest way to delete a group window and all its item icons is to:

   a. Delete each of the program item icons and then delete the group
   b. Maximize the group window and then delete the group
   c. Minimize the group window and then delete the group
   d. Group windows cannot be deleted while program item icons still remain in the group window

5. In what standard Windows group would you likely find the application "WordPerfect for Windows."

   a. Applications
   b. Main
   c. Accessories
   d. Games
   e. None of the above

6. Which Task List command organizes open windows into an overlapping stack?

   a. *Tile*
   b. *Switch To*
   c. *Arrange Icons*
   d. *Cascade*
   e. None of the above

7. Games are provided with Windows to:

   a. Decrease boredom
   b. Decrease computer anxiety
   c. Increase keyboarding skills
   d. Increase mouse skills
   e. c and d

8. Which method opens the Task List dialog box?

   a. Double-click on an empty portion of the desktop
   b. Press and hold the Ctrl key and then press Esc

c. Click on the control-box and
select *Switch To...*

d. a, b, or c

9. When adding a new program item icon, if you are unsure of the new program's starting command, you can use which Program Item Properties commands to search for the proper program command?

a. *Description*
b. *Command Line*
c. *Browse*

d. *Change Icon*
e. None of the above

10. If you position the mouse cursor on a program icon, press and hold down the Ctrl key, drag it to a different group window, release the mouse button, and then release the Ctrl key, you will have:

a. Moved an icon
b. Copied an icon

c. Deleted an icon
d. Changed an icon's properties

CHAPTER 4

Managing Files

● *Objectives*

Upon completing this chapter, you'll be able to:

1. View the directories and files on your disks.
2. Change the way file information is displayed.
3. Prepare and maintain disks for storing files.
4. Name, locate, select, rename, move, copy, and delete directories and files.
5. Start an application from File Manager.

OVERVIEW

File Manager is a Windows application that enables you to view and manipulate the work you store in files on a disk. It graphically represents the file structure of a disk, so you can easily comprehend and change it. Unlike DOS, File Manager provides the power to make alterations both easily and quickly. For example, to move files from one location to another using DOS, you must first copy the files to their new locale and then delete them from their old locale. In DOS, this typically requires a tiresome and frustrating series of repetitive keystrokes. With File Manager, you simply highlight the files you want to move and drag them to their new location!

In this chapter, we'll show you how to use File Manager to view files on a disk, prepare and maintain disks for storing them, locate specific files, and conveniently organize the way they are stored. In addition, we'll talk about how to start applications from File Manager and how to display and print text files.

LAB 4–1   VIEWING DIRECTORIES AND FILES

In Lab 4–1, we'll concentrate on the operations of File Manager that enable you to view files and directories. A **file** is either a program or a set of related data. Each file is identified by its filename and extension. You'll have the opportunity to experiment with filenames and extensions later in the chapter. For now, you may find it helpful to think of a filename as the file's first name and the file extension as its last name. Filenames may contain up to 8 alphanumeric characters. Extensions are separated from the filename by a period and may contain up to 3 characters (e.g., YOURWORK.WRI).

A **directory** is a collection of files stored at the same location on a disk. The name of the directory identifies its location. Directories make it possible to organize your files in a planned and logical manner. This helps you find, view, manage, and use your files in a more effective and efficient fashion. For instance, you can create a directory to hold all your word processing files so when you need to retrieve a certain document file, you'll know right where to look.

Viewing directories and files using DOS is a bit like being in a large maze. You can see your immediate surroundings (the current directory) but are blind to the size, organization, and contents of the rest of the maze (the number of directories, the way they're arranged, and the files residing in each directory). File Manager gives you a "bird's eye view" of your disk. It shows you all the directories and how they relate to each other. In addition, you can view the contents of multiple directories at the same time. You can even change the type and amount of information displayed about directories and their files. File Manager makes you the master of the maze.

Launching File Manager

You start File Manager by double-clicking its program icon in the Main group window of Program Manager.

1. Start Windows and display the Main group window in Program Manager.
2. Double-click the File Manager icon to launch the application.

The File Manager application window will appear, as portrayed in Figure 4–1. Within its workspace, File Manager displays a Directory window showing the contents of the current drive. Your Directory window will most likely contain items different from those shown in Figure 4–1.

Understanding a Directory Window

By default, a **Directory window** is split in two parts: The left half displays the Directory Tree, while the right half reveals the contents of

Figure 4–1. The File Manager window and its internal Directory window.

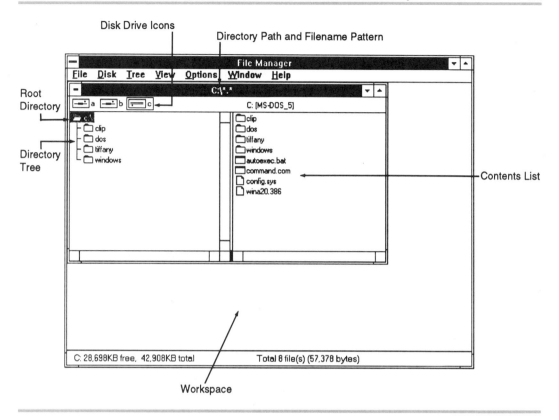

the current directory. The **Directory Tree** graphically illustrates the structure of the directories on any disk. Much like a real tree, it has a root and branches. Unlike an actual tree, the root of the Directory Tree is at the top, with branches or subdirectories extending downward. The branch directories are arranged in alphabetical order below it to aid you in locating a particular directory quickly.

Every directory is represented by an icon. You can easily identify a directory icon by its unique "file folder" graphic and adjacent title. The only exception is the root directory. The **root directory**, at the top of the tree, is the "parent" of all other directories and uses a disk drive designator (e.g., C) as its icon title. When a directory icon is highlighted, it is the active or current directory. The **current directory** is the collection of files presently targeted by File Manager for viewing or other file operations.

The **Contents List,** in the right half of the Directory window, displays the filenames and subdirectories in the current directory. The icons to the left of each filename signify whether the item is a directory, a program file, a document file, or a data file. A brief description of each type of icon is given below.

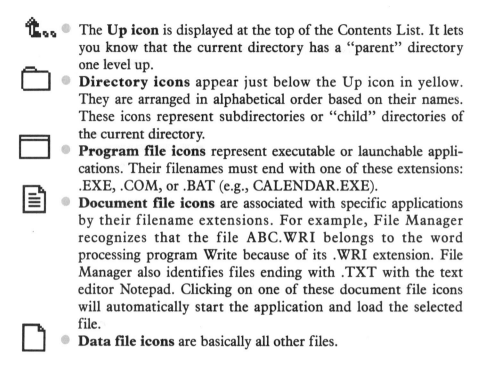

- The **Up icon** is displayed at the top of the Contents List. It lets you know that the current directory has a "parent" directory one level up.
- **Directory icons** appear just below the Up icon in yellow. They are arranged in alphabetical order based on their names. These icons represent subdirectories or "child" directories of the current directory.
- **Program file icons** represent executable or launchable applications. Their filenames must end with one of these extensions: .EXE, .COM, or .BAT (e.g., CALENDAR.EXE).
- **Document file icons** are associated with specific applications by their filename extensions. For example, File Manager recognizes that the file ABC.WRI belongs to the word processing program Write because of its .WRI extension. File Manager also identifies files ending with .TXT with the text editor Notepad. Clicking on one of these document file icons will automatically start the application and load the selected file.
- **Data file icons** are basically all other files.

The Directory window also includes a special title bar. The title bar in a Directory window displays the directory path (e.g., C:\WINDOWS) and filename pattern (e.g., *.*). A **directory path** or path name shows the directions for finding the current directory. It always begins with the root directory (e.g., C:\) and uses backward slashes (\) to separate any intervening directories leading to the current directory (e.g., C:\WPFILES\BACKUPS).

A **filename pattern** determines the types of files presented in the Contents List. For example, the filename pattern *.* will list every file in the active directory. This is because the asterisk symbol (*) is a wildcard that stands for any filename or extension—the period and three characters that appear after some filenames. Shortly, we'll show you how a filename pattern can be used to change the types of files that appear in your Directory window.

The disk drive icons are located just below and to the left of the title bar. **Disk drive icons** represent the disk drives installed in your computer system. These icons will be discussed further in Lab 4–2, *Working with Disks*.

Changing Directories

In the Directory Tree, a dotted box surrounding a highlighted icon marks the current directory. This dotted rectangle is called the **selection cursor** and is used to change directories. You can choose only one directory in the Directory Tree at a time. To select a different directory, simply click on the directory name you want.

1. If necessary, scroll the Directory Tree to expose the icon for the WINDOWS directory.
2. Click on it to make the WINDOWS directory the current directory.

The Contents List will change to display the items in the WINDOWS directory, as shown in Figure 4–2. Examine the **status bar** located at the bottom of File Manager. The right side of this indicator shows the total number and size of the files in the current directory. The left side provides information on the number of bytes free and the total capacity of the current disk drive.

Figure 4–2. Clicking a directory's icon makes it the current directory.

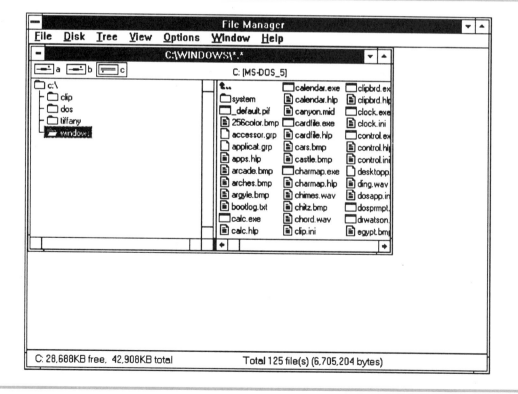

You can also use the Contents List to change directories by double-clicking on the name of the subdirectory in the Contents List you want to move to.

3. Point at the SYSTEM directory in your Contents List.
4. Double-click to make it the current directory.

The Contents List again alters to display the items belonging to the new current directory—SYSTEM. Notice that the Directory Tree expands to reveal this subdirectory's location. The next section will show you how to control the level of information displayed in the Directory Tree.

Expanding the Directory Tree

The main branches off a root directory often have additional branches so that you end up with multiple levels of directories. The Directory Tree makes viewing and working with these structures both convenient and easy. When File Manager is started, the Directory Tree will display only the first level of directories on the current disk drive, as shown back in Figure 4-1. However, you can use either mouse actions or the commands from the Tree menu to change the level of directory information shown.

You can determine whether a directory contains a subdirectory by first selecting a directory and then looking at the Contents List for a directory icon. To expand a directory one level down, double-click on its icon in the Directory Tree.

1. Since the WINDOWS directory is already expanded, find another directory with at least one subdirectory.
2. Double-click on its icon in the Directory Tree.

The Directory Tree will expand to display the subdirectories one level underneath the current directory, as shown in Figure 4-3. If deeper levels exist, you can repeat the above process to further extend the Directory Tree.

___ NOTE _____

You can also issue the **Indicate Expandable Branches** command from the Tree menu to display subdirectory information in the Directory Tree itself. This command will place a plus sign (+) on each icon in the Directory Tree that contains one or more subdirectories. When a directory is expanded, the plus will turn to a minus sign (−) to indicate that the directory can be collapsed.

Figure 4–3. Double-clicking on a directory icon in the Directory Tree will display its subdirectories one level down.

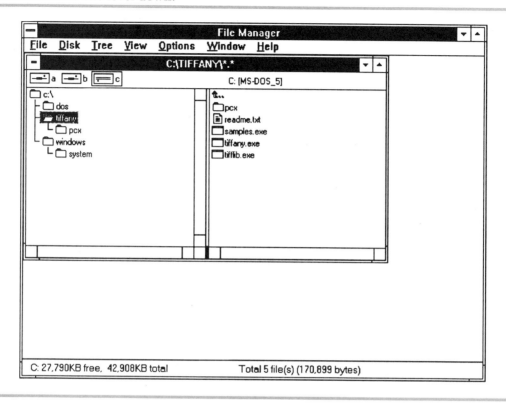

File Manager provides a quicker method for expanding all the branches in a Directory Tree. Simply select the **Expand All** command from the Tree menu (see Figure 4–4). The other commands in the Tree menu duplicate mouse actions for keyboard users.

3. Open the Tree menu from the menu bar in File Manager.
4. Select the *Expand All* command.

Figure 4–4.
The Tree
drop-down
menu.

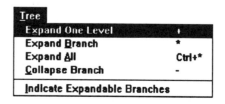

The Directory Tree will jump back up to the root directory. However, all the subdirectories will now be visible.

5. Use the scroll bar to examine all the branches in your Directory Tree.

Collapsing the Directory Tree

By double-clicking on a directory icon, you retract all the branches extending from it.

1. Scroll the WINDOWS directory into view.
2. Double-click its icon to collapse the directories below it.

To collapse all the branches of a Directory Tree, go to the top of the tree and double-click the root directory icon. You can double-click the icon again to expand the Directory Tree back to its original form, displaying only the directories immediately below the root.

3. Scroll to the top of the Directory Tree so that the root icon is visible.
4. Double-click the root directory icon (the directory icon at the very top of the Directory Tree).
5. Double-click the root icon again to expand the directories one level beneath it.

Opening Additional Directory Windows

You can display more than one Directory window at a time. As you'll see in Lab 4–3, it is highly desirable to have a second Directory window open when copying or moving files from one disk drive to another. To open another Directory window, either double-click a disk drive icon (covered in Lab 4–3) or issue the **New Window** command from the Window menu in File Manager.

1. Scroll the Directory Tree until the WINDOWS directory appears.
2. Choose the *New Window* command from the Window menu.

Once this is done, a Directory window similar to the one pictured in Figure 4–5 will materialize. It lists the same files and subdirectories as the previous active Directory window. The title bar in the new window displays a number after the directory path signifying that more than one Directory window is open for this disk drive and directory.

Figure 4–5. Issuing the *New Window* command from the Window menu opens another Directory window.

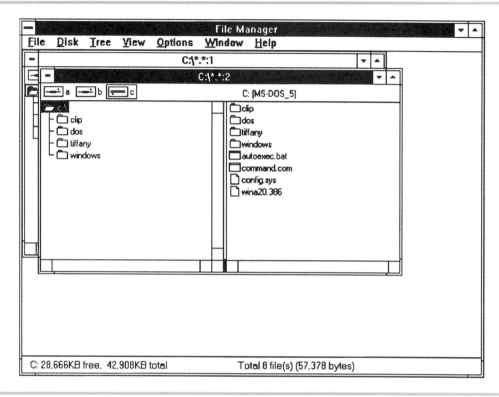

Selecting a Directory Window

When you open several Directory windows, you'll soon find it necessary to switch among them. You move to another directory window by clicking on it. This brings it into the foreground and makes it the active window. A Directory window must be active for you to work with its contents.

1. To select Directory window 1, click on its title bar, which is exposed above and behind Directory window 2.
2. To reactivate Directory window 2, click on any part of its exposed window. (If no portion is visible, select it from the Window menu.)

Your File Manager should again look like the one pictured in Figure 4–5. You can also activate a directory window by selecting it from the Window menu, much as you select a group window in Program Manager.

3. Open the Window menu.

4. Click on the option C:*.*:1.

After issuing this command, Directory window 1 will again become active and superimpose itself over Directory window 2.

Closing a Directory Window

As you open more Directory windows, File Manager's workspace will quickly become cluttered. Thus, as you finish working with a Directory window it is a good idea to close it. Closing a Directory window also frees up computer memory for other purposes. To close a Directory window, double-click on its control-menu box.

1. Select Directory window 2.

2. To close Directory window 2, double-click its control-menu box.

Your File Manager should resemble the one portrayed in Figure 4-6.

Figure 4-6. Double-clicking on the control-menu box of a Directory window closes it.

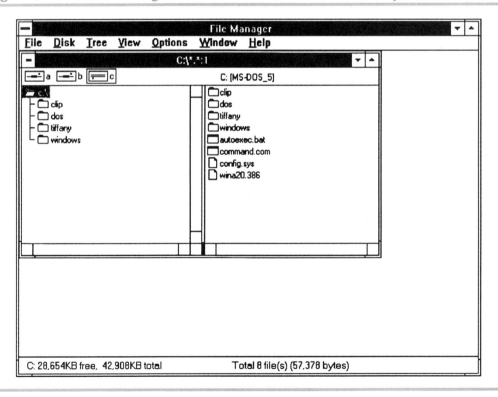

Changing the View

The View menu in File Manager lets you choose what is displayed in a Directory window (see Figure 4–7). These commands affect only the

Figure 4–7.

active Directory window. For example, when you first launch File Manager both the Directory Tree and Contents List are displayed. You can use the View menu to change the display of the active Directory window so that only the Directory Tree or the Contents List is shown. To view just the Directory Tree, select the **Tree Only** command from the View menu.

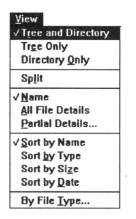

1. Select the *Tree Only* command from the View menu.

This action places a check mark in front of *Tree Only*, removes the check mark from the *Tree and Directory* command, and closes the View menu. Your Directory window will instantly change to show only the Directory Tree. This view is useful when you are working with directories exclusively. It provides a larger and clearer picture of the Directory Tree.

To see just the Contents List for the current directory, issue the **Directory Only** command from the View menu. When you open the View menu, notice that a check mark appears in front of the *Tree Only* command. Windows uses check marks to tell you which commands are presently enabled.

2. Choose the *Directory Only* command from the View menu.

The Directory window now lists only the contents of the current WINDOWS directory, as pictured in Figure 4–8. This fuller view gives you easier and faster access to the items in a directory.

To display both the Directory Tree and Contents List in the current Directory window, choose the **Tree and Directory** option from the View menu.

3. Select the *Tree and Directory* command from the View menu to return your Directory window to its original state.

The View menu also enables you to control the details, order, and types of files displayed in a Directory window. Let's see how these commands can be used to customize your view of directories and files.

Figure 4–8. Issuing the *Directory Only* command from the View menu displays just the Contents List of the current directory.

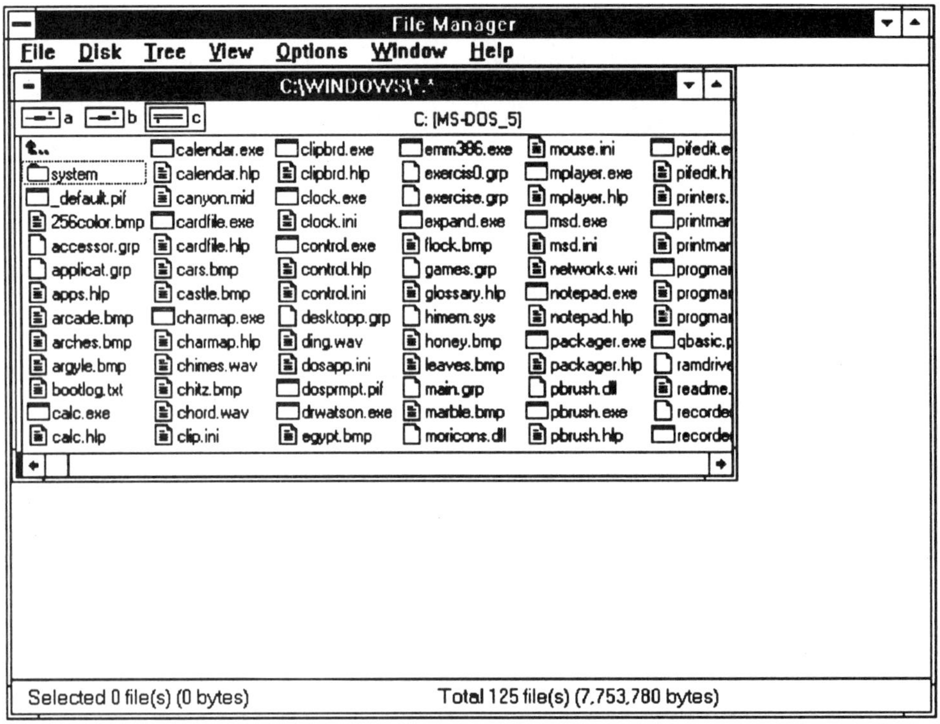

Showing Details

File Manager is capable of listing more information than is first shown in a Directory window. The middle set of options in the View menu **(Name, All File Details, Partial Details...)** let you tailor the kind of information displayed in a Contents List. File Manager is preset to list only filenames, but you can change this default setting to show the size of your files (in bytes), the last date and time they were modified (saved), and other special attributes.

To display all available information about the contents of a directory, select the *All File Details* command from the View menu.

1. With the WINDOWS directory selected, issue the *Directory Only* command from the View menu to provide additional space for displaying file information.
2. Choose the *All File Details* option from the View menu by clicking on it.

Figure 4–9. The WINDOWS Directory window with the *All File Details* option in effect.

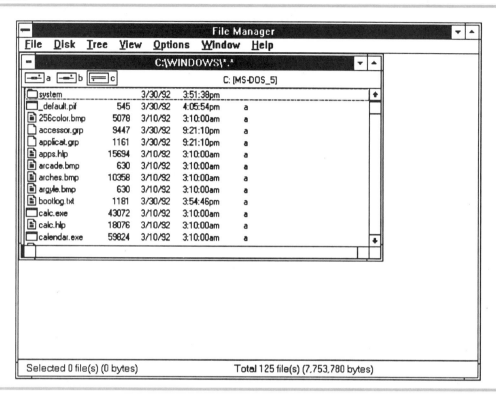

After giving these commands, your Directory window will look like the one exhibited in Figure 4–9. Each name now occupies a separate line, followed by details that further describe each directory element (when needed, you can use your horizontal scroll bar to view additional information). The second column tells you the size of a file in bytes; the third and fourth reveal the date and time a file was last modified (saved) or when a directory was created, and the final column displays a "flag" signifying the presence of a special file **attribute**. (For more information on special file attributes, see the Key Terms **Archive attribute, Hidden attribute, Read only attribute**, and **System attribute** at the end of this chapter.)

You can pick and choose what information is displayed about the elements in a directory. When you select the *Partial Details...* command from the View menu, a dialog box of viewing options appears (see Figure 4–10). Because you previously invoked the *All File Details* command, the check boxes for all four settings are currently toggled on. However, you are free to select any combination of these settings.

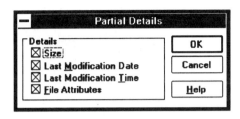

Let's say for the moment that you are only interested in the size of the files in the **WINDOWS** directory. To switch the other options off, all you need to do is click on their check boxes.

3. Select the *Partial Details...* command from the View menu.
4. Click on the check box for *Last Modification Date* to switch it off. The × in front of the setting will disappear.
5. Switch off the settings for *Last Modification Time* and *File Attributes,* then click the *OK* button.

File Manager will instantly reconfigure your active Directory window to reflect the new settings. The *Partial Details...* command will stay in effect for this and any additional Directory windows until you select either the *Name* or *All File Details* option from the View menu.

Sorting Files

When you first open a directory window, the contents are arranged alphabetically by name. However, you can also arrange your display so that items are listed by type, size, and the last date they were modified. The fourth set of commands in the View menu (**Sort By Name, Sort By Type, Sort By Size,** and **Sort By Date**) control the order in which files and directories are presented.

To sort files according to file type, select the *Sort By Type* command from the View menu. This will group the files based on their extension—the period and 3 characters that appear after some file-names. For example, files with an .EXE extension would be listed before those with a .WRI extension. Follow the instructions below to change the way your **WINDOWS** directory is displayed.

1. Issue the *All File Details* command from the View menu so you can see the effect of the following instructions.
2. Choose the *Sort By Type* command from the View menu.

If you look at your Directory window, you'll see the files are now listed alphabetically by extension. This is a convenient way of locating and working with groups of files based on their category. As with viewing file details, once a sorting format is selected it remains in effect until another is chosen. The sorting order also applies to any Directory window opened subsequently.

You can arrange the files in a Directory window from largest to smallest by choosing the *Sort By Size* command from the View menu.

3. From the View menu, pick the *Sort By Size* command.

File Manager will immediately reorganize the files so they are displayed in a descending order by size, with the largest at the top.

● **HINT**_____

When you begin to near the maximum storage capacity on your hard disk, you'll need to look for files you can erase. Displaying and sorting files by their size can help you quickly spot the ones that'll give you back the most storage space.

To display a directory sorted chronologically, choose the *Sort By Date* command from the View menu. The directories and files will be arranged separately by date, with the most recent appearing at the top of the list.

4. Select the *Sort By Date* command from the View menu.

Compare your Directory window with the one shown in Figure 4–11.

___**NOTE**_____

File Manager automatically updates the information displayed in a Directory window. However, in some situations File Manager will be unaware of changes. For instance, if you switch disks in the current floppy drive you'll need to issue the **Refresh** command from the Window menu to update the information shown in the Directory window. Also, the use of network directories may require periodic manual updates with the *Refresh* command.

Figure 4–11. The *Sort By Date* command from the View menu organizes the items in a Directory window by the date they were last modified.

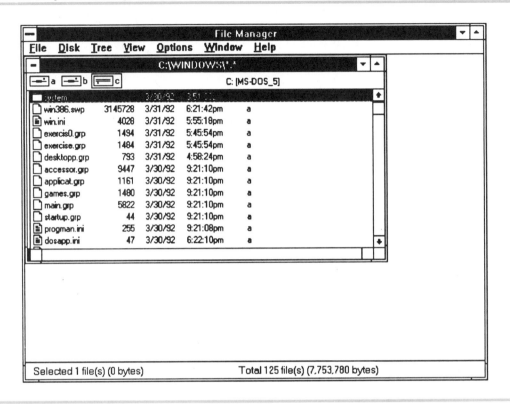

Selecting the Type of File to View

By default, File Manager shows you every subdirectory and file in a directory. But there will be occasions when you'll want to see only a specific set of subdirectories or files. For example, you might want to limit your view to just executable or launchable files while looking for a particular application. You can use the **By File Type...** command, from the View menu, to narrow the field of items displayed. The By File Type dialog box (see Figure 4–12) lets you specify a set of file types and a filename pattern that will "filter out" everything except those elements you want to view.

There are four File Type selections in the By File Type dialog box: *Directories, Programs, Documents,* and *Other Files.* These check boxes enable you to exclude entire groups from being displayed. For instance,

Figure 4–12.
The By File
Type dialog
box.

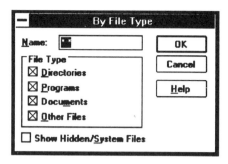

if you forgot the name and location of a letter you composed with Write, you could vastly reduce the number of files to look through by electing to view only document files.

The *Name* text box, located in the top portion of the dialog box, allows you to display files with similar names. All you have to do is enter a filename pattern to be matched and select *OK*. File Manager will include only the items in the active directory that match your pattern. When you specify your filename pattern, you can use an asterisk (★) to represent any series of characters and a question mark (?) to stand for any single character. For example, to list all the document files in your WINDOWS directory belonging to the word processing program Write, enter the filename pattern ★.WRI (WRI is short for WRIte) and select *OK*. Let's try it.

1. Select the *By File Type...* command from the View menu.
2. Type ★.WRI in the *Name* text box.
3. Click the *OK* button.
4. Use the vertical scroll bar to examine the files in your Directory window.

Check what you see against Figure 4–13. If you performed the above operations correctly, your window should contain only files ending with the extension .WRI. Also observe that the title bar of the Directory window has changed to reflect the new filename pattern.

Some programs hide files to prevent users from accidentally or intentionally modifying or deleting them. Selecting the *Show Hidden/ System Files* check box in the By File Type dialog box reveals these normally concealed files.

Figure 4–13. Changing the filename pattern in the By File Type dialog box lets you specify the type of file you want to view.

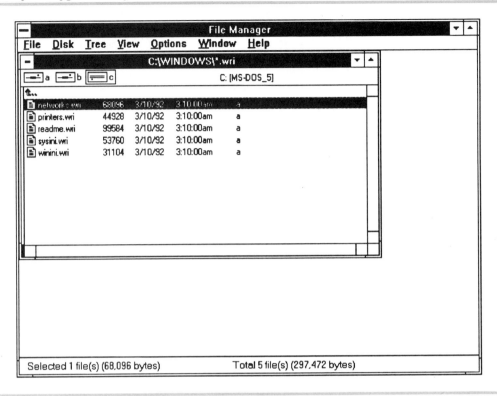

Arranging Directory Windows

You can control the Directory windows in File Manager by manually resizing and moving, maximizing and minimizing, and automatically rearranging them. By now, you should be quite familiar with manually resizing and moving windows, so we'll concentrate on the other methods available for manipulating windows in File Manager.

When you start File Manager, the Directory window is split into two sections by a bar. You can move the **split bar** to display more of either the Directory Tree or the Contents List.

1. Select *Tree and Directory* from the View menu in File Manager to return your Directory window to its default state.
2. Place the mouse pointer over the split bar between the Directory Tree and the Contents List so that it changes to the shape of a bar with two arrows.

3. Press and hold down the left mouse button, drag the split bar to the left 1 inch or so, and release the mouse button.

This action will expose a larger portion of the Contents List while showing less of the Directory Tree, as illustrated in Figure 4–14.

4. Now drag the split bar back the other direction so that all of the Contents List disappears, and release it.

The Directory Tree should now occupy your entire Directory window.

5. To restore the original split, issue the *Tree and Directory* command from the View menu.

Figure 4–14. The split bar lets you quickly adjust the space allotted to the Directory Tree and the Contents List.

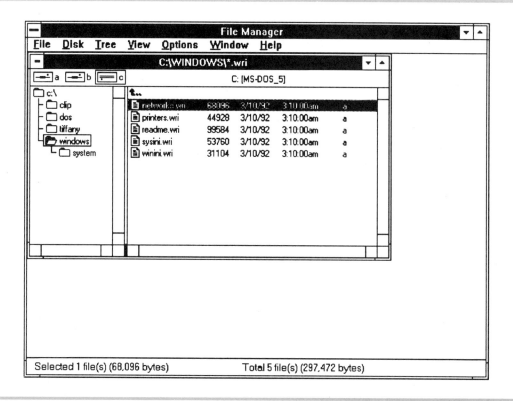

A Directory window can be expanded to fill the entire workspace in File Manager or reduced to an icon to conserve space. To see how this works, let's first maximize the Directory window and then reduce it to a document icon.

6. Click on the Directory window's maximize box.

File Manager enlarges the window so it fills the workspace. This is a quick and convenient way to view more of the information in a Directory window. It reduces the need to scroll around in search of a particular item or additional details.

If File Manager becomes cluttered with open Directory windows, you can shrink some of them to icons. This will make it easier for you to work with the remaining directories. When a window is minimized, its icon appears in the lower left corner of File Manager. Double-clicking on it expands the icon back into a window.

7. To shrink the maximized **WINDOWS** Directory window to an icon, first click on its restore box to return to the original window size.

8. Next, click the minimize box to reduce the window to an icon.

___NOTE_____

You can select the *Arrange Icons* command from the Window menu to organize the Directory window icons in File Manager.

_____

Check the appearance of your screen against the one portrayed in Figure 4–15. In the lower left corner, you should have an icon titled C:\WINDOWS*.WRI.

To arrange the windows in File Manager, you can use the Window menu's *Cascade* and *Tile* commands. These commands will organize all open Directory windows. As windows are opened in File Manager, they are stacked, starting in the upper left corner of the workspace, so that each window overlaps the last. This cascade arrangement enables you to see the title bar of each window.

You can also arrange Directory windows so that each one receives an equal amount of the available workspace in File Manager. Simply select the *Tile* command from the Window menu.

9. Issue the *New Window* command from the Window menu to open a second Directory window.

Figure 4–15. Clicking the minimize box of a Directory window reduces the window to an icon.

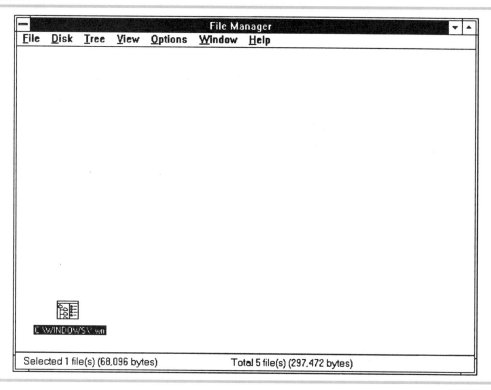

10. Use the Directory Tree in the second window to find and select your DOS directory. (If you are unable to locate a directory titled DOS, it may be listed under a different name. Check with your instructor for the correct name.)
11. To expand the C:/WINDOWS/*.WRI icon, double-click on it.
12. Reorder your window stack by choosing the *Cascade* command from the Window menu.
13. Select the C:\DOS*.WRI Directory window by clicking on its title bar.
14. To see all the files in the DOS directory, select the *By File Type...* command from the View menu and change the filename pattern in the *Name* text box back to *.*.
15. Select the *Sort By Name* command from the View menu to arrange the files alphabetically.

Notice that selecting a different Directory window partially obscured the first one. You could reorganize File Manager by selecting the *Cascade* command again, but this can clearly become a very tedious process.

The tile format is a more practical arrangement for working with multiple windows. It resizes and arranges the windows so they are displayed in their entirety. Selecting a window to work with does not conceal other windows as with the cascading.

16. Choose the *Tile* command from the Window menu to restack the Directory windows in File Manager.

Your screen should look like the one shown in Figure 4–16.

17. Close the C:\DOS*.* Directory window.

The only drawback to tiling Directory windows is the fact that File Manager will continue to cascade newly opened windows. Thus, you'll

Figure 4–16. The *Tile* command rearranges Directory windows so that they are entirely visible.

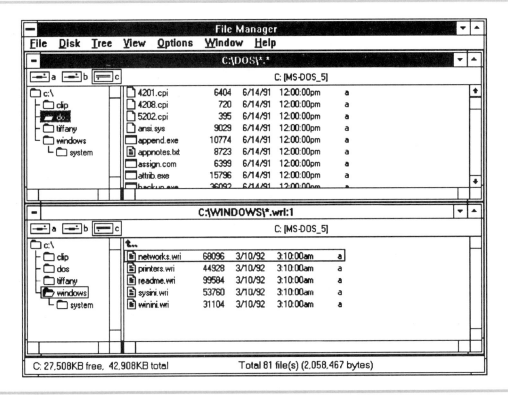

need to reissue the *Tile* command each time after you open a window. Nevertheless, this is still preferable to the cascade format where you must rearrange the windows practically every time you select a different one to use.

Exiting File Manager

To quit File Manager, select the *Exit* command from the File menu. By default, File Manager will automatically save the changes you made to the environment. Next time you or someone else runs File Manager, those changes will become the default settings for presenting directory information. This could obviously become very confusing. To prevent your alterations from being saved, verify that there is *not* a check mark in front of the *Save Settings on Exit* command in the Options menu before exiting File Manager.

1. Open the Options menu and look to see if a check mark appears in front of the *Save Settings on Exit* command. If there is a check mark, select the command to toggle it off; otherwise, go on to the next instruction.
2. Select the *Exit* command from the File menu to leave File Manager.
3. You may end your Windows session after verifying that the *Save Settings on Exit* command in the Options menu of Program Manager is toggled off.

LAB 4–2   WORKING WITH DISKS

In this lab, we'll introduce the facilities in File Manager for maintaining your storage media. These facilities are easy to use and provide many safeguards for preventing unintentional erasure of your work. We'll begin by showing you how to prepare a floppy diskette for storing data. You'll then learn to select a disk drive, name your disks, and make duplicate disks for backing up important files. You will need two blank high density diskettes to complete these exercises.

Formatting Disks

Before you can work with a disk, it must be formatted. **Formatting** prepares the diskette so it can hold information. When you use File Manager to format your disks, it erases any existing data, maps out locations for storing new data, and checks for damaged or unusable areas. Beyond preparing fresh disks, formatting also provides a handy way to erase all the files on a disk at once.

⊘ **HAZARD**_____

For all practical purposes, formatting a disk permanently removes all the existing data from it. So be extremely careful to make sure you know what you're formatting. Accidentally formatting the wrong disk can be a very painful experience!

Figure 4–17.

To format a disk, begin by inserting your disk in a drive and selecting the **Format Disk...** command from the Disk menu in File Manager (see Figure 4–17).

1. If you quit Windows after the previous lab, you'll need to launch it again and start File Manager.
2. Before you start the next portion of the lab, you need to attach the self-adhesive labels that came with your diskettes. Label one disk EXERCISES and the other PRACTICE, and stick them in the upper left-hand corner on the front side of your new diskettes.
3. Place your EXERCISES disk in a floppy disk drive. Make sure you insert it correctly and close the drive door. (You might want to go back and review the section in Chapter 1 that deals with handling disks.)
4. Choose the *Format Disk...* command from the Disk menu.

The Format Disk dialog box, shown in Figure 4–18, will appear. This dialog box contains several options. It lets you specify the location

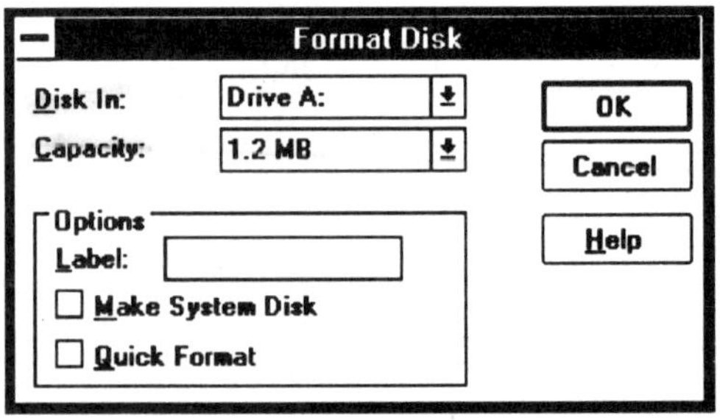

Figure 4–18.
The Format
Disk dialog
box.

of the disk to be formatted, the capacity of the disk, and a disk label (name). If you want to use a drive different from the one shown, click the down arrow button in the *Disk In* box and select the appropriate drive from the drop-down list box. You can perform the same procedure to select a different disk capacity.

The *Label* text box makes it possible to label or name the disks you format. (You can use the **Label Disk...** command from the Disk menu to name or rename already formatted disks.) A well-chosen name, or **volume label,** helps you quickly identify the contents of a disk. You create a volume label by simply entering a name, up to 11 characters in length, in the *Label* text box of the Format Disk dialog box.

Once you are satisfied with the entries in this dialog box, select the *OK* button to proceed. You can click the *Cancel* button to abort the operation altogether and return to File Manager. If necessary, the *Help* button provides additional information on formatting.

Since we're going to use drive A as the source and destination drive, all that you need to do before continuing is to label your disk.

5. Click on the *Label* text box and type: EXERCISES
6. If you have only one floppy drive, skip to step 7. If you have multiple floppy drives and need to use a drive different from the one shown in the dialog box, click the down arrow button in the *Disk In* box and choose the drive you want to use.
7. Select the *OK* button in the Format Disk dialog box to format and label your disk. (Choosing *Cancel* will abort the operation and return you to File Manager.)

___ NOTE ___

The two check boxes in the Format Disk dialog box let you quickly format a disk and create a **system disk** to start or "boot" your computer. The *Quick Format* check box makes it possible to format a disk rapidly by skipping the normal scan for bad sectors. This can lead to problems if the disk has defective spots, and it should only be used when urgency is paramount.

When you select the *Make System Disk* check box, File Manager copies a set of system files onto your floppy disk. (The *Make System Disk...* command from the Disk menu will add system files to an already formatted disk.) However, because your hard disk already contains these system files and placing them on your disk reduces the storage space available, it is both unnecessary and unwise to choose this option.

After you select *OK*, the Confirm Format Disk dialog box will appear to warn you that formatting will erase all data from your disk. Clicking the *Yes* button confirms the command. If you select *Cancel*, the process is aborted and you are returned to File Manager.

8. Click the *Yes* button to complete the operation.

The Formatting Disk dialog box will replace the previous dialog box to inform you that your disk is being formatted. It will also report on the progress of formatting by showing you the percentage of the disk completed (see Figure 4–19). You may halt the process at any time by selecting the *Cancel* button in the dialog box. You'll then be returned to File Manager.

Figure 4–19.
A dialog box informs you of progress.

When the formatting is complete, File Manager will display the Format Complete dialog box. The total storage size of the newly formatted disk is shown along with the bytes available for use. Clicking the *Yes* button in this dialog box takes you back to the Format Disk dialog box so you can prepare another disk. The *No* button ends the format operation and returns you to the File Manager window.

9. Click the *No* button to signal that you are finished formatting for now.

Selecting a Disk Drive

File Manager employs disk drive icons, like the ones illustrated in Figure 4–20, to represent the drives installed in your computer system. Disk drive icons are located to the left and just below the title bar in a Directory window. The number and type will vary depending upon your system configuration.

Figure 4–20.

Floppy drives are depicted by icons that look like miniature floppy drive faceplates and are usually labeled drive A and B. Hard drive icons resemble the front of a typical hard drive and use designators such as C and D. A rectangular box surrounding a drive icon indicates it is the active or **current drive**. For example, in Figure 4–20 the current drive is C.

To select a drive, you simply point at its icon and click.

1. Your newly formatted EXERCISES disk should be in drive A. If you used a different drive (say, drive B) to format it, you'll need to substitute that drive letter whenever you see drive A in the instructions.
2. Point at the drive A icon and click.

This action will place a rectangular box around the icon for drive A, signifying it is the current drive. Notice the disk now has a volume label. File Manager displays it in brackets right above the Contents List, as shown in Figure 4–21. You can always find the name of the disk

Figure 4–21. The volume label for a disk will appear above the Contents List in the first Directory window.

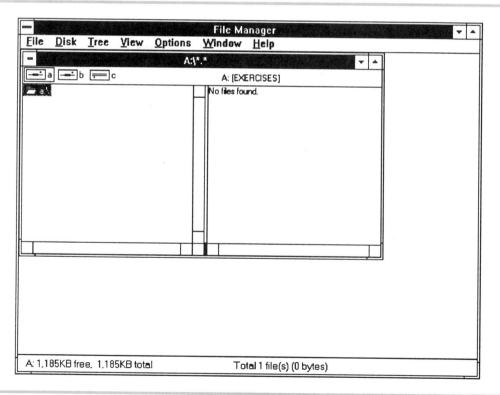

in the current drive (assuming it has one, of course) by checking this spot.

3. Select drive C and remove your disk.

⊘ **HAZARD**_____

If you try to choose a drive without a disk properly inserted, you'll get an error message telling you the drive is not ready. If this happens, click *OK* to signal you've read the message, check the disk and drive door, and then try the operation again.

Copying Disks

To make an exact duplicate of all the contents on a disk, use the **Copy Disk...** command from the Disk menu in File Manager. This command provides a quick and accurate way to back up an entire diskette. It copies everything on your source disk to a destination disk. A **source disk** is the disk you are copying from, while the **destination disk** is the disk you are copying to. The destination disk doesn't even need to be formatted; File Manager will format it as it copies. However, both disks do need to be the same size and density. For example, you can't use a 5¼″ disk, with a capacity of 1.2 Mb, to duplicate a 3½″ 1.44 Mb disk.

Let's step through the process of duplicating a disk. We can use the one you labeled in the previous exercise. (Even though your disk is empty at this point, the duplication process is the same for a full or empty disk.)

To copy a disk, insert it into a drive and issue the *Copy Disk...* command from the Disk menu.

1. Place your formatted EXERCISES disk in drive A.
2. Choose the *Copy Disk...* command from the Disk menu.

If your computer system has dual floppy drives, File Manager will prompt you to pick a source and a destination drive. Click on the down arrow to display a list of drives and choose the ones you want. If your machine has two differently sized floppies, you'll need to designate the same drive as both the source and destination.

3. If prompted for a source and destination drive, click the *OK* button to accept the default drive designations.

The Confirm Copy Disk dialog box will appear. It warns that all contents on the destination disk will be erased and asks if you're sure you really want to proceed with duplicating the disk. Click on the *Yes* button to continue or choose *Cancel* to abort the operation.

4. If prompted click on the *Yes* button.

Figure 4–22.

File Manager will display a Copy Disk dialog box prompting you to insert the source disk, as shown in Figure 4–22. This message box furnishes you with a chance to make sure you've inserted the right disk. It also offers yet another opportunity to cancel the process. If you choose *OK*, File Manager will begin reading data from your source disk into memory. After a few moments, you'll be asked to insert the destination disk.

5. Click on the *OK* button to start copying the source disk.
6. When prompted for the destination disk, remove the source disk, replace it with the unformatted **PRACTICE** disk, and select *OK*.

___NOTE_____

If the amount of free memory in your system falls below the capacity needed to store the entire contents of the disk, you'll be asked to swap the source and destination disk several times in order to copy all the information. During this procedure, File Manager will keep you apprised of its progress by showing the percentage completed. Continue to exchange the disks in accordance with the messages from File Manager until you're notified the duplication is complete.

You now have two identical disks with the same volume label. Although no files were transferred in this practice run, the time will come when this backup technique will prove invaluable. As you accumulate files on your disks, periodically use the *Copy Disk...* command to make a backup copy. The effort it takes to duplicate a disk is relatively small in comparison to the work required to recreate the information stored on it, should it be lost.

7. Select C as the active drive.
8. Exit File Manager and Windows after making sure the *Save Settings on Exit* check boxes are switched off for both applications.

___NOTE_____

If you're on a network, the Disk menu will also contain commands
for working with network servers, volumes, drives, and directories.
Consult your Windows Help facility for information on these
commands.

LAB 4–3   WORKING WITH DIRECTORIES AND FILES

Now that you're able to view directories and files, arrange the workspace in File Manager, and maintain the media (disks) necessary to
store files, you're ready to start using File Manager to perform directory and file operations. In this lab, you'll learn to name, select, search,
rename, copy, move, and delete directories and files. You'll see how to
create directories, start an application from File Manager, and print a
text file.

Some file operations require that you name or rename directories and
files. You must adhere to these DOS rules when naming directories or
files.

- **RULE 1:** As mentioned earlier in the chapter, a **filename** can
  consist of up to 8 characters, followed by an optional **extension**
  with up to 3 characters. The name and extension must be
  separated by a period. For example, MEMO.WRI is a permissi-
  ble filename, because MEMO is fewer than 8 characters and
  WRI complies with the 3-character limit.
- **RULE 2:** The first character in a filename or extension must be
  a letter or number. Thereafter, any character can appear in a
  filename or extension with these few exceptions.

period	.	quotation marks	"
comma	,	brackets	[ ]
colon	:	vertical bar	|
semicolon	;	forward slash	/
backward slash	\	equal sign	=

● **RULE 3:** DOS restricts certain names for use as commands and for addressing hardware devices. These are not available for use as filenames.

CON	COM3	LPT3
AUX	COM4	PRN
COM1	LPT1	NUL
COM2	LPT2	

Searching for Directories and Files

When you want to work with a directory or a file, but have forgotten where it's stored, you can use the **Search** command to find it. You can search for a particular item, or for all the items with a similar filename or extension, and you can search either the current directory or all directories on the current disk.

Figure 4–23.

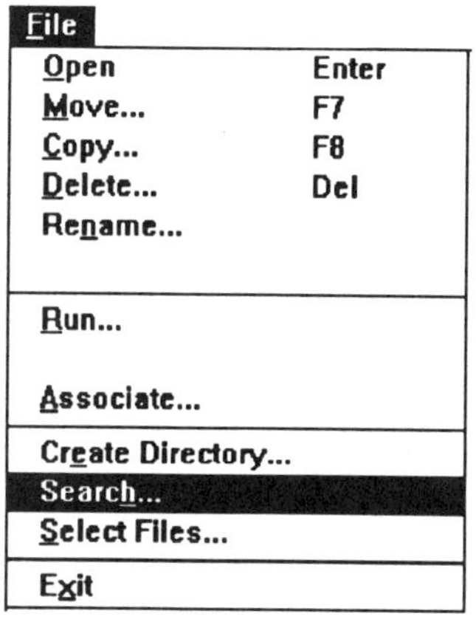

```
┌─────────────────────────┐
│ File                    │
├─────────────────────────┤
│ Open            Enter    │
│ Move...         F7       │
│ Copy...         F8       │
│ Delete...       Del      │
│ Rename...                │
├─────────────────────────┤
│ Run...                   │
├─────────────────────────┤
│ Associate...             │
├─────────────────────────┤
│ Create Directory...      │
│ Search...                │
│ Select Files...          │
├─────────────────────────┤
│ Exit                     │
└─────────────────────────┘
```

When you choose the *Search...* command from the File menu (see Figure 4–23), File Manager will present the Search dialog box shown in Figure 4–24. If you know the name of the item you are looking for, all you have to do is enter it in the *Search For* text box, and select *OK*. File Manager will, by default, search through the entire disk for the item.

The *Start From* text box displays the current directory. This is the location where the search will begin unless you enter a different starting point in the *Start From* text box. You can limit the search to the current directory by toggling off the *Search All Subdirectories* check box.

Let's experiment with the *Search...* command by having it find the WRITE.EXE application file.

1. Start Windows and File Manager.
2. Choose the *Search...* command from the File menu.
3. Type the filename WRITE.EXE in the *Search For* text box (as you begin typing, the wildcards *.* will disappear).
4. Make sure the *Search All Subdirectories* check box is toggled on, then click *OK* to start the search.

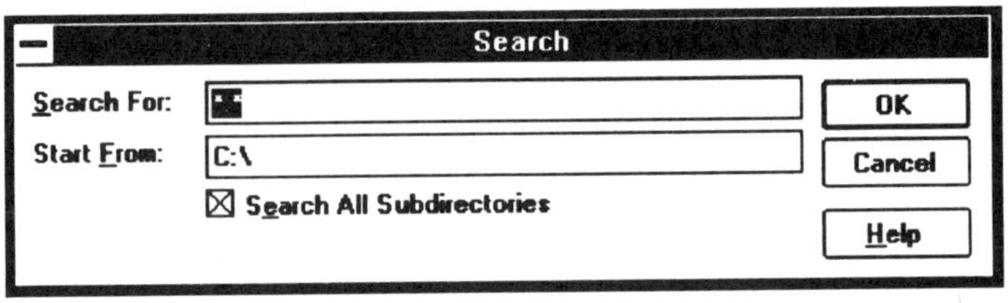

Figure 4–24.
The Search
dialog box.

File Manager will look through the entire contents of the current disk for matches to the name you specified in the Search dialog box. Whatever it finds will be displayed in a special Search Results window. Figure 4–25 shows what your search should have produced. Each item in the Search Results window will appear as an icon with its complete directory path. From this information, you know the WRITE.EXE file is located in the C:\WINDOWS directory.

If you are uncertain about the name of a directory or a file, you can use wildcards to help you search for likely matches. For example, let's assume you want to find a Write document file but can't remember its name. You know, however, that it is somewhere in the WINDOWS directory. Fortunately, it has a .WRI extension, so you can use the filename pattern *.WRI to search for it. The asterisk (*) is a wildcard that stands for any filename.

5. Close the Search Results window by double-clicking on its control-menu box. Then issue the *Search* command again.
6. Enter the filename pattern ***.WRI** in the *Search For* text box.

Figure 4–25.
The Search
Results
window
displays the
items
matching
your search
criteria.

Since you're only going to search the WINDOWS directory, you'll need to specify it as the starting point in the *Start From* text box.

7. Click the *Start From* text box and change it to read: C:\WINDOWS

8. Toggle off the *Search All Subdirectories* check box, and click *OK*.

File Manager will again display the Search Results window. This time the window lists several files that match your search pattern. Also note that the status bar at the bottom of the File Manager window has changed to indicate the number of files found.

You can select, open, and use most other File Manager commands with the items appearing in a Search Results window. However, you can't copy or move items into the window (see *Copying Directories and Files* and *Moving Directories and Files* later in this lab). You can also reposition, resize, maximize, and minimize a Search Results window.

9. After you finish studying the Search Results window, double-click its control-menu box to close it.

Selecting Directories and Files

Before you can tell File Manager what operation to perform on a directory or file, you must select it. To choose a directory or a file, all you have to do is click on it. When you are in the Directory Tree, you can only choose one directory at a time. However, in the Contents List you can choose multiple directories and files at the same time.

To extend the selection of items beyond one, you simply click on the first and then press the Ctrl key each time before you click on an additional item. Each selected item will be highlighted. To cancel a selection, you hold down the Ctrl key and click on the item again. The highlighting will vanish.

We can practice these techniques by selecting the Write document files in your WINDOWS directory.

1. Go to the Directory Tree and choose the WINDOWS directory.

2. Find the first filename in the Contents List ending with .WRI and click it.

3. After you find the next file with a .WRI extension (you may need to use the scroll bars), hold down the Ctrl key and click it. This highlights the second element without canceling the first selection.

4. Repeat step 3 until all the filenames ending with .WRI have been highlighted.
5. Now go back and cancel your selections by holding down the Ctrl key and clicking on each highlighted file. (We'll show you a much easier way to cancel all the selections in a directory window in a moment.)

You'll no doubt readily agree that selecting files scattered throughout a directory window is both a time-consuming and an irritating process. However, if the items you want to choose are in a continuous sequence, all you have to do is click on the first one and then, while holding down the Shift key, click on the last item. This combination of actions will highlight the whole group at once. To discontinue the selection, you simply click on the first item again.

To see how much easier this method of selection is, we'll use it to again choose the Write document files in the WINDOWS directory. Before we can proceed, you'll need to group the text files together. You can use the *Sort By Type* command from the View menu to display these items sequentially.

6. Issue the *Directory Only* command from the View menu to provide a better view of the Contents List.
7. Choose the *Sort By Type* command from the View menu and scroll across to the filenames ending in .WRI.
8. Click on the first element in the group.
9. Move down to the last file with the extension .WRI, hold down the Shift key, and click on it.

Compare your directory window to the one shown in Figure 4–26. Notice that the status bar indicates the number of files selected, their total size, and the total number and size of all the files in the directory. (This is a handy feature for determining if your selection is too big to be copied or moved to another disk drive.)

At this point, you can issue a number of different commands to manipulate or even erase these files. We'll be exploring these commands in the following exercises. But for now, let's drop this selection and change the view so we can look at one final method for selecting a group.

10. Click on the first element in the group to cancel the selection.
11. Issue the *Sort By Name* command from the View menu to return the Contents List to its original order.

Figure 4–26. Selecting a continuous group of items is much easier than choosing elements scattered throughout a directory.

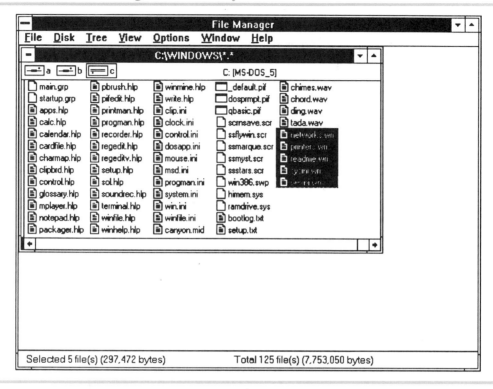

You can make the selection process even more effortless by using the **Select Files...** command from the File menu to both find and mark the files you want selected.

12. Choose the *Select Files...* option from the File menu.

Figure 4–27.

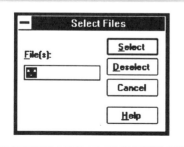

The Select Files dialog box shown in Figure 4–27 will materialize. The *File(s)* text box, located to the left of the buttons, lets you specify which files to find and mark. After entering a filename pattern, click the *Select* button to complete the operation. The *Cancel* button, which aborts the operation, will change to the *Close* button to let you exit the dialog box with the selection intact. The *Deselect* button allows you to change your mind and unselect the marked items. Clicking the *Help* button brings additional assistance on using this dialog box.

13. In the *File(s)* text box, type *.WRI and then click the *Select* button.
14. Exit the dialog box by choosing the *Close* button.

File Manager will have highlighted every file in the current directory that matches the file pattern you specified (see Figure 4–28). You can scroll through the Contents List to confirm this fact.

15. When you are satisfied, nullify the selection by issuing the *Select Files...* command from the File menu and clicking the *Deselect* button in the Select Files dialog box.
16. Click on the *Close* button to exit the dialog box.

File Manager will remove the highlighting from the previously selected files in the WINDOWS directory. You can use the *Deselect*

Figure 4–28. You can both find and select groups of files with the *Select Files...* command from the File menu.

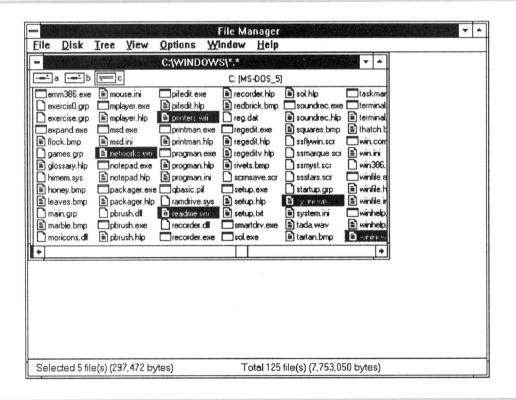

button to negate selections regardless of the technique used to establish them.

17. Issue the *Tree and Directory* command from the View menu to restore the original Directory window display format.

___NOTE_____

To select multiple groups of items, follow these instructions: (1) Use the Shift-click method to highlight the first group. (2) Hold down the Ctrl key while you click on the first item in the next group, then hold down both the Ctrl and Shift keys when you select the last item in the second group. (3) Repeat step 2 until all the groups are marked.

Creating Directories

You can add new directories to both hard and floppy drives by using the *Create Directory...* command in the File menu. To create a directory, you must first select a parent directory to place it under. This is done from the Directory Tree.

Once a parent directory is chosen, the next step is to issue the *Create Directory...* command, which produces the Create Directory dialog box pictured in Figure 4–29. This dialog box displays the current directory and prompts you to enter a name for the subdirectory you want to add below it. Directory names must conform to the same conventions as filenames. They can be up to 8 characters in length with a 3-character extension. After you type the name and click the *OK* button, File Manager will build the subdirectory immediately below the parent directory.

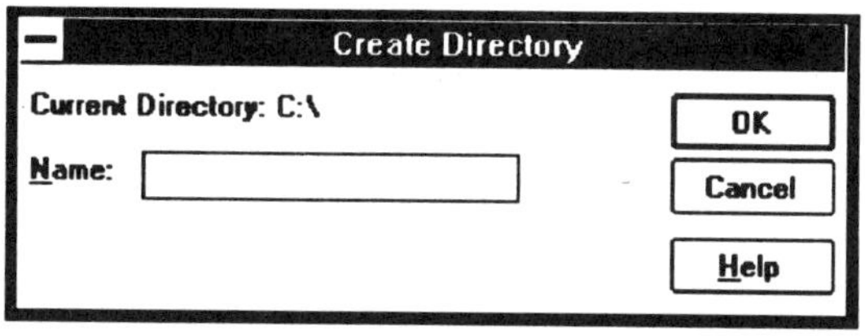

Figure 4–29.
The Create Directory dialog box lets you name a new directory.

Create Directory

Current Directory: C:\

Name: _____

OK
Cancel
Help

Directories are an excellent way to organize your files. It's a good idea to create a separate directory for each of your major applications and subdirectories for their associated data files. Placing data files in a directory below their parent application makes saving and retrieving them a faster and more convenient process. This way, you'll always know exactly where to look for a particular file.

Let's make some directories to store the data files you'll be generating in later chapters. We'll start by creating a directory to hold the word processing files belonging to the Write application.

1. Check to be sure your EXERCISES floppy disk is in drive A, then make it your current drive.
2. Open the File menu and select the *Create Directory...* command.
3. In the *Name* text box, type: WPFILES (short for Word Processing FILES).

If you make a mistake while typing the name, use the Backspace or Delete key to correct it. The *Cancel* button will abort the entire operation and send you back to File Manager. The *Help* button provides information on creating directories.

4. Click *OK* to confirm the creation of the directory.

Your Directory Tree will sprout a new branch titled WPFILES. Let's add another subdirectory below WPFILES. We'll call it BACK-UPS. In the next exercise, you'll use BACKUPS to store a group of Write document files copied from your hard disk.

5. Select the WPFILES directory from the Directory Tree.
6. From the File menu, choose *Create Directory...*
7. Enter the directory name: BACKUPS

● **HINT**_____

When creating subdirectories, you should avoid adding more than three levels. Deep directory structures result in long and awkward path names (e.g., C:\LEVEL1\LEVEL2\LEVEL3\LEVEL4 *.*) that are confusing both to use and to maintain.

We'll create one final directory to hold the drawings you'll be producing with Paintbrush. When you finish with the instructions below, your Directory Tree should look like the one exhibited in Figure 4-30.

Figure 4–30. Your disk should contain three directories.

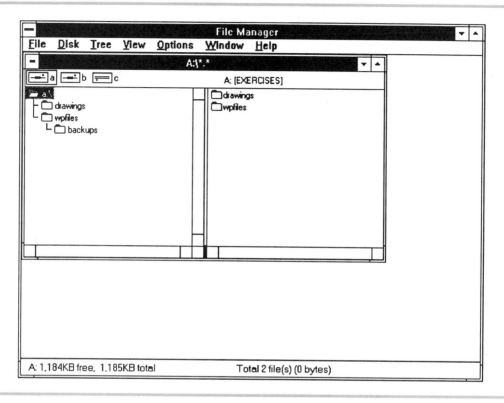

8. Select the root directory icon (A:\) from the Directory Tree.
9. Create a directory and name it DRAWINGS

Renaming Directories and Files

To change the name of a directory or a file, you can use the *Rename...* command from the File menu. To rename a directory, first select it from either the Directory Tree or the Contents List. Then issue the *Rename...* command to summon the dialog box illustrated in Figure 4–31. The Rename dialog box displays the old directory name in the *From* text box. You simply type the new name in the *To* text box and click the *OK* button. If you accidentally choose a filename that belongs to another file, File Manager will alert you to the problem and give you a chance to abort the operation.

Let's say you've changed your mind about the DRAWINGS directory and want to rename it PBFILES. PBFILES seems to be a

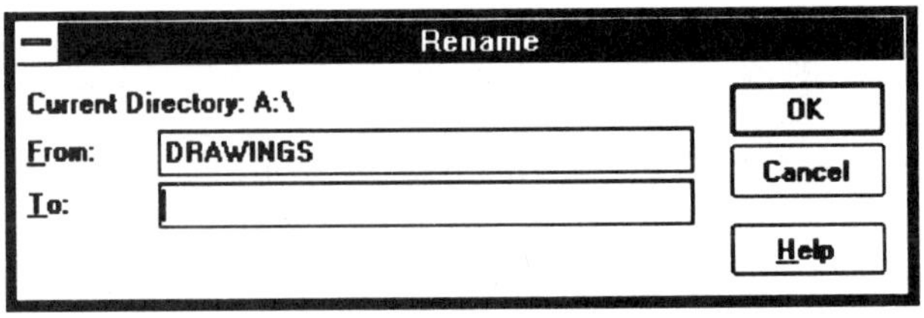

Figure 4–31.
The Rename
dialog box.

better "fit" with the other directory names and it more accurately reflects the type of files you plan to store there.

1. With your disk in drive A, use the Directory Tree to select DRAW-INGS.
2. Choose the *Rename...* command from the File menu.
3. In the *To* text box, type: PBFILES
4. Click *OK*.

File Manager will change the title of the directory icon from DRAWINGS to PBFILES.

The ability to rename directories and files makes it possible to reorganize your disks. You can customize items so that their names better reflect the files, applications, and data they represent.

⊘ HAZARD

OR MAPS
MAIN DIRS

Under no circumstances should you rename the WINDOWS directory or any of the files in it. Ignoring this warning may cause Windows to cease running. You should rename only those directories and files you have created. Never rename any directory created by a program's installation process.

Copying Directories and Files

You'll typically copy directories and files between different drives; however, occasionally you'll find it necessary to copy items between directories on the same drive. Before you copy, you must first display both the source and destination directories. The **source directory** is the location you plan to copy items from, while the **destination directory** is the location you intend to copy them to. These directories can be in either the Directory Tree or the Contents List.

With the source and destination visible, select the items you want to copy, place the pointer anywhere on the selection, press and hold down the Ctrl key, press and hold down the left mouse button, drag the pointer to the destination directory, release the mouse button, and then release the Ctrl key. As you are copying the selection, the pointer will change shape to reflect the type of items you're carrying (e.g., if you're moving a directory, the pointer assumes the shape of a folder).

When you are copying between directories on different disks, the *Tile* command is handy for rearranging Directory windows so that the directories are in clear view. Let's use this technique to copy a group of files from the WINDOWS directory on your hard disk to the subdirectory BACKUPS on your floppy disk.

1. To display the source items, select the C drive and the WINDOWS directory.
2. To display the destination directory, double-click on the icon for drive A to open a second Directory window, then double-click on the WPFILES directory to expose BACKUPS.
3. From the Window menu, select the *Tile* option (see Figure 4–32).
4. Click on the C:\WINDOWS*.* directory to make it active. Then use the *Select Files...* command to mark all the text files in the WINDOWS directory ending with .WRI.
5. Place your pointer on any part of the highlighted area in the WINDOWS directory.
6. While holding down the Ctrl key, press the left mouse button, and drag the selection to the BACKUPS directory icon in either the Directory Tree or the Contents List (a rectangular box will surround the icon when the pointer is in the correct position).
7. Release the mouse button and then release the Ctrl key.

⊘ **HAZARD**_____

Be careful when dragging a selection into a Directory window that you don't release it over the wrong directory icon. If you do, cancel the operation or the items will be placed in a subdirectory other than the intended one.

_____

Once you've released the selection, a dialog box will appear requesting confirmation on copying the selected files to the A:\WPFILES\BACKUPS subdirectory. Answering *Yes* will cause File Manager to copy the files. Responding *No* aborts the operation and prevents any items from being copied.

Figure 4–32. The *Tile* command arranges the source and destination windows so they are both visible for copying or moving items between them.

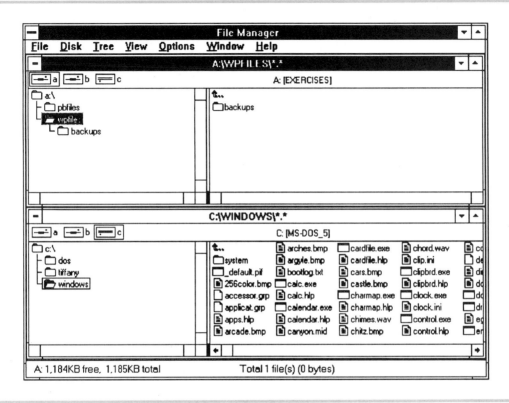

8. If the dialog box specifies the correct subdirectory, choose *Yes* to confirm the copying operation.

File Manager will display the name of each item as it's being copied from the source to the destination directory. You can abort the copy operation at any time by clicking the *Cancel* button. When File Manager finishes, BACKUPS will contain a duplicate of every .WRI file in the WINDOWS directory.

9. To see these files, select the BACKUPS directory in the upper Directory window (see Figure 4–33).

Let's repeat the copy operation, except this time you'll use the Contents List as your destination instead of a directory icon.

Figure 4–33. The BACKUPS directory on drive A now contains a copy of every Write file in the WINDOWS directory on drive C.

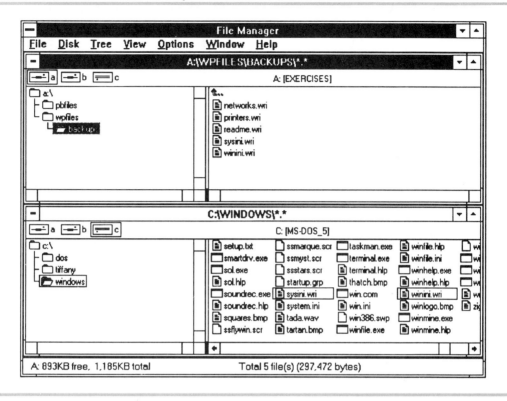

10. To provide a better view, make the A:\WPFILES\BACKUPS*.* the active window and issue the *Directory Only* command from the View menu.

11. All the items with a .WRI extension should still be highlighted in the WINDOWS directory. If not, reselect them.

12. Point at any one of these files, press and hold down the Ctrl key, drag the selection to any location in the Contents List of BACK-UPS (except over the Up icon), release the mouse button, and then release the Ctrl key.

13. When the Confirmation dialog box appears, choose *Yes*.

    After affirming your intentions to copy the chosen items, a dialog box like the one pictured in Figure 4–34 will appear. It alerts you that the file shown already exists and checks to see if you really want to replace it. To help with this decision, the dialog box provides information showing which version of the file is most recent.

Figure 4–34.
The Confirm
File Replace
dialog box.

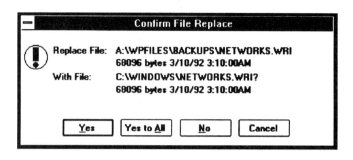

If you decide to continue, click *Yes* and File Manager will replace the existing file with your copy. Choosing this option means you will be questioned about each file replacement remaining in your selection. Choosing the *Yes to All* button will allow you to avoid these repeated prompts by pre-approving any replacements necessary to complete the copy operation. If you respond *No,* File Manager will keep the original and discard the copy. It will then continue to the next file to be copied. You can choose *Cancel* to abort the whole operation.

14. Click *Yes* to replace the first existing file in the BACKUPS directory.

Since every file in your selection matches a filename in the destination directory, File Manager will show you the replace prompt each time it attempts to copy a file.

15. To copy the remaining files without confirming each replacement, click the *Yes to All* button.

___ **NOTE** _____

To disable this verification procedure altogether, issue the **Confirmation...** command from the Options menu and toggle off the *Confirm on File Replace* check box. You can also suppress several other verification requests from the Confirmation dialog box. However, we recommend you do this only for specific file operations and, afterward, switch the confirmation back on. These safeguards will help prevent serious accidents—accidents that can end up costing you far more than the time lost in responding to a prompt.

To copy a directory, select it from either a window or an icon, press and hold down the Ctrl key, drag the selection to the destination directory, and release the mouse button and then the Ctrl key. These actions will duplicate the entire directory, contents and all.

Let's copy BACKUPS to another location on your floppy disk. This will provide you with a copy of all the files in the original BACK-UPS directory. File Manager will allow you to use the same name for both directories, as long as you choose a different parent directory for the duplicate. When you finish the steps below, your Tree should look like the one portrayed in Figure 4–35.

16. Close the C:*.* Directory window.

17. To make the Directory Tree for drive A visible again, select the *Tree and Directory* command from the View menu.

18. For even better visibility, maximize the remaining Directory window and select the *Tree Only* command from the View menu.

Figure 4–35. After you copy the original BACKUPS directory to the root directory, your Tree displays two identical directories.

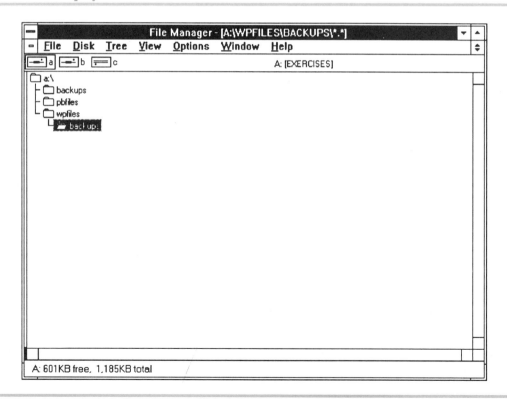

19. Click on BACKUPS to select it from the Directory Tree.

20. Point at the highlighted icon and hold down the Ctrl key, then press the left mouse button.

21. To copy BACKUPS to the root directory, drag the icon to the top of the Tree (when the mouse pointer is in the correct position a rectangular box will appear around the A:\ icon), release the mouse button, and then release the Ctrl key.

22. Confirm the copy operation.

___NOTE_____

When copying items from a destination on one disk drive to a source on a different drive, you can simply drag them with the mouse. You don't need to use the Ctrl key.

Moving Directories and Files

As we remarked in the beginning of this chapter, moving files or directories with File Manager is much easier than with DOS. You move items between directories and drives by simply dragging them from one visible location (source) to another (destination). If you think this sounds a lot like the way you copy elements, you're right. The difference is that moving doesn't create a second set of identical items.

To move directories or files, display the source and destination, select the element(s) to move, point anywhere in the selection area, press and hold down the Alt key, drag the item(s) to the new location, release the mouse button, and then release the Alt key.

Let's use this technique to move the contents of the BACKUPS directory up to WPFILES.

1. To display the source, select the BACKUPS directory located below WPFILES in the Directory Tree. Then issue the *Tree and Directory* command from the View menu.

2. Select all the files in the BACKUPS Directory window.

3. Point anywhere in the highlighted area, press and hold down the Alt key, and press the left mouse button to grab the selection.

4. Drag it to the WPFILES directory icon in the adjacent Directory Tree (when the mouse pointer is in the correct position a rectangular box will appear around the icon), release the mouse button, and then release the Alt key. (Be sure to release it over the correct directory icon, or File Manager will attempt to move the files to the wrong subdirectory.)

These actions will cause a dialog box to appear prompting you to verify the move. After doing so, File Manager will use another dialog box to keep you apprised of its progress in moving the selection. You can click *Cancel* in this dialog box to abort the operation at any time.

5. Once you have made sure the destination A:\WPFILES is specified in the Confirm Mouse Operation dialog box, click *Yes* to verify your intentions to relocate the items.
6. Select the WPFILES directory.

Your File Manager window should match the one pictured in Figure 4-36. The items in A:\WPFILES\BACKUPS have been transferred to WPFILES, leaving BACKUPS empty. You can check this by displaying the A:\WPFILES\BACKUPS directory.

One advantage of using the Contents List to select from is that you can choose more than one directory for moving or copying. With the

Figure 4–36. WPFILES now holds the items previously stored in the subdirectory BACKUPS.

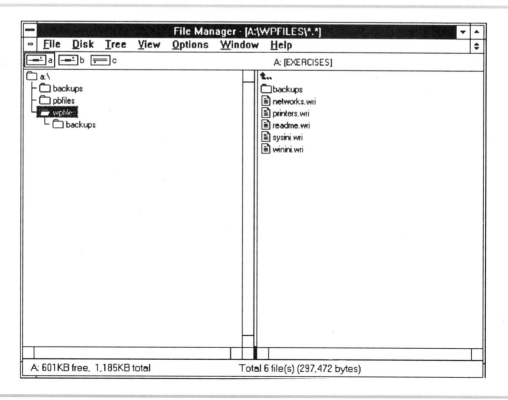

Directory Tree, you are able to select just a single directory at a time. Whatever the source, you are still free to use either a Contents List or a Directory Tree as your destination.

Moving a directory with File Manager relocates everything in the directory, even its subdirectories. This makes it both easy and fun to reorganize your disk. To reposition a directory in DOS, you must create a new directory, copy all the files to it, delete the original files, and then remove the original directory. Fortunately, with File Manager, all you have to do is drag the directory, contents and all, from one place to another.

We'll practice this technique by moving the BACKUPS directory from the root to beneath WPFILES. Since it is, after all, a backup directory, placing it next to the original makes more sense. However, File Manager will not allow two identically named directories to exist adjacent to each other and share the same parent. So, we'll first rename the directory and then move it. When you complete the instructions below, check your screen against Figure 4–37.

7. To provide a better view, issue the *Tree Only* command from the View menu.
8. Make sure all the branches of the tree are visible by choosing the *Expand All* command from Tree menu.
9. Select the A:\BACKUPS directory immediately below the root and rename it STORAGE.
10. With the STORAGE directory selected, press and hold down the Alt key, and drag the selection over the WPFILES icon (a rectangular box will form around the WPFILES icon when the mouse pointer is in the correct place).
11. Release the mouse button and then release the Alt key.
12. Answer *Yes* when asked to confirm the move.

___NOTE___

When moving items from a destination to a source on the same disk drive, you can simply drag them with the mouse. You don't need to use the Alt key.

Starting an Application from File Manager

To activate an application from File Manager, just double-click on its filename in the Contents List. Application filenames usually have a

Figure 4–37. The BACKUPS directory has been relocated below WPFILES.

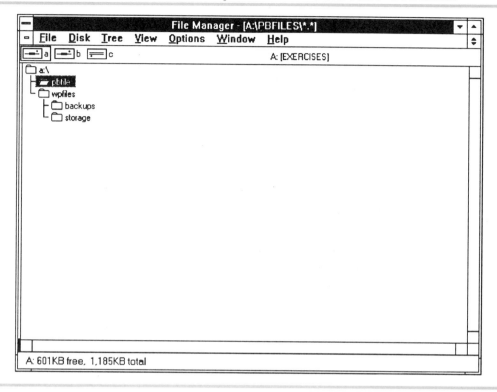

.COM, .EXE, .PIF, or .BAT extension. To see how this works, let's activate the Write accessory from File Manager.

1. Double-click on the C drive icon to open a second Directory window and choose the *Tree and Directory* command from the View menu.
2. Select the WINDOWS directory from the Directory Tree.
3. Locate the filename WRITE.EXE in the Contents List and double-click it to launch the accessory program.
4. Close the Write window by double-clicking on its control-menu box.

Two other methods also exist for launching an application from File Manager. Both have the added benefit of opening a file at the same time the application is launched. The first method consists of double-clicking on a file associated with a particular program. For example, files ending with the .WRI extension are associated with the executive word processor Write. Double-clicking on a .WRI file automatically starts Write and opens the file.

The second procedure involves dragging a file over a program and releasing or dropping it. This method also starts the application and opens the selected file.

Let's try the first method.

5. Find the filename README.WRI in the Contents List.
6. Double-click on it to activate the Write program and load the document.

The Write application window will appear with the README.WRI file visible. In Chapter 5, you'll learn all about Write. But for now, we'll just use it to print the document README.WRI.

7. Make sure your printer is ready and then choose the *Print...* command from the File menu of Write.
8. Since this is a very long document, you'll only print the first page of it. When the Print dialog box appears, click on the *Pages* radio button to print just page 1. Then select the *OK* button.
9. To quit Write, select the *Exit* command from the File menu in Write.

___NOTE_____

Some applications include text files as a way of giving you the latest information about the software. **Text files** are written in a standard format called *ASCII* (American Standard Code of Information Interchange). These files typically have titles such as README.TXT (the .TXT extension is optional). File Manager provides a *Print...* command to produce a hard copy of a text file. If you attempt to print a non-ASCII file, the output will most likely be illegible. To print any text file, you first select it and then issue the *Print...* command from the File menu. File Manager will present a dialog box like the one in Figure 4–38. The selected document will appear in the *Print* text box. To print it, all you have to do is click *OK*. The Print dialog box will remain visible during printing to give you the option of canceling the operation at any time.

Deleting Directories and Files

As your computing needs change over time, you'll find that a file or even a whole directory is no longer of any use. To remove a file or files

Figure 4–38.
The Print
dialog box.

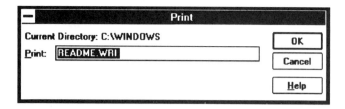

from your disk, you first select them in a directory window, then choose the *Delete...* command from the File menu, and confirm the deletion in the dialog boxes that follow. When you delete a directory, all of its contents are erased. The potential for disaster in this situation is obvious. Fortunately, File Manager provides a number of safeguards against unintentional deletions. Let's step through erasing some files and then an entire directory to see how these safety measures come into play.

1. Select all the files in your WPFILES directory. Be very careful to highlight only the files and not the two subdirectories STORAGE and BACKUPS.
2. Select the *Delete...* command in the File menu.

When you attempt to remove files or directories, File Manager displays a Delete dialog box similar to the one in Figure 4–39. The Delete text box lists the elements you've chosen for deletion. At this point, you have several options. You can edit the items in the text box, either adding to or removing them, click *Cancel* to end the operation, get additional help, or continue by selecting *OK*.

3. Click the *OK* button to verify your intention to remove all the listed files.

Figure 4–39.
The Delete
dialog box.

```
┌─────────────────────────────────────────────────────┐
│ [─]                     Delete                    ,   │
│ Current Directory: A:\WPFILES              ┌──────────┐│
│                                            │   OK     ││
│ Delete:   [WRI README.WRI SYSINI.WRI WININI.WRI]   ┌──────────┐│
│                                            │  Cancel  ││
│                                            ┌──────────┐│
│                                            │  Help    ││
│                                            └──────────┘│
└─────────────────────────────────────────────────────┘
```

File Manager will then require you to confirm the deletion of each selected file (see Figure 4–40). This is a further protection against accidental erasure. If you are certain about removing everything in the selection, you can avoid these repeated prompts by choosing the *Yes to All* button. To skip deleting a particular item, just click the *No* button. Clicking *Cancel* aborts the operation and leaves the remaining files intact.

Figure 4–40.
File Manager
requires
confirmation
for each file.

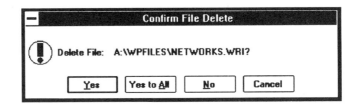

4. Click *Yes to All* to delete all the marked items.

File Manager will display a dialog box showing which files are being erased. When the dialog box vanishes, the WPFILES directory will be empty except for the Up icon and the two directories STORAGE and BACKUPS.

To remove a directory from your disk, you first select it from either a Directory Tree or a Contents List, then issue the *Delete...* command from the File menu. The Delete dialog box will appear, but this time it will contain only the name of the directory to be eliminated. Clicking the *OK* button confirms your intention to remove the directory and its contents.

If the directory contains files or other directories, File Manager will present a dialog box for you to validate the deletion of each element in the directory. If you skip deleting even one item, File Manager will not let you remove the directory. You must erase or relocate everything in a directory before you can eliminate it.

5. Select the STORAGE directory from the WPFILES directory window.
6. Choose the *Delete...* command from the File menu.
7. When you're prompted, verify your intention to delete the directory by choosing *OK* and then click the *Yes to All* button in the follow-up dialog box to confirm the uninterrupted erasure of all the items in the directory.
8. Now delete the subdirectory BACKUPS.

___NOTE___

You can mark more than one directory for deletion. However, you must make the selections from a Contents List since the Directory Tree only allows you to highlight one icon at a time.

When you are done, compare your Directory Tree with the one shown in Figure 4–41. It should contain only the root and the two subdirectories: WPFILES and PBFILES.

9. You may exit Windows. As always, be sure the *Save Settings on Exit* check box in the Options menu is toggled off before exiting.

COMING ATTRACTIONS . . .

Chapter 3 taught you to use Program Manager to organize and run applications. In this chapter, you learned to use File Manager to view,

Figure 4–41. The Directory Tree now shows only two subdirectories.

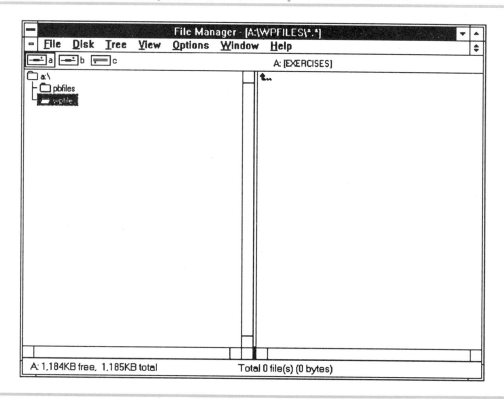

prepare and maintain, and organize disks. These skills are a prerequisite for effectively working with applications and the files they create and modify. Now that you've mastered these systems, you are ready to launch and use the two most powerful applications included with Windows, Write and Paintbrush.

Write is a fairly full featured word processor, while Paintbrush is a graphics application for drawing pictures. In Chapter 5, you'll be creating, editing, formatting, and printing a document with Write. Then, in Chapter 6, you'll try your hand at drawing a simple diagram with Paintbrush.

KEY TERMS

All File Details   File Manager View menu command that expands the listing in a directory window to include the filename, extension, size, date, time, and attributes of each file.

Archive attribute   A special code DOS assigns to a file indicating it has been changed. When you create or modify a file, it displays an "a" for archive. (To view file attributes in a directory window, you must first select the *All File Details* command from the View menu in File Manager.)

Associate...   File Manager File menu command that lets you associate a file type with a particular application. Clicking on a file associated with a program will activate the program and automatically load the selected file.

Attribute   A special code that DOS attaches to a file. This special code determines how users can access the file. There are four attribute types: Read Only, Archive, Hidden, and System. File Manager allows you to view and change these special attributes. Changing a file's attributes is a task best left to advanced Windows users.

By File Type...   File Manager View menu command that produces a dialog box with options to specify the items you want displayed in the Contents List of a Directory window. Default options include directories, programs, documents, other files, and hidden/system files.

Confirmation...   File Manager Options menu command that produces a dialog box with options to control whether or not confirmation prompts appear during file operations such as deleting and copying.

Contents List   The half of the directory window that displays filenames and subdirectories in the current directory.

Copy Disk...   File Manager Disk menu command that makes an exact duplicate of another disk.

Create Directory   File Manager File menu command for making a new directory.

Current directory   The directory that is presently targeted by File Manager for viewing or other file operations.

Current drive   The presently selected or active drive. All File Manager commands affect the current drive.

Data file icons   Icons used to represent all files that are not program or document files.

Delete...   File Manager File menu command that erases selected items from a disk.

Destination directory   In a copying operation, the directory you are copying to.

Destination disk   In a copying operation, the disk you are copying to.

Directory   A collection of files stored under the same name. Directories make it possible to organize your files in a planned and logical manner.

Directory icons   Images that graphically represent the directories on a disk.

Directory Only   File Manager View menu command that displays just the Contents List in a Directory window.

Directory window   The File Manager window that displays the Directory Tree and the Contents List.

Directory path   Shows the location of a directory on a disk.

Directory Tree   A graphical illustration of the structure of the directories on a disk.

Disk drive icons   Icons in the Directory window that represent the disk drives installed on your computer.

Document file icons   Images that represent data files associated with specific applications. The association is based on the filename extension.

Expand All   File Manager Tree command that displays all the branches in a Directory Tree.

Extension   The 3-character abbreviation following a filename that identifies the file's type (e.g., a Write document file has the extension .WRI).

File   A program or a set of data stored under the same name.

File Manager   A Windows application that enables you to view and manipulate the work you store in files on a disk.

Filename   The name given to a particular file. A filename can consist of up to 8 characters followed by an optional extension. The name and extension must be separated by a period.

Filename pattern   The example name used to determine the types of files presented in a directory window.

Font...   File Manager Options menu command that lets you specify the font type, font size, and case used to display information in Directory windows.

Format Disk...   File Manager Disk menu command that prepares a disk to hold information.

Formatting   A process for preparing a disk to hold information.

Hidden attribute   The special code "h" DOS attaches to a file signifying it will not appear in a normal directory listing. Files are often hidden for copy protection or security reasons. It is important to note that a file is always hidden for a reason. Never arbitrarily change the attributes of a file.

Indicate Expandable Branches   File Manager Tree menu command that displays subdirectory information in a Directory Tree. After you issue the command, any directory containing a subdirectory will display a plus sign (+), which will turn to a minus sign (−) when the directory is expanded.

Label Disk...   File Manager Disk menu command that lets you name or rename a disk. A well-

chosen name (volume label) can help you quickly identify the contents of a disk.

Minimize on Use   When using File Manager to launch applications, it is handy to use this Options menu command to minimize File Manager automatically to an icon each time you launch an application. This will save on desktop space.

Name   File Manager View menu command that lists only the filenames in the Contents List of the current Directory window.

New Window   File Manager Window menu command that causes another Directory window to open.

Partial Details...   File Manager View menu command that lets you determine the information shown in a Contents List. You can elect to display the size of your files, the last date and time they were modified, and other special attributes.

Print...   File menu command that prints a copy of a selected file.

Program file icons   Icons that represent executable or launchable applications.

Read Only attribute   The special code "r" DOS assigns to a file indicating you will be unable to modify it. You can look at a Read Only file but you can't change it.

Refresh   File Manager Window menu command that is used to update a Directory window. It instructs File Manager to rescan the current drive. The new scan will reflect the latest changes made to the directories or files. (E.g., when you change disks in the current drive and want an updated listing, use the *Refresh* command.)

Root directory   The "parent" of all other directories on a disk.

Search...   A Help option that lets you easily locate a directory on file.

Select Files...   File Manager File menu command that lets you quickly find and select a group of files.

Selection cursor   The dotted rectangle used to change directories in File Manager.

Sort By Date   File Manager View menu command that arranges the items in the Contents List of a Directory window according to the last date they were modified.

Sort By Name   File Manager View menu command that arranges the items in the Contents List of a Directory window alphabetically by their filenames.

Sort By Size   File Manager View menu command that arranges the items in the Contents List of a Directory window from the largest to smallest.

Sort By Type   File Manager View menu command that arranges the items in the Contents List of a Directory window by file type.

Source directory   In a copying operation, the directory you are copying from.

Source disk   In a copying operation, the disk you are copying from.

Split bar   The split bar can be moved to display more of either the Directory Tree or the Contents List.

Status bar   An indicator showing information about the current drive and directory, such as the number of bytes free, and the files presently selected.

System attribute   The special code "s" DOS attaches to a file indicating that it is essential to the operation of the computer. Files marked this way are part of the computer's operating system.

System disk   A disk that has been formatted and prepared by DOS for use as a startup disk. Sys-

tem disks can be used to boot, or start, the computer. The *Make System Disk...* command in the Disk menu will create a system disk from any empty but formatted disk. The disk must not contain files or an error message will appear.

Text files   Files written in a standard format called ASCII (American Standard Code of Information Interchange). Many applications use this standard text format as a means of sharing files between otherwise incompatible programs.

Tree and Directory   File Manager View menu command that arranges the items in the Contents List of a Directory window by file type.

Tree Only   File Manager View menu command that displays just the Directory Tree in a Directory window.

Up icon   The icon in Contents List that lets you know the current directory has a parent directory.

Volume label   The name of the disk in the current drive. Volume labels let you easily identify the contents of a disk. Volume labels can be up to 11 characters in length and, unlike filenames, can contain spaces. For example, you might label a disk TEXT BACKUP and then use this disk to keep backup copies of all your text files.

EXERCISES

4-1. The instructions below will give you a chance to practice the material presented in Lab 4–1. In addition, you'll use the Windows accessory program, Notepad, to create and print a short document.

    a. Start Windows and launch File Manager.

    b. Select the WINDOWS directory and double-click its icon to expand it.

    c. Open a second Directory window.

    d. In the new Directory window, select the subdirectory SYSTEM.

    e. Select the Tile command from the Window menu.

The two Directory windows should now be completely visible, as shown in Figure 4–42.

Figure 4-42. File Manager with two Directory windows displayed in a tiled format.

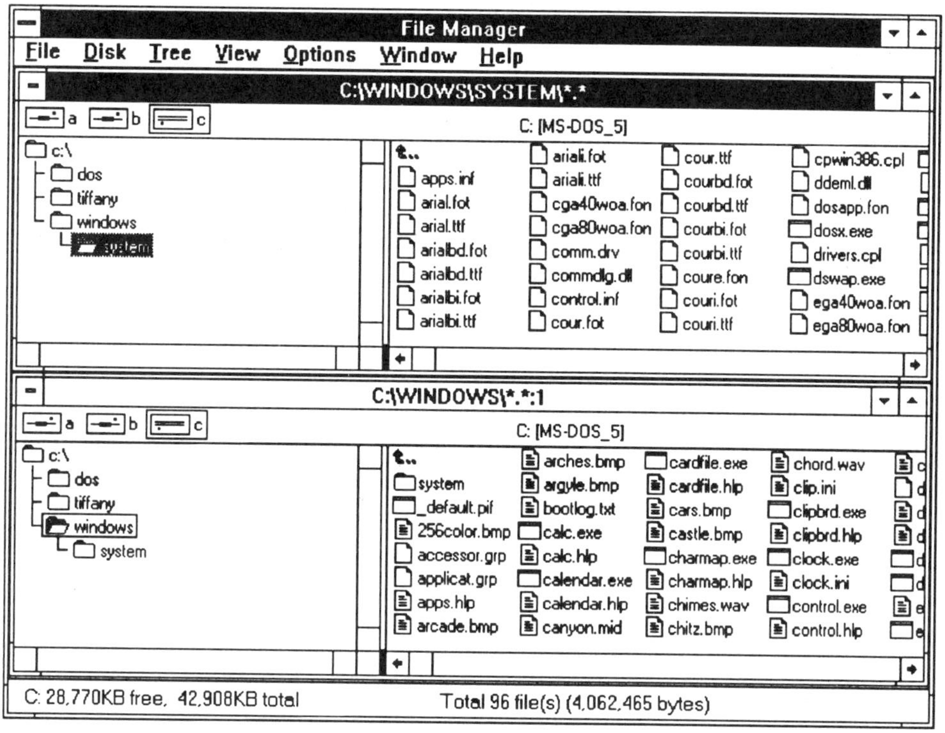

f. Select the C:\WINDOWS*.* Directory window, and then issue
the *Cascade* command from the Window menu.

g. Use the *By File Type...* and *Directory Only* commands from the
View menu to display only the files with .EXE extensions.

Print Screen / Paste & Print New Word Doc

Your screen should closely resemble the one illustrated in Figure 4-43.

h. Locate the program NOTEPAD.EXE in the Contents List.

i. Double-click on the filename to launch the application.

j. Type the following text in the Notepad workspace. Use the Backspace and Delete key to correct any typographical errors.

Windows 3.1 Tutorial
Chapter 4
Exercise 4-1
[Your Name]
[Today's Date]

Figure 4–43. The Contents List of the active Directory window shows only the files ending with .EXE.

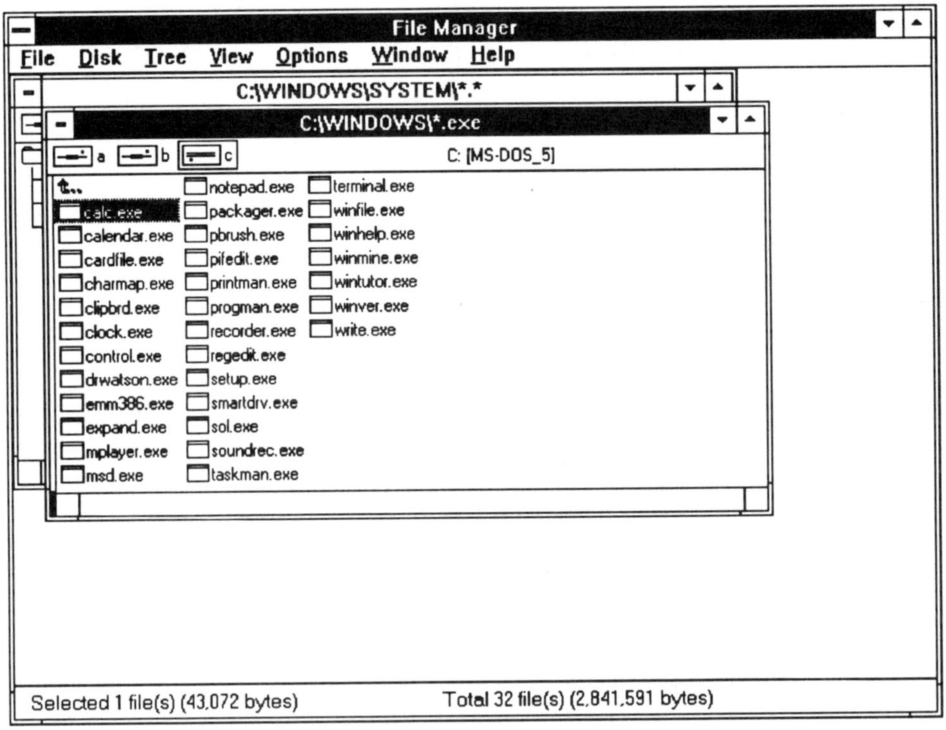

k. Type the names of the section headings for Lab 4–1. Put each section heading on a separate line. There are 12 headings. The first one is Launching File Manager. As you type each heading, take a moment to review the information in the section.

Figure 4-44 displays Notepad with the first two section headings entered.

l. When you finish entering all 12 section headings, print the document by selecting the *Print...* command from the File menu in Notepad.

m. Exit Notepad without saving the document.

n. If you are stopping here, exit File Manager and Windows after making sure the *Save Settings on Exit* commands are toggled off for both applications.

Figure 4-44. Notepad, with the beginning of an outline for Lab 4-1.

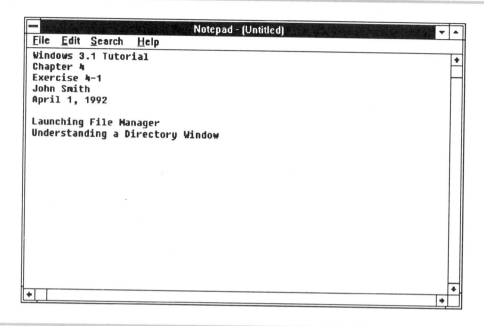

4-2. This exercise reviews the material presented in Lab 4-2. You'll practice formatting, labeling, and copying diskettes. You'll also use the Windows accessory program, Notepad, to create and print a record of your work.

Notepad has the ability to create an automatic time log. We'll use this feature to track how long it takes you to complete this exercise. Many professionals use time logs to track their progress while working on a specific task or project. Accountants, lawyers, consultants, and salespeople often record how they spend their time. Windows' Notepad makes this process simple.

To use the time log feature, place the .LOG command on the first line of the document you intend to use as a time log. LOG must be capitalized and a period must appear directly in front of it. Each time you open this file, Notepad will insert the time and date at the bottom of the document and then place the cursor on the line below the Date/Time stamp.

In the next two exercises, you'll use Windows' ability to multitask. You will switch between File Manager and Notepad using Task List.

    a. Start Windows and launch File Manager.
    b. Use the Directory Tree to locate and select the WINDOWS directory on drive C.

    c. Launch Notepad by double-clicking on the filename NOTE-PAD.EXE.

    d. On the first line of the Notepad workspace, type **.LOG** and press the Enter key.

    e. Type the following information in the document on the lines below the Notepad .LOG command.

        Windows 3.1 Tutorial
        Chapter 4
        Exercise 4-2
        [Your Name]
        [Today's Date]

    f. Insert a blank line below the date. Then press the F5 function key to insert the first Date/Time stamp. On the line beneath the Date/Time stamp, type: Created the time log.

    g. To save the document on your EXERCISES disk, first insert the disk in drive A.

    h. Issue the *Save* command from the File menu in Notepad. When the Save As dialog box appears, click the arrow button in the *Drives* drop-down list box and then click on the a: icon. (This will make drive A the active drive.)

    i. Next, double-click on the WPFILES directory in the *Directories* list box to make it the active directory.

    j. Check the path name located just above the *Directories* list box to make sure it displays the correct path—A:\WPFILES. **If it doesn't, carefully repeat steps h and i until it does.**

    k. Now, click on the *File Name* text box, use the Backspace or Delete key to erase the *.TXT, and type: TIME.TXT. (The filename extension .TXT is short for TeXT.)

    l. Finally, select the *OK* button to save the document.

Compare your screen with the one pictured in Figure 4–45.

    m. To remove the TIME.TXT document from Notepad's workspace, choose the *New* command from the File menu of Notepad.

    n. Remove your EXERCISES disk and insert your PRACTICE disk.

    o. Activate Task List by holding down the Ctrl key and pressing the Esc key. Activate File Manager by selecting it from Task List.

    p. Make sure you have the PRACTICE disk in the disk drive, then format and label it PRACTICE.

    q. Activate Task List and select Notepad.

Figure 4–45. A time log document created using Notepad.

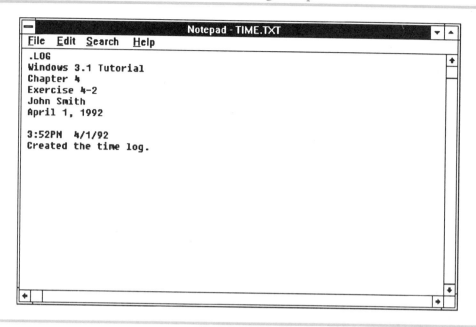

r. Insert the EXERCISES disk in your drive. Use the *Open* command from the File menu to retrieve the file TIME.TXT created earlier.

s. Beneath the new Date/Time stamp, type: Formatted the PRAC-TICE disk.

t. Save the document using the *Save* command from the File menu.

u. Print the document.

v. Exit Notepad using the *Exit* command from the File menu.

w. If you are stopping here, exit File Manager and Windows only after verifying that the *Save Settings on Exit* commands are toggled off in both applications.

4–3. The instructions below review the concepts and procedures covered in Lab 4–3. You'll create and manipulate directories and files and, in addition, use the time log feature of Notepad to track your work. (For an explanation of how the time log in Notepad functions, see the beginning of Exercise 4–2.)

a. Insert the EXERCISES disk and load Windows and File Manager.

b. Use File Manager to launch Notepad.

c. On the first line of the Notepad workspace, type .LOG and press the Enter key.

d. Type the following information on the lines below the Notepad .LOG command.

Windows 3.1 Tutorial
Chapter 4
Exercise 4-3
[Your Name]
[Today's Date]

e. Insert a blank line below the date, then press the F5 function key to insert the first Date/Time stamp. On the next line, type: Created this time log.

f. Save the file to the WPFILES directory on your EXERCISES disk in drive A. (If necessary, see Exercise 4–2 for instructions on saving a Notepad document.) Use the name TIME2.TXT

g. Select the *New* command from the File menu.

h. Switch to File Manager and select drive A.

i. Create two new directories, BACKUPS and TIMEFILE, so your directory structure matches Figure 4–46.

Figure 4-46. New directory structure of the EXERCISES disk.

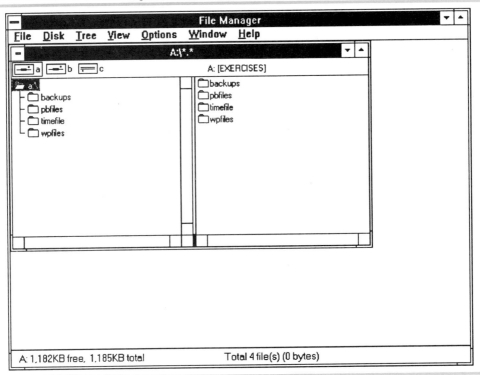

j. Switch to Notepad. Open the TIME2.TXT file, and beneath the newest Date/Time stamp, type: Created two new directories.

k. Save the file, issue the *New* command, and switch to File Manager.

l. Copy the BACKUPS directory below each of the other three directories.

m. Maximize the Directory window and delete the original BACKUPS directory.

Your directory structure should match Figure 4–47.

n. Switch to Notepad, open TIME2.TXT, and below the new Date/Time stamp, type: Copied the BACKUPS directory beneath PBFILES, TIMEFILE, and WPFILES. Save the file, issue the *New* command, and switch to File Manager.

Figure 4–47. Three BACKUPS directories have been copied below the three main directories.

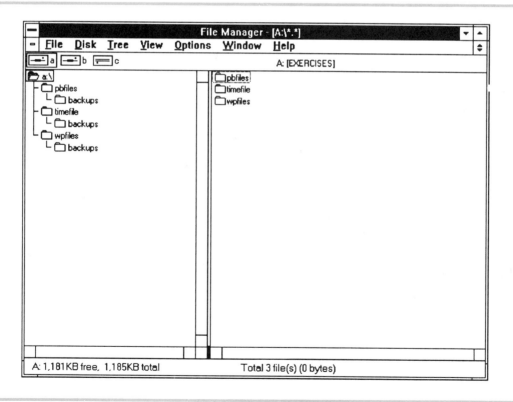

o. Rename the BACKUPS subdirectories so they match the directory names shown in Figure 4–48.

p. Switch to Notepad, open TIME2.TXT, and beneath the latest Date/Time stamp, type: Renamed the BACKUPS directories. Save the file.

q. Select the *Exit* command from Notepad's File menu.

r. Select the WPFILES directory of the EXERCISES disk.

s. To load Notepad and the time log file automatically, double-click on the filename TIME2.TXT. Below the new Date/Time stamp, type: Loaded Notepad and TIME2.TXT using File Manager. Save the file, select *New*, and switch to File Manager.

t. Restore the Directory window to its original size. Maximize the File Manager window.

u. Double-click on the drive A icon to open a second Directory window. Select the PBBACK directory in the Directory Tree. Now minimize the Directory window to a directory icon. Open a third Directory window for drive A, select the TIMEBACK directory,

Figure 4–48. The Directory Tree with the renamed backup directories.

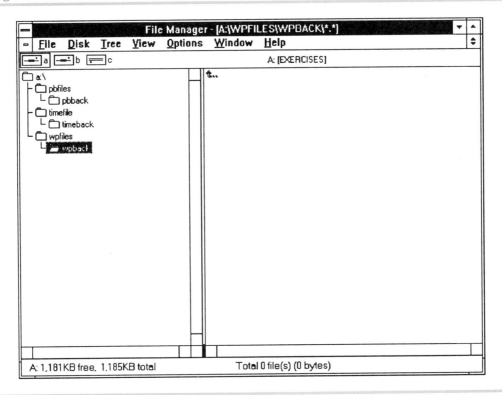

and minimize the Directory window. Open a fourth Directory window for drive A, select the WPBACK directory, and minimize the window.

Your desktop should closely resemble the one pictured in Figure 4–49.

v. Copy TIME.TXT to each of the backup directories (PBBACK, TIMEBACK, and WPBACK) by dragging the file down to each minimized directory icon and dropping it in.

w. Switch to Notepad, open TIME2.TXT, and on the line below the latest Date/Time stamp, type: Copied TIME.TXT to the backup directory icons. Save the document, select *New*, and switch to File Manager.

x. Delete each of the backup directories. Be careful to delete only the backup directories (PBBACK, TIMEBACK, and WPBACK). When asked about deleting the copies of TIME.TXT, respond *Yes*.

Figure 4–49. File Manager displaying three directory icons in its lower workspace.

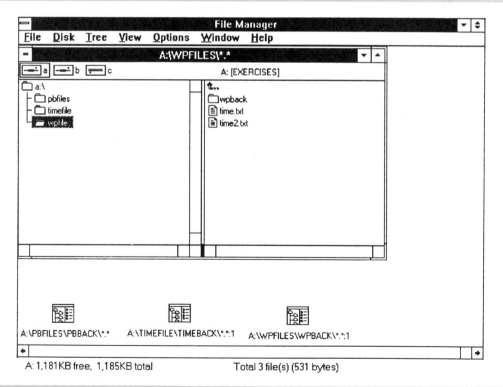

y. Switch to Notepad, open TIME2.TXT, and on the next line below the newest Date/Time stamp, type: Deleted the backup directories. Save and print TIME2.TXT. Exit Notepad. Use File Manager to move TIME.TXT and TIME2.TXT into the TIMEFILE directory.

z. Exit File Manager and end your Windows session after making sure the *Save Settings on Exit* commands are switched off for both applications.

REVIEW QUESTIONS

True or False Questions

1. **T   F**   By default, a Directory window displays a Directory Tree and a Contents List.

2. **T   F**   Formatting a disk removes all data previously stored on the disk.

3. **T   F**   The Directory Tree graphically illustrates the structure of the directories on any disk.

4. **T   F**   A source disk is the disk you are copying to, while the destination disk is the disk you are copying from.

5. **T   F**   File types are determined by filename extensions.

6. **T   F**   You may select more than one file in a Directory window by using the Ctrl key and the mouse.

7. **T   F**   A file is a collection of directories stored under the same name.

8. **T   F**   When you delete a directory, all of its contents are also erased.

9. **T   F**   Under no circumstances should you rename the WINDOWS directory or any of the files in it.

10. **T   F**   A directory pattern determines the types of files presented in a directory window.

Multiple Choice Questions

1. To open another Directory window, you would issue the command

   a. *New Directory*
   b. *Open Window*
   c. *Second Window*
   d. *New Window*
   e. c or d

2. To collapse all the branches of a Directory Tree, click on the

   a. Minimize box
   b. Control-menu box
   c. Root directory icon
   d. Program file icon
   e. None of the above

3. You can change the name of a directory by issuing this command.

   a. *Rename...* from the File menu
   b. *Rename...* from the Disk menu
   c. *Rename...* from the Directory menu
   d. You can't change the name of a directory

4. To use the *Copy Disk...* command to duplicate a 1.2 Mb diskette, you need:

   a. Any capacity disk will work
   b. A 360 Kb or a 1.2 Mb diskette
   c. A 1.44 Mb or 1.2 Mb diskette
   d. Another 1.2 Mb diskette

5. Which of the following is an acceptable filename?

   a. FILE NAME.TXT
   b. FILENAME.TEXT
   c. FILENAME.TXT
   d. TXT.FILENAME
   e. None of the above

6. The name of a disk is also called a

   a. Directory tree
   b. Volume label
   c. Directory path
   d. Source drive

7. When you want to copy between windows, this command is handy because it arranges the windows so they are both in clear view.

   a. *Copy...*
   b. *Move...*
   c. *Arrange icons*
   d. *Cascade*
   e. None of the above

8. To display files by their file extension, you must sort by

   a. Name
   b. Date
   c. Type
   d. Size
   e. a and d

9. Using File Manager to move a directory will cause which of the following to be relocated?

   a. Subdirectories of the directory being moved
   b. Files in the directory being moved
   c. a and b
   d. None of the above

10. How many characters may a filename contain?

    a. 11
    b. 3
    c. 8
    d. 16

Using Write

● *Objectives*

Upon completing this chapter, you'll be able to:

1. **Create and navigate within a document.**
2. **Save and retrieve a document.**
3. **Edit a document.**
4. **Print a document.**
5. **Format a document.**

OVERVIEW

Write is an "executive" word processor. It earns the label "executive" because it is tailored for the tasks executives typically perform, such as writing memos, reports, and letters. Although Write lacks some of the more advanced features of expensive and complex word processors (e.g., a spell checker, a thesaurus, and mail merge capabilities), its ease of use and flexibility make Write ideally suited for most business correspondence.

The labs in this chapter are structured around the creation, modification, and printing of a Write document. You can use Write's sophisticated editing and formatting capabilities to create a professional looking hard copy of your work. Because Write takes full advantage of Windows' integrated environment, both text and graphics can be combined in the same document to produce a persuasive and effective product.

LAB 5–1   CREATING A DOCUMENT

In this first lab, we'll introduce you to the basics of word processing. You'll learn to start Write, create a document, save it, print it, and safely exit Write. You'll also get a chance to practice moving around in Write and using some of its menus.

Be especially careful to follow the instructions in this lab precisely. The document you create here will serve as the foundation for the activities you perform over the next two chapters. You'll continue to embellish and improve upon it until you have a polished and professional-looking product. This document or a later version of it will provide the means to illustrate many of the features of Write, as well as those of Paintbrush and Clipboard (Chapters 6 and 7, respectively). So take your time and double-check your work.

Using a Word Processor

Before we explore Write's features, we'll pause to examine some concepts that are fundamental to all word processors. The most logical place to start this investigation is with your computer keyboard.

You've probably noticed the striking similarity between the typical typewriter keyboard and your computer keyboard. The keys are placed in the same standard "QWERTY" layout, making it easier for those familiar with a typewriter to use a computer. However, to tap the full power of a word processor, you'll need to go well beyond the basic typing skills required to use a typewriter. We think you'll find the journey well worth your time.

Write is one of a growing number of WYSIWYG word processors. As you learned in Chapter 1, WYSIWYG means that the text you see on your computer's screen closely approximates the final printed output. This feature simplifies word processing because you can see what the document will look like before it's actually printed. In fact, you'll find it indispensable in exploring the different ways you can alter the appearance of your documents.

Write and most other modern word processors share a feature called *word wrap*. **Word wrap** lets you type a stream of text without having to stop and press the Enter key (carriage return on a conventional typewriter) at the end of each line. When you reach the end of a line, Write automatically moves you down to the next line.

The only time you'll need to move manually to the next line is when you're starting a new paragraph. When you press the Enter key, you create a **hard return**. Write also refers to hard returns as *paragraph markers*. Write considers the text between two paragraph markers to be a paragraph. Thus, if you press the Enter key at the end of each line, you'll be making each line a separate paragraph. Instead, you should simply let word wrap move you down to the next line automatically. Press Enter only when you really want to start a new paragraph.

Formatting a document refers to changes made to the text. Formatting changes include adjusting the margins of your document, as well as bold printing or underlining areas of text, choosing the font (style of printing) of the text, and altering the line spacing. These are but a few of the capabilities you will have at your fingertips after mastering Write.

When you use a typewriter, you are forced to perform all formatting as you type. For example, you must set your margins before you begin a letter. Formatting mistakes or changes are time-consuming to correct or implement. This approach lacks flexibility, requires much forethought, and is quite inefficient.

Word processing, on the other hand, is best done in the following sequence.

- Type the text into the computer's memory.
- Correct any spelling and grammatical errors.
- Read the text for clarity and comprehension.
- Make any structural changes that are necessary, rearranging the text to enhance accuracy.
- Begin the formatting process, starting with changes made to individual words or small blocks of text. Examples of this type of formatting are bold printing and underlining of words or sentences.
- Format larger areas of text, working up to those formatting changes that are global (changes that affect the entire document). Global changes include page numbering, headers, and footers. Headers are typically one- or two-line titles, messages, or page numbers that appear at the top of most pages of a document. Footers provide the same function, except they are displayed at the bottom of each page.

This sequence guarantees efficiency and allows you to focus your attention on just one task at a time. You can also easily go back and change the work done in any earlier stage, as you cannot with a typewriter where formatting decisions are set in stone. Simply put, a word processor complements your creative processes.

Before we begin the lab, you should know one very important thing about entering work in a computer. Until you save it on disk, it is very vulnerable to being partially or completely lost. Whether from mistakes, accidents, power failures, or some other mishap, data loss is all too common. So, for the sake of your sanity, *save your work frequently*. Never allow more than 15 minutes to pass between saves. Saving your work is simple and takes only a moment. Reconstructing it is not so simple.

Starting Write

Write is accessed from the Windows Accessories group. As you may recall, we briefly discussed this application in Chapter 3. Write's program icon looks like a fountain pen. To launch Write, you double-click its icon in the Accessories group window of Program Manager. After starting Write, you'll see a screen similar to the one displayed in Figure 5-1.

1. Start Windows.
2. Select the Windows Accessories group. Activate Write by double-clicking on its icon. Maximize the Write window.

Notice the familiar window elements such as the title bar, scroll bars, control-menu box, and menu bar. Obviously, Write conforms to the Windows' environment standards. As you learn to use Write, you'll also be increasing your working knowledge of Windows. In addition to the familiar window elements, you'll see a few new elements that are

Figure 5-1. The opening screen of Write with the filename, end-of-file marker, text cursor, and page status bar labeled.

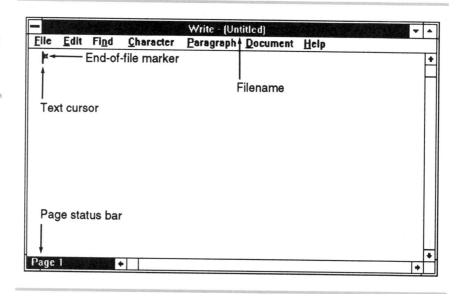

specific to Write. The menu bar contains some menu headings that are unique to Write. We'll introduce you to each of these in more detail as they become relevant to the task at hand. For now, let's concentrate on the four elements labeled in Figure 5–1.

The name of the current document file appears just to the right of the window title in the menu bar. By default, the filename **Untitled** is given to every new document until you save it. When you save a file, you have the option of renaming it. When you save and change a file's name or retrieve another document, the new name will appear in the menu bar. You can always determine which document is loaded by checking this display.

The **end-of-file marker** can be seen in the workspace area of Write, just below the menu bar and to the far left. This marker is in every Write document and indicates where the document ends. When you type text, you'll notice the marker will move to the right and down. However, it is impossible for you to enter text either below or to the right of the marker.

The **text cursor** is the blinking vertical line resting directly in front of the end-of-file marker. The text cursor is also called the *insertion point* because it indicates where the text you type will appear on the screen. You'll also notice that the mouse pointer changes to the shape of an I-beam when you move it into the workspace of the Write window.

The **page status bar** is located in the lower left portion of the Write window. It reveals the number of the page where the text cursor is presently residing. Because Write waits to organize your document into pages until printing, the page status bar is not always accurate. The document must be "paginated" before the page status bar can be relied on to locate the text cursor.

Pagination is the process of assigning page breaks to a document. A *page break* tells the printer where one page ends and the next begins. Pagination normally occurs only when you print; however, you can force Write to paginate a document at any time by issuing the *Repaginate...* command from the File menu.

Entering Text

You now know enough about Write to enter some text. For fun, let's assume you're the personnel manager of a fast-growing business called Norm's Neurosurgery and Chainsaw Supply, Inc. You've been assigned to produce a memorandum to help employees become acquainted with the company's new building. The memo will eventually incorporate both text and a map to explain the layout of the building. You'll use Write to create and enhance the text portion of the memo.

As you type the text below, remember to use the Backspace or Delete key to correct any typographical errors. When you finish, your screen should resemble the one shown in Figure 5-2. Don't worry if your text lines have a length different from the ones shown in the figure.

1. To enter the first paragraph, type:

> **Welcome Aboard!!! We are happy to have you join our team. Norm's is the premier firm in its market niche. From scalpels to splitting mauls, we service the entire spectrum of cutting needs for both the brain surgeon and lumberjack.**

Figure 5-2. The Write window after the first four paragraphs of text have been entered.

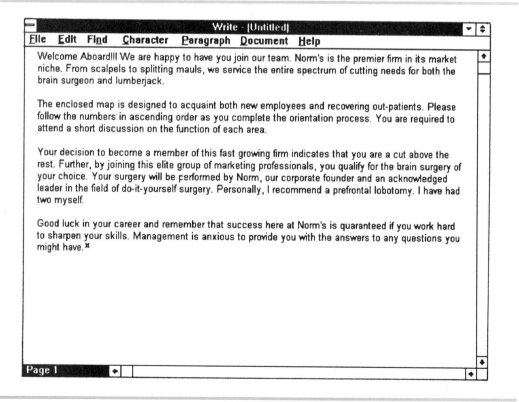

2. After the word "lumberjack," press the Enter key twice to create a blank line between paragraphs. Then type:

The enclosed map is designed to acquaint both new employees and recovering out-patients. Please follow the numbers in ascending order as you complete the orientation process. You are required to attend a short discussion on the function of each area.

3. Press Enter twice, and type:

Your decision to become a member of this fast growing firm indicates that you are a cut above the rest. Further, by joining this elite group of marketing professionals, you qualify for the brain surgery of your choice. Your surgery will be performed by Norm, our corporate founder and an acknowledged leader in the field of do-it-yourself surgery. Personally, I recommend a prefrontal lobotomy. I have had two myself.

4. Finally, push Enter twice again, and type:

Good luck in your career and remember that success here at Norm's is guaranteed if you work hard to sharpen your skills. Management is anxious to provide you with the answers to any questions you might have.

Saving a Document

Figure 5–3.

To save a Write document, you begin by choosing the File menu from the menu bar in Write. The menu exhibited in Figure 5–3 drops down. From the File menu, you can click the **Save** command. The first time you save a document, Write will display the Save As dialog box shown in Figure 5–4. This dialog box contains a *File Name* text box, a *File Name* list box, a *Directories* list box, two drop-down list boxes, a check box, and the *OK* and *Cancel* buttons.

The *File Name* text box lets you name your document. You can use any legal filename (the rules for legal filenames were covered in Chapter 4). However, do not enter a file extension, because Write adds its own extension (.WRI).

Figure 5–4.
The Save As
dialog box.

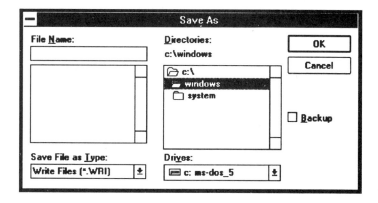

1. Select the *Save* command from the File menu.
2. Click on the *File Name* text box, and type: EX5-1A

   Clicking the arrow in the *Drives* drop-down list box displays the available disk drives in your system. You can select a drive from this list. We'll use your EXERCISES floppy to save all your work.

3. Insert your EXERCISES disk in drive A.
4. Click the arrow in the *Drives* drop-down list box, and click on the drive a: icon (if drive A is not visible, use the scroll bar to find it).

   The *Directories* list box will now display the directories on drive A. Notice the subdirectories PBFILES and WPFILES listed there. To select a different directory, double-click on it in the *Directories* list box.

5. To make WPFILES the current directory, double-click on it in the *Directories* list box.
6. Check the path name, located just above the *Directories* list box, to make sure it displays the correct path—A:\WPFILES. If it doesn't, carefully repeat steps 4 and 5 until it does.

   After a file has been saved once, selecting the *Save* command again will automatically replace it with the document currently displayed in Write. The computer will not prompt you for a new name.
   If you want to retain a backup copy of the original file, you have two alternatives: Either rename the current file using the *Save As...* command, or when you save the document, switch on the *Backup* check

box. When you save with the *Backup* option engaged, Write changes
the extension of the original file from .WRI to .BKP, thus preventing
you from overwriting it. For example, a file initially saved as
ESSAY.WRI would also be saved as ESSAY.BKP.

7. To ensure a backup copy every time you save EX5-1A, click the
   Backup check box.

The *Save File as Type* drop-down list box lets you save a Write
document in another file format. This allows your file to be opened by
applications other than Write. The options include: *WRITE (WRI),
WORD (DOC), WORD/TEXT ONLY (DOC),* and *TEXT (TXT).
WRITE (WRI)* is the default file format. The *WORD (DOC)* and
WORD/TEXT ONLY (DOC) options will convert your Write document into a file acceptable to the popular word processor Microsoft
Word for Windows. If you choose this option, your document retains
all its formatting when it is opened in Word.

The *TEXT (TXT)* option is a generic format that can be read by
most other word processors. Unfortunately, a document saved with this
option loses all its special formatting such as boldfacing and underlining. This option is typically used to share a file with a friend or colleague who has a different word processing program such as WordPerfect or WordStar.

At this point, your Save As dialog box should match the one
shown in Figure 5-5. You are now ready to complete the naming and
saving process by choosing the *OK* button.

Figure 5-5.
The Save As
dialog box.

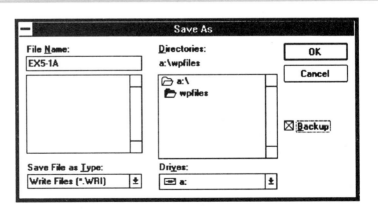

8. Click the *OK* button in the Save As dialog box to save your document to the floppy in drive A. The light on the drive will glow briefly as the file is being stored on your disk.

9. Once again, choose *Save* from the File menu. Notice that the process takes only a moment and requires no further input.

___NOTE___

Although you'll be given specific instructions to save your work throughout this chapter, you should carry out the practice on your own from here on. Get in the habit of saving every 15 minutes and you'll vastly reduce the chances of losing your work.

Moving around in Write

The mouse lets you move the text cursor anywhere in a document (except, of course, beyond the end-of-file marker). To position the text cursor, you simply point at the spot where you plan to work and click the mouse button. The text cursor immediately relocates to that exact position.

Navigating in Write with the keyboard usually requires more effort, but, on occasions, the keyboard can offer a more expedient option. Figure 5–6 lists the most useful keystrokes for cursor movement. To familiarize you with using the mouse and these keystrokes, we'll take a moment to practice moving around your document.

Figure 5–6. Keystrokes for moving around in a Write document.

Keystroke	Movement	Keystroke	Movement
↑	Up one line	*[Goto] →	Next sentence
↓	Down one line	*[Goto] ←	Previous sentence
→	Right one character	*[Goto] ↓	Next paragraph
←	Left one character	*[Goto] ↑	Previous paragraph
[Ctrl] →	Right one word	*[Goto][PgUp]	Previous page
[Ctrl] ←	Left one word	*[Goto][PgDn]	Next page
[Home]	Go to beginning of line	[PgUp]	Up one window
[End]	Go to end of line	[PgDn]	Down one window
[Ctrl][Home]	Go to beginning of document	[Ctrl][End]	Go to end of document

*[Goto] refers to the 5 key on the numeric keypad.

Num Lock OFF

• Hold 5/press second key

1. Press and hold down the Ctrl key and press the Home key to send the text cursor instantly to the top of your document.
2. Press and hold down the Ctrl key and press the End key to send the text cursor back to the bottom of the document.
3. To move to the top of the document once again, scroll to the first sentence and click anywhere on it.
4. Practice moving the cursor one word, one sentence, and then one paragraph at a time using the mouse and then the keystrokes in Figure 5-6.

Printing a Document with Write

To print a document, you choose the *Print...* command from the File menu, pick the print options you want from the dialog box that appears, and click *OK*.

1. Select the *Print...* command from the File menu.

The Print dialog box pictured in Figure 5-7 will materialize. It contains a Print Range area with the radio buttons *All, Selection,* and *Pages*. A **radio button** is like check box: If the circle in front of the label contains a dot, the option is switched on. The radio buttons in the Print Range area let you specify all or a portion of your document to be printed.

The *All* radio button is the default setting. However, you can use the *Pages* button to designate a selected portion of your document for printing. The *From* and *To* text boxes let you specify a range of pages to print (e.g., from page 2 to page 8). This option comes in handy if your

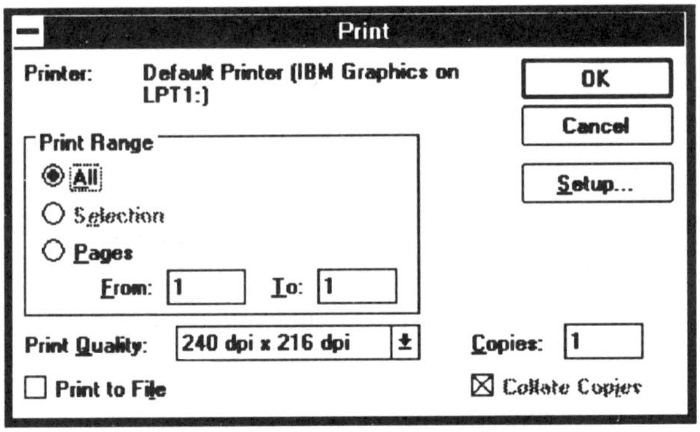

Figure 5-7.
The Print
dialog box.

printer has jammed or run out of paper. You can use it to print just the remaining pages of your document.

If your printer supports it, the *Print Quality* drop-down list box provides the means to change the resolution of your printout. Choosing a lower resolution will cause the printer to print at a faster speed but with less than the optimal print quality.

The *Copies* text box permits the printing of multiple copies of the same document. For example, if you wanted to print an extra copy of your document, you would enter a 2. Selecting the *Cancel* button aborts the operation and returns you to Write.

2. To print two copies of your document, click on the *Copies* text box, erase the existing number, and type: 2
3. After making sure your printer is ready, click *OK* to print.

___NOTE_____

The Print dialog box also offers options for changing the printer setup, printing to a file instead of the printer, and (when the printer supports it) collating the multiple copies. For additional information on these topics refer to the Windows *User's Guide*.

Quitting Write

Always quit any Windows application by choosing the *Exit* command from the File menu. Never quit a program by turning off your computer—you may lose valuable information.

1. To quit Write, select the *Exit* command from Write's File menu.
2. You may end your Windows session after verifying that the *Save Settings on Exit* command in the Options menu of Program Manager is switched off.

LAB 5-2   EDITING A DOCUMENT

In this lab, we'll begin to explore the power of Write to arrange and rearrange the text in a document. The ability to edit selected portions of your documents provides you with an incredible amount of freedom and flexibility. As new ideas occur or better ways to state things come to mind, you can quickly and easily reorganize your work to incorporate those improvements.

We'll put the power of editing to work to refine the company memo you began in the last lab. First, however, you'll need to restart Write and retrieve your file.

Opening a Write Document

To retrieve or open a Write file, choose the *Open...* command from the File menu, select the filename from the Open dialog box, and click *OK*.

1. If necessary, start Windows.
2. Launch the Write program.
3. To provide the greatest work area, maximize the Write window.
4. Select the *Open...* command from the File menu.

After issuing this *Open...* command, the Open dialog box will appear, as shown in Figure 5–8. If your document is displayed in the *File Name* list box, you can click on it and then choose *OK* to open it. A faster method of opening a file is to simply double-click its name.

If the document is not listed in the *File Name* list box, you must use the *Drives* drop-down list box and/or the *Directories* list box to change to the drive and/or directory where the file is stored. To change drives, click on the arrow in the *Drives* drop-down list box and select the drive you want. To choose a different directory, double-click on it in the *Directories* list box. Once the filename appears in the *File Name* list box, you can open it by double-clicking it.

In this case, we'll need to switch to drive A and directory WPFILES.

Figure 5–8.
The Open dialog box lets you retrieve your Write files.

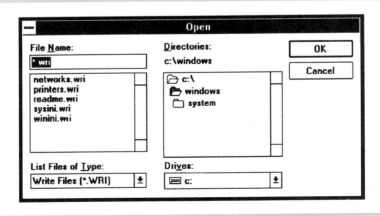

5. To make drive A current, open the *Drives* drop-down list box and click on the a: icon.
6. To select the WPFILES directory, double-click on it in the *Directories* list box.

Before proceeding, check the path name, located just above the *Directories* list box, to make sure it now displays the correct path— A:\WPFILES. If not, carefully repeat steps 5 and 6 until it does.

7. To open your document, double-click on EX5-1A.WRI in the *File Name* list box.

After completing the above actions, your document will appear in the workspace of the Write application window. You are now ready to begin editing it.

___NOTE_____

You can also open a Write file by typing the directory path and filename in the *File Name* text box and clicking *OK*. For example, to open the file EX5-1A, you would type **A:\WPFILES\EX5-1A.WRI** in the *File Name* entry area and click *OK*.

Selecting Text

The first step in editing a document is to select the text you want to edit. **Selecting** or **blocking** text highlights it. The block will display in *inverse video*, where characters appear white and the background becomes black. Once text is blocked, you can issue commands and carry out actions to modify that portion of your document.

The mouse makes selecting text fast and easy. Depending upon the amount of text you want to highlight, you can choose one of five blocking actions summarized in the list below. The first three require only mouse movements, while the last two involve using the mouse in concert with your keyboard.

To Select	Do This
By the character	Move to the first character to be selected. Press and hold the mouse button while you drag the cursor over the text to be selected. Release the button to complete the selection.

By the line	Move to the selection area (the column that borders the left margin) and point next to the line to be selected. Click the mouse button once to select the line.
By the paragraph	Move to the selection area (the column that borders the left margin) and point next to any line in the paragraph. Double-click to select the entire paragraph.
Between points	Move to the first character to be selected and click the mouse button. Move to the last character in the block. Hold down the Shift key and click the mouse button.
Entire document	Move to the selection area (the column that borders the left margin), hold down the Ctrl key, and click the mouse button.

You'll need to become familiar with each of these blocking techniques to edit your documents efficiently. The following exercises will let you practice using these procedures to block various-sized segments of your document.

Blocking by the Character

To block text by the character, you position the mouse pointer on the first letter you want to mark, press and hold the left mouse button, drag the pointer over the area you want to highlight, and release the mouse button. This method lets you block an area as small as one character or as large as the entire document.

Let's use this method to block the second paragraph of your document. When you finish, compare your screen to the one shown in Figure 5-9.

1. Point at the first letter of the second paragraph.
2. Press and hold down the mouse button.
3. Drag the pointer down until the entire second paragraph is highlighted in inverse video, and release the button to complete the selection.

Blocking by the Line

To select an entire line of text at a time, you begin by moving the pointer to the selection area of the Write window. The **selection area** is the blank column located between the left window frame and the left

Figure 5-9. The mouse selection technique for blocking text by character lets you mark various sized segments of your document.

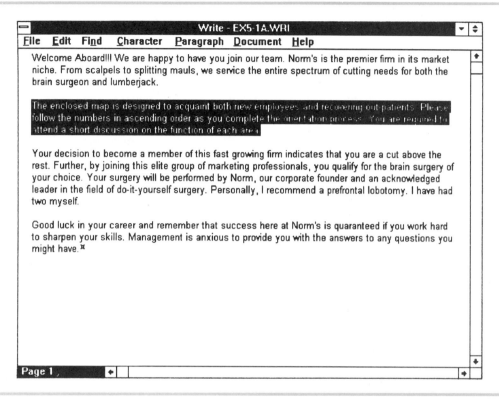

margin of your text, as shown in Figure 5-10. When your pointer is in this area, it assumes the standard arrow shape. You can then point at the line of text you want blocked and click.

To extend the blocking, simply hold down the mouse button, drag the pointer down (or up) the selection area, and release the button when you have highlighted all the text you want blocked. You can deselect a block by clicking anywhere in the workspace.

Let's use the "by the line" method to mark a single line of text and then extend the selection to several lines.

1. Deselect the second paragraph by clicking anywhere in the body of the document.
2. Position the pointer in the selection area to the left of the first line of text in the second paragraph. If you're in the selection area, the pointer will look like an arrow.
3. Click the mouse button to highlight the line.

Figure 5–10.
This window
indicates the
location of
the selection
area on the
left side of
the work-
space.

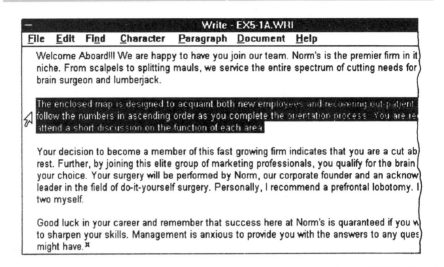

4. To extend the block, again position the pointer in the selection area next to the first line in the second paragraph.
5. Hold down the mouse button and drag the pointer down the selection area until all of the second paragraph is blocked. Release the button.
6. Deselect the text by clicking anywhere in the document.

Blocking by the Paragraph

To select an entire paragraph instantly, move the pointer to the selection area, position it next to any line in the paragraph you want to highlight, and double-click.

Let's select the second paragraph again using the method described above.

1. Move the pointer to the selection area next to any line in the second paragraph.
2. Double-click to highlight the entire paragraph instantly.
3. Deselect the paragraph.

Blocking between Points

To mark text between any two points in your document, point at the first character you want to block, click once, then point at the character where you want the block to end, press and hold down the Shift key, and press the left mouse button. All the text between the two characters immediately displays in inverse video.

Let's use the "between points" method to mark the text from the second sentence in the second paragraph to the end of the third paragraph. After you complete the steps below, check your work against Figure 5-11.

1. Position your pointer in front of the first letter of the second sentence in the second paragraph and click once.
2. Move the pointer to the last character in the third paragraph. When your pointer is just beyond the period of the final sentence, press and hold the Shift key and click once.

● **HINT**

Like the drag and release method, blocking between points lets you select an area as small as one character or as large as the entire document. However, when you block between points, your mouse is free for rapid scrolling through your document. This makes blocking multiple pages of a long document a much faster and easier operation. Instead of dragging the mouse down page after page, you mark the top of the intended block, quickly scroll to the end, and Shift-click to complete the selection. For shorter documents, you'll still find blocking by the character a more efficient technique because it requires fewer steps and no keyboard interaction.

Blocking the Entire Document

To select an entire document, move the pointer to the selection area, hold down the Ctrl key, and click the mouse button. All the text in your document will immediately be highlighted. This is without doubt the fastest way to select an entire document. It's especially handy because you can invoke the technique anywhere inside the selection area. Let's try it on your document.

1. Move your pointer to the selection area so that it assumes the shape of an arrow.
2. Press and hold the Ctrl key and then click the left mouse button.
3. Deselect the text.

Figure 5–11. The selection technique for blocking between points lets you quickly mark portions of a large document.

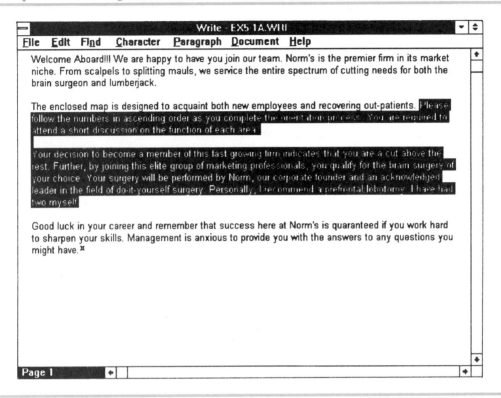

Armed with this arsenal of techniques for selecting text, you are ready to learn about the commands available for editing your document. As you use these commands, remember that only the highlighted section(s) of your text will be affected; the rest of your document will remain unchanged.

You can quit now or proceed to the next section. If you choose to stop, exit Write without saving your file. Select the *No* button when the dialog box appears asking if you want to save your changes. Be sure the *Save Settings on Exit* command in the Options menu of Program Manager is toggled off before exiting Windows.

Moving and Copying Text

The commands in Write's Edit menu (see Figure 5-12) make it possible for you to move and copy text. **Moving** a block of text involves

temporarily removing or cutting it from your document and then inserting or pasting it back in. **Copying** leaves the original block in place but creates a duplicate to be inserted elsewhere.

Before you can move or copy text, you must select it. Once a portion of your document has been selected, you can issue either the *Cut* or *Copy* command from the Edit menu. The **Cut** command removes the block of text and places it in **Clipboard**— a temporary storage area for text and graphics. You then move the cursor to the location in the document where you want to insert the text stored in Clipboard. Choosing the **Paste** command from the Edit menu inserts the text at that spot.

When you choose the *Copy* command, Write duplicates the highlighted text and places it in Clipboard. The original block of text remains untouched in your document. You then position the cursor at the spot where you want the text inserted and select *Paste* from the Edit menu. The contents of Clipboard are instantly copied to that location.

You can reverse your last command or action by issuing the *Undo* command from the Edit menu. **Undo** can be a life saver. It gives you a way to recover from both minor and major mistakes. For example, if you accidentally delete 50 pages of text, you can use Undo to cancel the deletion and return your document to its previous condition.

The *Undo* command changes to alert you to the type of command or action it will reverse. When you cut, copy, or paste text, the *Undo* command becomes *Undo Editing;* during typing it appears as *Undo Typing;* and while you are formatting it changes to *Undo Formatting.* You'll get a chance to use the *Undo* command shortly.

The *Paste Special...*, *Paste Link*, *Links...*, *Object*, and *Insert Object...* commands work together to let you embed (paste) objects (data) from other applications in a Write document. We'll explore these commands in Chapter 7, *Transferring Data Between Applications.*

The final commands in the Edit menu, *Move Picture* and *Size Picture*, let you manipulate objects (data) that have been embedded (pasted) into your document. We'll also delay discussion of these commands until Chapter 7, where you'll learn to use Write to rearrange data imported from other applications.

To gain some practice in using the rest of these editing commands, we'll move and copy portions of the memo you created earlier. Let's start by repositioning the second paragraph to the end of the memo.

1. If necessary, start Windows, load Write, and open the file EX5-1A.WRI.
2. Select the second paragraph of your document.
3. Next, choose the *Cut* command from the Edit menu.

The second paragraph will disappear, as pictured in Figure 5-13. It has been placed in Clipboard. Clipboard will hold this text until you cut or copy another selection. The new selection will replace the previous one because Clipboard can contain only one block at a time. Also, if you exit Windows before inserting the text into your document, it will be lost. We'll cover Clipboard in greater detail in Chapter 7.

With the block cut, you are now free to reposition your text cursor and paste the selection back into your document.

4. To insert the second paragraph at the bottom of your document, click at the end-of-file marker.

Figure 5-13. Blocking the second paragraph and issuing the *Cut* command removes it from your document and transfers it to Clipboard.

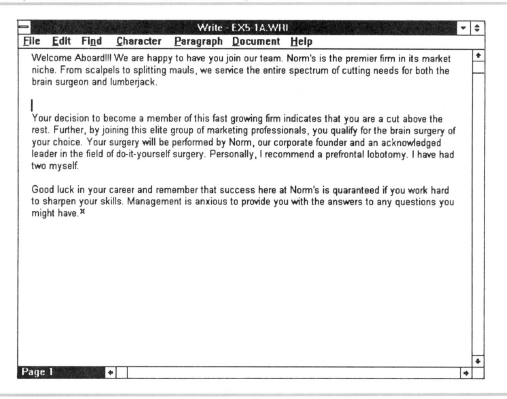

5. Press the Enter key twice to create a blank line below the final paragraph of text.

6. Choose the *Paste* command from the Edit menu.

The block of text will be inserted immediately following the present position of the text cursor.

7. Reposition the cursor to the top of your document.

Check your screen against the one portrayed in Figure 5–14. What was formerly the second paragraph now appears at the bottom. Even though you have pasted it back in, Clipboard will continue to hold a copy of the text, unless you displace it with another selection. You can issue the *Paste* command as many times as you like to create multiple copies of the same block. Write will insert each one immediately after the current location of the text cursor.

Figure 5–14. Reissuing the *Paste* command places another copy of the contents of Clipboard into your document.

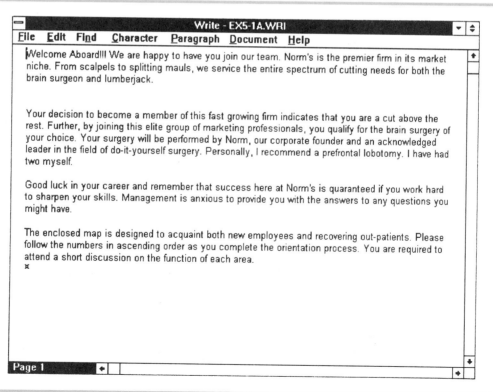

To demonstrate how this works, we'll paste another copy of the text directly above the first paragraph.

8. Position the text cursor at the top of your document and to the left of the first character.
9. Choose the *Paste* command again.

The *Undo* command returns your document to its former state before the last action or command. Since the most recent command was *Paste*, issuing *Undo Editing* will remove the inserted paragraph at the top of your document.

10. Choose the *Undo Editing* command from the Edit menu.

Your screen should once again match Figure 5–14.
We can use the *Copy* command to replicate the greeting in your document for more emphasis. Follow the steps below and compare your results with those pictured in Figure 5–15.

Figure 5–15. The *Copy* and *Paste* commands have been used to replicate the greeting phrase.

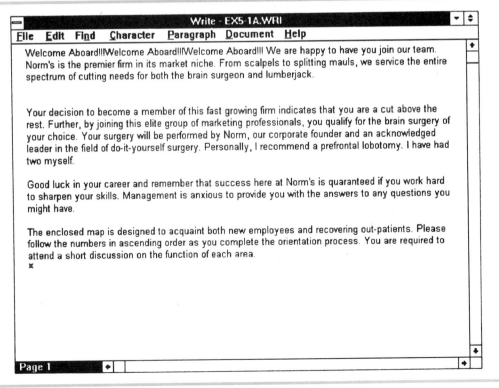

11. Block the greeting in the first paragraph: **Welcome Aboard!!!**
12. Choose the *Copy* command from the Edit menu.
13. Deselect the block of text by clicking in front of the first character of the greeting.
14. Choose *Paste* to create a second copy.
15. Select *Paste* again to insert one more copy of the greeting.

Deleting and Undeleting Text

You can quickly erase portions of your document by simply blocking them and pressing the Delete key. If you press the Delete key without selecting any text, the character immediately to the right of the text cursor will be erased. Pressing Delete repeatedly or holding the key down will cause it to erase a steady stream of characters.

You can use the Backspace key to delete characters directly to the left of the text cursor. If the cursor is positioned at the beginning of a line, pressing Backspace will delete the last character on the line above. Backspace will also erase any selected text.

To undelete text, use the *Undo Editing* command from the Edit menu. It returns the text most recently deleted to its previous location in the document.

We'll use these commands to make some modifications to your document. Follow the instructions below carefully.

1. Block the two extra copies of the greeting you inserted in the last exercise and push the Delete key to erase them.
2. To reverse the last command, choose *Undo Editing* from the Edit menu.

___**NOTE**_____

You can speed up the editing process in a long document by using the commands in the Find menu to locate and replace text rapidly. To get more information on the Find menu, check Windows' Help facility.

_____

The two greetings will reappear in the same location in your document. Note that they remain highlighted.

3. Delete the block again.
4. To remove the extra blank line between the first and second paragraphs, move the text cursor to the first empty line and press Delete.
5. Choose *Undo Editing* from the Edit menu to recover the blank line.

Blank lines created by pressing the Enter key are actually not empty. They contain unseen codes that represent the hard returns created by the Enter key. When you delete one of these invisible codes, you remove the line. You can also use the Backspace key to delete a "blank" line.

6. To delete one of the extra lines between the first and second paragraphs, place your cursor right before the first character of the second paragraph and push the Backspace key.

Check your document against the one shown in Figure 5–16. Make any corrections necessary so that it matches this illustration and then issue the following commands to print a copy of it.

Figure 5–16. The Delete and Backspace keys have been used to erase the two additional greetings you inserted earlier and the extra space between the first and second paragraphs.

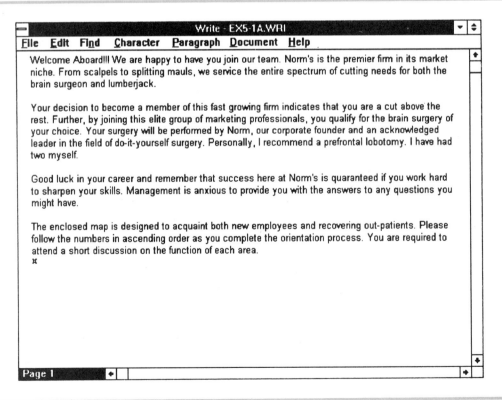

7. Choose the *Print...* command from the File menu and click *OK*.

8. Choose the *Save As...* command from the File menu and rename the file EX5-2A.WRI. Check to make sure the *Backup* option is selected and the current directory is WPFILES.

9. Click *OK* after you finish entering the new filename.

10. You may end your Windows session after verifying that the *Save Settings on Exit* command in the Options menu of Program Manager is switched off

LAB 5-3   FORMATTING A DOCUMENT

Once you have typed, corrected, and edited a document, you are ready to begin the formatting phase. Formatting enables you to enliven and clarify your text. You've no doubt heard the timeworn adage "you only get one chance to make a first impression." The printed appearance of your documents often creates that all-important first impression. By making wise formatting choices, you can improve the chances that your documents will elicit a favorable response.

This is where the WYSIWYG capability of Write really comes into play. It lets you immediately evaluate the impact of a formatting decision. Because your screen displays an accurate reflection of what the printed document will look like, you can quickly try a wide variety of formatting options without ever printing. This makes it much easier to find the right combination of options to fashion dynamic and awe-inspiring documents.

● HINT

It is quite typical, when confronted with all the formatting choices available in a modern word processor, to go a bit "crazy" and format everything in sight. However, the paramount rule of formatting is to use restraint. Many good documents are ruined by excess.

Write has an impressive list of formatting commands. They are grouped into three menus: Character, Paragraph, and Document. In the first portion of this lab, you'll learn how to use the options in the Character menu. As you might guess by the menu name, these commands are primarily intended for use with smaller amounts of text. The next section of the lab deals with the formatting choices in the Paragraph menu. These commands are normally used to format larger portions of your document. Finally, the Document menu features the options that affect your entire document.

Formatting with the Character Menu

Character menu commands can affect a block of text as small as one character or as large as the entire document. However, they are typically directed at individual words and phrases. Figure 5-17 displays the choices available in this menu. To use these options, you should first select the text you want to format and then issue the desired command from the Character menu. (You may want to refer back to the selection techniques covered in the preceding lab.)

Figure 5-17.

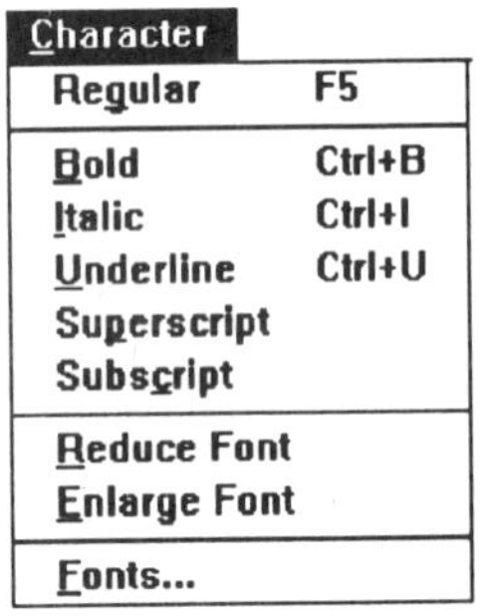

Character	
Regular	F5
Bold	Ctrl+B
Italic	Ctrl+I
Underline	Ctrl+U
Superscript	
Subscript	
Reduce Font	
Enlarge Font	
Fonts...	

● **HINT**

Write provides speed keys for its most commonly used commands. They appear on the menu beside the command. Using these speed keys can accelerate the formatting process.

Using Character Styles

Character commands are broken into three categories: styles, fonts, and sizes. **Styles** are the options that change the appearance of text without changing its font. (A font is the actual design or shape shared by a set of characters.) Write offers the following style choices: regular, bold, italic, underline, superscript, and subscript. Character styles give emphasis to your documents.

Let's use the options in the Character menu to dress up your memo document. First, we'll add a title and heading.

1. If necessary, start Windows.
2. Then open Write and maximize it.
3. Retrieve the file EX5-2A.WRI from the WPFILES directory on your EXERCISES disk.
4. Insert two blank lines above your first paragraph by positioning your cursor at the top of the document and pressing the Enter key twice.

5. Type the following title at the very top of your memo: **Norm's Neurosurgery and Chainsaw Supply, Inc.**

6. To insert another two blank lines after your new title, press Enter twice.

7. Next, type To: and press the Tab key. Then, type: Our New Employees. Again, insert two more empty lines by pressing Enter twice.

8. Type From: and push Tab. Now type: [your name]. Press Enter once to insert a blank line.

9. Press Tab, and type: Personnel Director

Now, let's emphasize several sections of your new title and heading.

10. To boldface the title, select it and choose *Bold* from the Character menu. Note that selected text remains highlighted even after a format command is issued.

11. Next, select the text Our New Employees and issue the *Underline* command from the Character menu.

12. Highlight your name and italicize it.

After these embellishments, your document should look like the one shown in Figure 5–18.

● **HINT**_____

You can combine styles by selecting additional style options. Avoid making the formatting obtrusive with too many style options. If you incorrectly format a block of text or just change your mind about its appearance, you can remove the formatting by again selecting the block (if it's no longer highlighted) and issuing the *Regular* command from the Character menu.

_____

Changing the Font Type

In addition to modifying the style, you can actually alter the underlying font. The colloquial definition of a **font** is the design or shape shared by a set of characters. Characters that belong to a particular font are easily recognized because they share common elements of the same base design. There are two categories of fonts available for printing text with

Figure 5–18. Your memo with the new heading inserted and embellished.

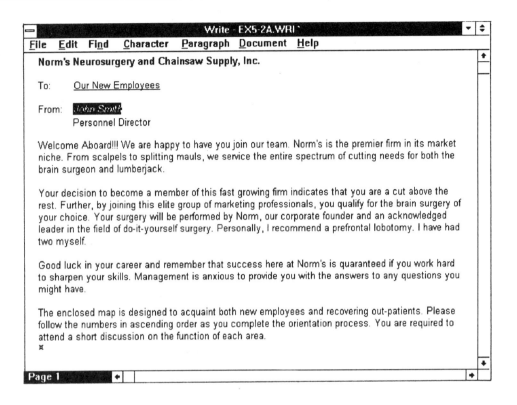

Windows' applications: TrueType and printer fonts. **TrueType fonts** print pretty much as they look on the screen. They are also scalable to any size. **Printer fonts** are printer dependent so their appearance on the screen may vary from the way they look when printed. In addition, printer fonts have a very limited number of pre-defined sizes.

Selecting the *Fonts...* command from the Character menu will display the available list of fonts, as shown in Figure 5–19. For quick and easy identification, all the TrueType fonts are preceded by the letters TT.

To alter the font type of part or all of a document, first block the portion you want to alter. Then issue the *Fonts...* command from the Character menu. The Font dialog box will appear with a list of available fonts. If you pick a character design from the Font dialog box, you'll have to click the *OK* button to complete the command.

Figure 5-19.
The Font
dialog box
lets you select
from all the
available font
options.

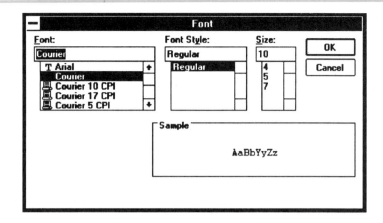

To gain some experience in using these commands, follow these steps.

1. To change the base font of your first paragraph to Times New Roman, block it, and then choose the *Fonts...* command from the Character menu.
2. When the Font dialog box appears, scroll to the *Times New Roman* font in the *Font* list box, and click on it.

The *Sample* area in the Font dialog box will change to display a set of characters formatted with the new font. These sample characters provide a convenient way for you to evaluate the effect of a font before implementing it in your document. The *Font Style* text and list boxes directly above the *Sample* area give you the ability to incorporate font type and style changes simultaneously. To pick a font style for the text currently selected, either type it in the *Font Style* text box or click on it in the *Font Style* list box.

3. Click on the *Italic* option in the *Font Style* list box to italicize the entire first paragraph, then select the *OK* button.
4. Next, select the second paragraph, and click on the *Fonts...* command from the Character menu.
5. Click on the *Times New Roman* option in the *Font* list box, and select *OK*.
6. Block the third paragraph, issue the *Fonts...* command from the Character menu, and select the *Courier New* font from the *Font* list box.

7. Once the new font is chosen, click *OK*.

8. Deselect the third paragraph.

Your screen should now look similar the one portrayed in Figure 5–20. The first paragraph is displayed in Times New Roman and italics, the second paragraph in Times New Roman, and the third paragraph is shown in Courier New. The remaining text is formatted in the default font Arial.

Adjusting a Font's Size

In addition to altering the font and style of text, you can adjust its size. For example, you can enlarge a title for emphasis or reduce a passage of text to set it off from the rest of your document. The measurement used to adjust the size of text is called **point size**. A *point* is equal to $1/72$ of an inch. A larger point size increases the size of text, while a smaller number reduces its dimensions.

Figure 5–20. Your memo after the font change.

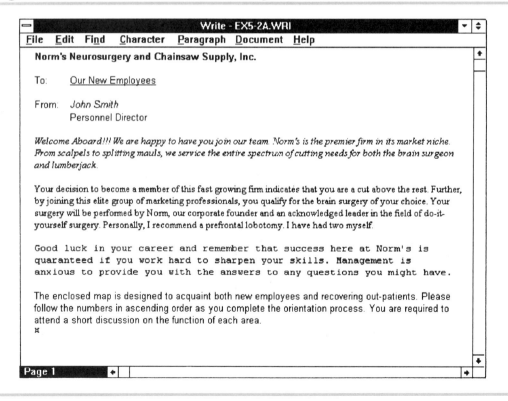

To change the size of part or all of your document, you must first block the portion you want to adjust. Then, select either the *Reduce Font* or *Enlarge Font* commands from the Character menu. Each time you click on one of these options you'll increment the block's size by two points. Of course, this assumes you are using TrueType fonts or a printer font that is capable of supporting such adjustments. Some printer fonts only allow a single point size. If you attempt to increment beyond the dimensions permitted by a printer font type, the text will simply remain the same size.

1. Block your name in the memo.
2. To increment the point size of your name by a factor of 6, select the *Enlarge Font* option in the Character menu three times.

● **HINT**_____

If the size of your name doesn't change, your font type may not support a larger point size. In this case, switch to a font capable of displaying a bigger point size and then repeat the above instructions to enlarge the title text.

If you want to make size alterations rapidly, use the *Size* text and list boxes in the Font dialog box. First, block the text you want to resize, then choose the *Fonts...* command from the Character menu. When the Font dialog box appears, enter the desired font size in the *Size* text box (if you are using a TrueType font) or choose one of the available sizes from the *Font* list box. Click the *OK* button to implement the adjustment.

3. Block the title of your memo.
4. Choose the *Fonts...* command from the Character menu.
5. Type 24 in the *Size* text box and select *OK*.
6. Deselect the title.

Compare your screen with the one pictured in Figure 5-21. The title should be slightly larger than your name because it has a point size of 24 and your name's point size is only 18.

7. Save your memo as EX5-3A.WRI to the WPFILES directory.
8. Print the document. All of your character formatting should be present on the printout.

Figure 5–21. The title of the memo has been enlarged to 24 points.

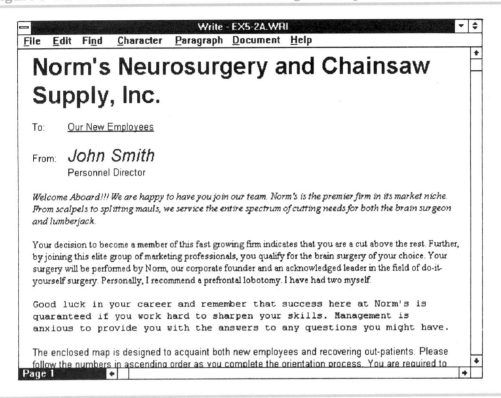

9. You may stop here. If you do, exit Write and end your Windows session only after verifying that the *Save Settings on Exit* command in the Options menu of **Program Manager** is switched off.

Formatting with the Paragraph Menu

The formatting commands for the Paragraph menu fall into three categories: justification, spacing, and indents. Figure 5–22 shows the formatting options available from the Paragraph menu.

Using the Alignment Options

The first category of Paragraph commands are used for text alignment. **Text alignment** is the way your text is arranged on a page. You can choose to left, center, or right align part or all of a document. When you type text in Write, it is automatically left aligned.

Figure 5–22.

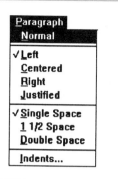

Left aligned text is evenly arranged down the left side of a page but has an uneven or jagged right edge. Text that is **centered** appears in the middle of a page. For example, titles are commonly centered. **Right** aligned text has a rough left side and a smooth right margin. This setting is commonly used for positioning names and addresses along the right margin of your document.

You can also align text so that both of its margins are uniform. The **Justified** command in the Paragraph menu adjusts the spacing between words so that each line is exactly the same length. This arranges text evenly along the left and right sides of a document.

To practice using these alignment commands, follow these steps.

1. If they're not already running, start Windows and launch Write.
2. Open file EX5-2A.WRI from the WPFILES directory.

Since the default setting for text alignment is left, your entire document is currently left aligned.

3. Place the text cursor at the beginning of the document, press Enter twice, move up to the first blank line, and type: Draft Memo
4. To center the new title, position the cursor anywhere on it and choose the *Centered* command from the Paragraph menu.

The whole line is instantly centered. Note that you didn't have to block it first. Actually, any paragraph containing the text cursor is automatically affected when a paragraph command is given. To indicate an area larger than a paragraph, simply block the section you want to change and then issue the desired paragraph command.

5. Block the third and fourth paragraphs and choose the *Justified* command from the Paragraph menu.
6. Position your text cursor in the second paragraph and choose the *Right* command from the Paragraph menu.

Your four paragraphs of text should closely resemble those pictured in Figure 5–23.

7. Save your work as EX5-3B.WRI to the WPFILES directory.
8. Print the document.

Figure 5–23. The memo with the text aligned four different ways.

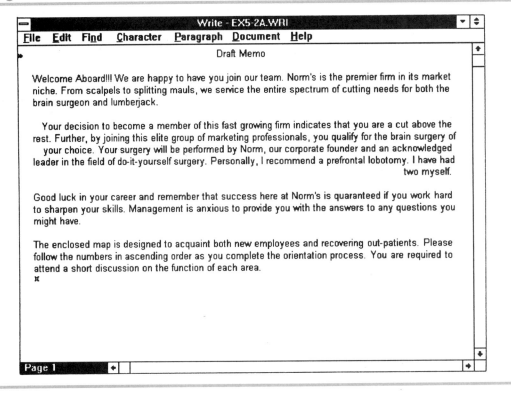

Using the Spacing Options

The second category of Paragraph commands controls space between the lines of text in your Write documents. There are three **line spacing** options: *Single Space, 1 1/2 Space,* and *Double Space.* The *Single Space* option is the default setting you normally see, while the *1 1/2 Space* option increases the space between text lines by an area equal to half the height of a row of text. The *Double Space* command inserts a full blank line between each line of text.

1. Open file EX5-2A.WRI from the WPFILES directory on your EXERCISES disk.
2. To increase the space between the lines of text in your second paragraph, position the text cursor in the paragraph and then choose the *1 1/2 Space* command from the Paragraph menu.
3. Now, block the third and fourth paragraphs and choose the *Double Space* command from the Paragraph menu.

Your document should resemble the one pictured in Figure 5–24.

Figure 5-24. The memo with the spacing options in effect.

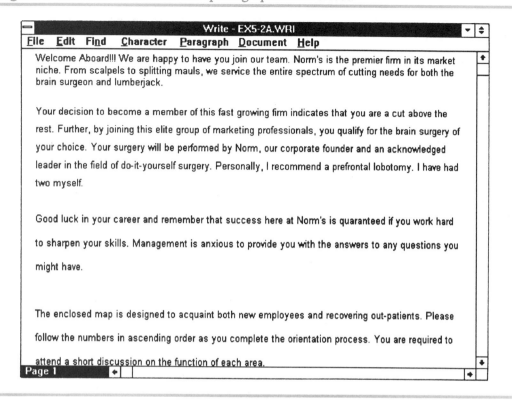

4. Save your work as EX5-3C.WRI to the WPFILES directory.
5. Print the document.

Using the Indents Options

If you choose the final option in the Paragraph menu, the *Indents...* command, the dialog box shown in Figure 5-25 will materialize. The Indents dialog box lets you automatically indent the first line of a paragraph and change the margins of selected portions of your text.

A common way of setting off paragraphs in a document is to **indent** their first lines. However, instead of pressing the Tab key at the beginning of each new paragraph, you can tell Write to perform the indents. All you have to do is choose the *Indents...* command from the Paragraph menu and, when the Indents dialog box appears, enter a value of .05 inches in the *First Line* text box, and click *OK*.

If you perform these actions before entering text in a new document, the beginning line of each paragraph will automatically be

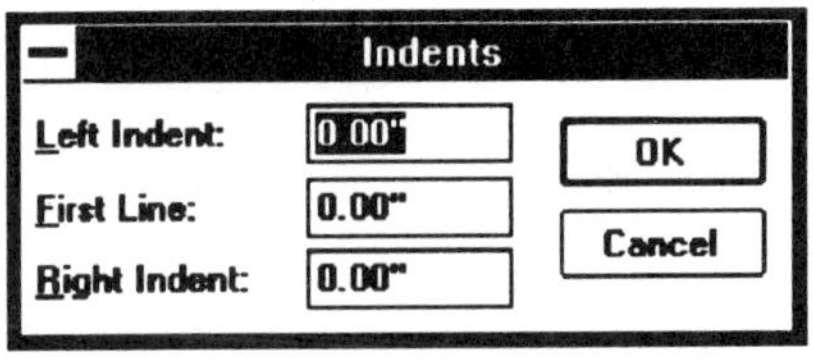

Figure 5–25.
The Indents
dialog box.

```
┌──────────────────────────────────────────┐
│ ▬            Indents                      │
├──────────────────────────────────────────┤
│ Left Indent:   ┌0.00"┐      ┌─────────┐   │
│                └─────┘      │   OK    │   │
│ First Line:    ┌0.00"┐      └─────────┘   │
│                └─────┘      ┌─────────┐   │
│ Right Indent:  ┌0.00"┐      │ Cancel  │   │
│                └─────┘      └─────────┘   │
└──────────────────────────────────────────┘
```

indented. In an existing document, you must first block the paragraphs to be affected, then issue the *Indents...* command.

1. Open the document EX5-2A.WRI, block all of it, and choose the *Justified* command from the Paragraph menu. (This will make your indented text stand out more clearly. Of course, you can indent a document without justifying it.)
2. Position your cursor in the second paragraph, choose the *Indents...* command from the Paragraph menu, type *.5* in the *First Line* text box, and click *OK*.
3. Next, use the same procedure to indent the third paragraph.

Your second and third paragraphs immediately reform to display indented first lines. The other options in the Indents dialog box, the *Left Indent* and *Right Indent* text boxes, allow you to change the **margins** for the entire paragraph (or any block of text). Once a paragraph or block of text has been specified, you simply enter a value in each of these text boxes equal to the distance in inches you want the margins reduced. This is an especially handy feature for setting off a passage from surrounding text, such as in the case of a quote.

To reduce the margins of your third paragraph, follow these steps.

4. Place the text cursor in the third paragraph and choose the *Indents...* command from the Paragraph menu.
5. To move the left margin by 1 inch, type 1 in the *Left Indent* text box.
6. Type 1 in the *Right Indent* text box to bring in the right margin by an inch.
7. Click *OK*.

The third paragraph immediately reforms to fit within these narrower margins. Of course, you can change just one margin of a passage.

   8. Position your cursor in the first paragraph and choose the *Indents...* option.
   9. Type 1 in the *Left Indent* text box and click *OK*.

   Your document should now match the one portrayed in Figure 5–26.

   10. Save your work as EX5-3D.WRI to the WPFILES directory.
   11. Print the document.

Formatting with the Document Menu

The last set of formatting options are contained in the Document menu. These items generally affect your whole document. They include the *Header...*, *Footer...*, *Ruler On/Off*, *Tabs...*, and *Page Layout...*

Figure 5–26. Indenting a paragraph focuses the reader's attention on the passage.

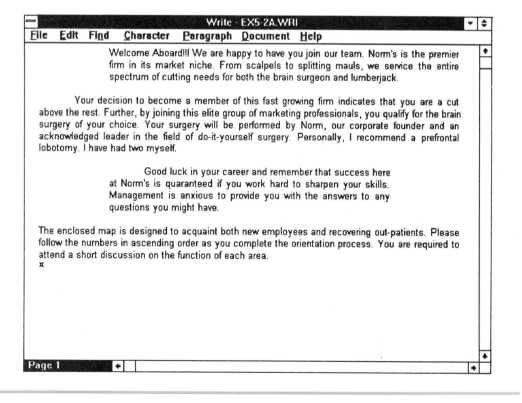

Figure 5–27.

commands, as shown in Figure 5-27. We'll take a close look at all of these formatting facilities except one—the *Ruler On/Off* command. This option provides an icon-driven menu for many of the formatting commands we've already covered. (If you're interested in learning more about the *Ruler On/Off* option, you can consult Windows' *User's Guide*.)

Inserting Headers and Footers

Header... is the first command on the Document menu. A **header** is a line of descriptive text that is typically placed at the top of every page in a document. Headers often display information such as the title of a paper, the author's name, and the current page number. Choosing the *Header...* command from the Document menu will open both a document window called HEADER and a dialog box, as shown in Figure 5-28.

The text for the header is typed in the HEADER document window, and you can format it using any of the character or paragraph formatting options. Notice the *Distance from Top* text box in the Page Header dialog box. It lets you set the space between your header and the top of the page. This is not the distance from the top margin but the distance from the edge of the page itself to where the header will appear. Normally, the default setting of 0.75" is sufficient for most headers.

The dialog box also contains an *Insert Page #* button. Choosing this button will enter a page number code in the text of your header. This code will automatically display the current page number in your header. However, this option only inserts the actual page number. If you want a label, such as "Page," to precede the number, you must type the label first, followed by a space, and then select the *Insert Page #* button.

By convention, headers are seldom used on the cover page of a document. However, you may occasionally want to violate this convention. You can use the *Print on First Page* check box in the Page Header dialog box to print your header on every page including the first one. The Page Header dialog box also includes a *Clear* button to erase a header and a *Return to Document* button to accept the header and exit the dialog box. The headers (and footers) you add to your text will remain invisible until you print.

Figure 5-28. The HEADER window lets you add a repeating text line to the top of every page in your document.

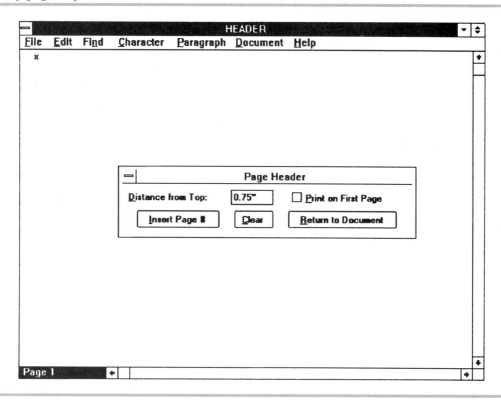

To add a header to your memo, follow these steps.

1. Open EX5-2A.WRI and choose the *Header...* command from the Document menu.
2. To enter the text for your header, type: This header created by [your name]
3. Click on the *Print on First Page* check box.

Compare your screen with the one illustrated in Figure 5-29.

4. To activate the header and return to your document, click the *Return to Document* button.

The *Footer...* command works exactly the same way as the *Header...* option, except it places the descriptive text line at the bottom of each page. **Footers** are typically used to display page numbers.

Figure 5-29. The HEADER window displays an example header, while the dialog box shows the *Print on First Page* check box selected.

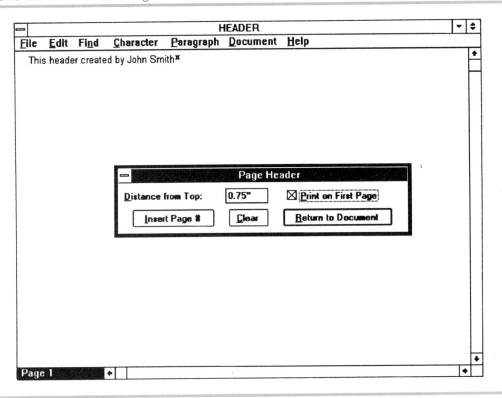

When you issue the *Footer...* command from the Document menu, a new document window called FOOTER is opened and the same dialog box used for creating headers appears.

5. Select the *Footer...* command from the Document menu.
6. Type: Page
7. Press the Spacebar once to create a blank space after the word "Page."
8. To insert a number code following the label "Page," click the *Insert Page #* button.
9. To center the footer, first block the text and the page number code you just entered. Then choose the *Centered* command from the Paragraph menu.
10. Place a check in the *Print on First Page* check box.

Check your footer against the one pictured in Figure 5-30.

Figure 5–30. A footer often serves to display page numbering.

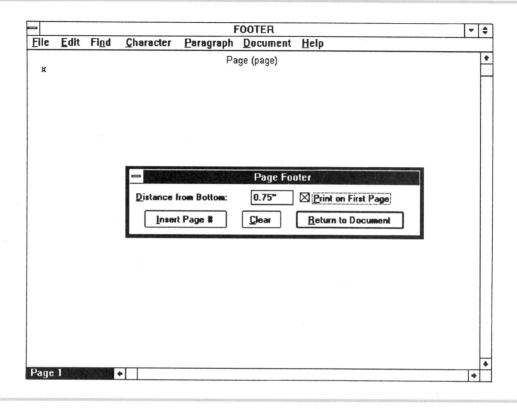

11. Select the *Return to Document* button.
12. Save your work as EX5-3E.WRI to the WPFILES directory.
13. Print the document.

Changing Tab Settings

Write gives you complete control over the tab settings in your document. **Tab settings** are invisible predefined markers that your text cursor will advance to each time the Tab key is pressed. They are very convenient for creating straight columns of text or numbers. There are two kinds of tab settings: left-aligned and decimal. When you tab to a left-aligned setting and begin to type, your first character will line up directly on the tab marker. By default, Write comes with left-aligned tab markers spaced every half inch across your document. Changing to a decimal tab lets you create a straight column of numbers aligned by their decimal points.

To alter or delete the current tab settings, choose the *Tabs...* command from the Document menu. The dialog box portrayed in Figure 5-31 will appear. You can enter up to 12 tab markers using the *Positions* text boxes. Each marker is a location, in inches, from the left margin of your document. For example, if you want your first tab setting to be positioned 1 inch from the left margin, type 1 in the first *Positions* text box. To make the marker a decimal tab, simply place an X in the *Decimal* check box below it. Once you're satisfied with the new settings, click the *OK* button.

Figure 5-31.
The Tabs
dialog box
lets you
customize
your tab
settings.

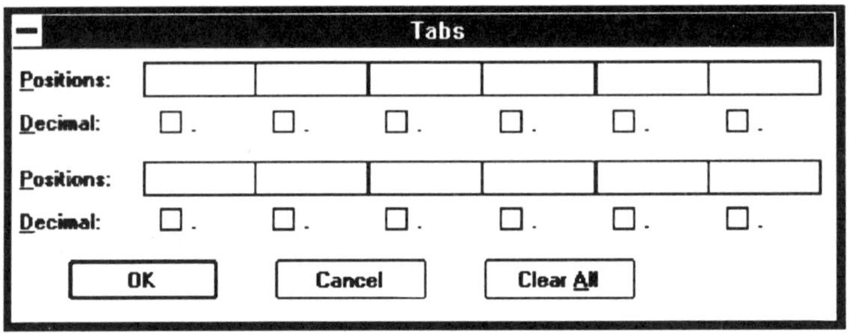

To duplicate the customized tab settings pictured in Figure 5-32, follow these steps.

1. To clear the current document from Write's workspace, choose the *New* command from the File menu.
2. To create custom tabs, select the *Tabs...* command from the Document menu.

Figure 5-32.
The Tabs
dialog box
with Custom
Settings.

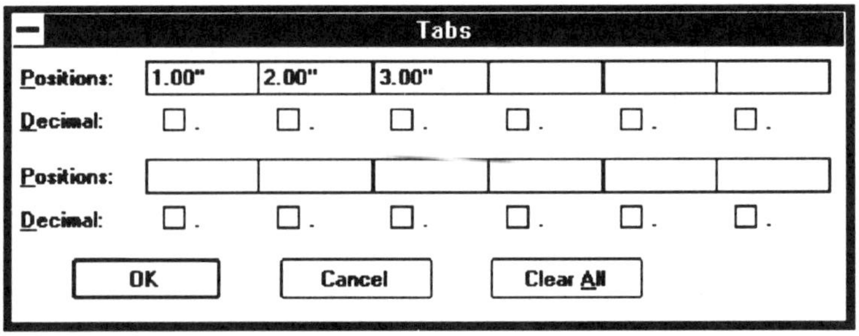

3. When the Tabs dialog box materializes, type 1 in the first *Positions* text box, type 2 in the second box, and type 3 in the third. It's unnecessary to enter the shorthand symbol for inches (″) because Write will do it automatically when you click *OK*.

4. Click *OK* when you are done.

The new tab settings took effect as soon as you clicked *OK*. Now, each time you press the Tab key, the text cursor will advance to the next custom marker.

To see these new tab settings at work, follow these steps.

5. Push the Tab key once, and type: This tab is set at 1.0″. Then tap the Enter key twice to start a new line.

6. Next, push the Tab key twice, and type: This tab is set at 2.0″. Press Enter twice again to begin another line.

7. To enter some text 3 inches from the left margin, push the Tab key three times, and type: This tab is set at 3.0″. Press Enter twice more.

The first line of text is now positioned at the 1″ tab, the second at the 2″ marker, and the third at 3″.

If you want to remove a custom tab marker, open the Tabs dialog box, click on the tab you want to remove, and push the Delete key. To delete all the custom settings and restore the default tab markers, open the Tab dialog box, and click the *Clear All* button followed by the *OK* button.

8. Select the *Tabs..*: command from the Document menu.

9. To erase all your custom tab markers at once, click the *Clear All* button.

10. Click *OK* to return to the original default tab settings.

Recall that Write, by default, places a tab marker every half inch (.5″). When you removed the custom tab settings, your text shifted to comply with these original settings. Notice the first line of text is now indented .5″, the second line 1″, and the third 1.5″.

Changing the Page Layout

The *Page Layout...* command enables you to set the starting page number, margins, and units of measurement for your document. When you issue the *Page Layout...* command from the Document menu, it activates the dialog box found in Figure 5–33.

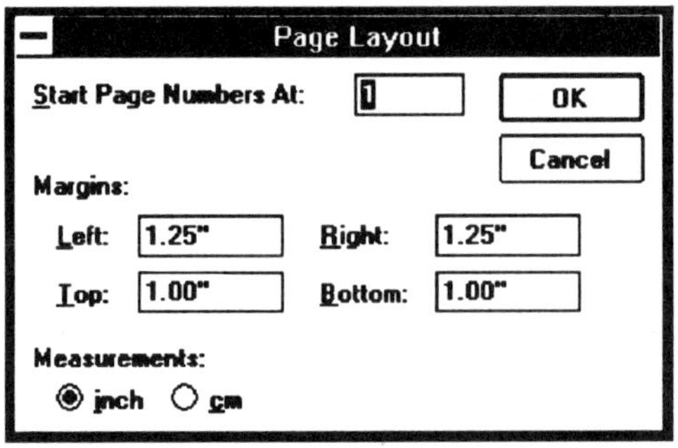

Figure 5–33.
The Page
Layout dialog
box.

The *Start Page Numbers At* text box is located in the upper part of the dialog box. You can use it to begin page numbering at a number other than 1. This feature is beneficial when you're storing portions of a large document in separate files but want to print all of the sections with consecutive page numbers. For example, if you're writing a long paper, it's often a good idea to break up the project into more manageable parts by using separate files. When you're ready to print these files, you can use a different starting page number for each file so the combined printout will appear as if it were printed from a single file.

The Page Layout dialog box also contains text boxes to set the *Left, Right, Top,* and *Bottom* margins for your entire document. Figure 5–33 displays the defaults for these options. The left and right margins are set in 1.25″ from the sides, while the top and bottom margins are indented by 1″. These measurements are made from the edges of the paper.

The Measurements buttons, in the lower portion of the Page Layout dialog box, allow you to display your settings in either inches *(inch)* or centimeters *(cm)*.

In order to gain some experience with the page layout options, let's change the starting page number and margins of your memo document.

1. Open EX5-3E.WRI and when prompted to save the previous untitled document respond *No*.
2. Choose the *Page Layout...* command from the Document menu.
3. To assign the page number 10 to the first page in your document, type 10 in the *Start Page Numbers At* text box.
4. Make the following changes to your margins.

Left	2.5	Right	2.5
Top	1.5	Bottom	2.5

5. Click *OK* to activate the settings and return to your document.

6. Save your work as EX5-3F.WRI to the WPFILES directory.

7. Print a copy of the document.

Your printout should display a footer with a page number of 10 and conform to the new narrower margins settings.

8. Exit Write and end your Windows session after checking to make sure the *Save Settings on Exit* command in the Options menu of Program Manager is toggled off.

COMING ATTRACTIONS . . .

This chapter has introduced you to Write, a word processing program that takes full advantage of Windows' graphical environment. You've learned to use Write to enter, edit, and format text. In addition, you now know how to save, retrieve, and print the documents you create.

In the next chapter, we'll take you on a tour of Paintbrush, a powerful graphical drawing tool. We'll show you how to use it to develop an image to enhance the company memo you created here. In Chapter 7, we'll complete the project by having you combine the Paintbrush image with your Write document to produce an impressive visual communiqué.

KEY TERMS

Center alignment   Placing text in the middle of a line.

Clipboard   A temporary storage area for text and graphics that allows you to transfer data within and between application packages.

Copy   Edit menu command that duplicates a text selection and places it in Clipboard.

Cut   Edit menu command that removes a text selection from your document and places it in Clipboard.

End-of-file marker   The indicator signaling the bottom of a document. It is impossible to enter text below or to the right of the end-of-file marker.

Font styles   Options that change the appearance of text without altering its basic shape or font (e.g., bold, italic, underline, superscript, and subscript).

Font types   A basic design or shape shared by a set of characters.

Footer   A line of descriptive text typically appearing at the bottom of every page in a document.

Formatting   Arranging and altering the appearance of text in a document.

Hard return   A marker indicating the end of a paragraph. You insert a hard return by pressing the Enter key.

Header   A line of descriptive text typically appearing at the top of every page in a document.

Indent   The space text is moved in from the margin of a document.

Justified alignment   Text evenly spaced between left and right margins of a page.

Left alignment   Text evenly arranged down the left side of a page but with an uneven or jagged right edge.

Line spacing   The Paragraph menu commands that control spacing between the lines of text in a Write document. There are three spacing options: *Single Space, 1 1/2 Space,* and *Double Space.*

Margins   The page borders of a document.

Moving   The technique for relocating a block of text within a document.

Page status bar   Bar located in the lower left portion of the Write window that displays the number of the page where the text cursor can be found. However, the document must first be paginated for this feature to work properly.

Pagination   The process of assigning page breaks to a document. A page break tells the printer where one page ends and the next begins. Pagination normally occurs only when you print; however, you can force Write to paginate a document at any time by issuing the *Repaginate...* command from the File menu.

Paste   Edit menu command that copies the contents of Clipboard to the current location of the text cursor.

Point size   The unit of measurement used to adjust the size of text. One point is equal to $\frac{1}{72}$ of an inch.

Printer fonts   A category of fonts included with Windows that lack true WYSIWYG capabilities. Printer fonts also have a very limited range of point sizes.

Radio button   An option appearing in some dialog boxes. You select a radio button by clicking on the circle in front of the button's label. When a dot appears in the circle, the option is toggled on.

Right alignment   Text with a rough left margin and a smooth right margin.

Save   File menu command that stores a copy of your document on disk.

Save As...   File menu command that lets you store your document using a different name, location, or file format.

Selecting (blocking)   The process of marking or highlighting the text you want to work with. A block will display in inverse video, where characters will appear white and the background black.

Selection area   The blank column, along the left window frame of a Write document window, that lets you quickly highlight a block of text.

Tab settings   Invisible predefined markers that your text cursor will advance to each time the Tab key is pressed. Tab settings are very convenient for creating even columns of text or numbers.

Text alignment   The manner in which text is arranged along the borders of a page. By default, Write automatically left aligns the text you enter. However, you can choose to center or right align part or all of a document.

Text cursor   A blinking vertical line used to indicate where text will be entered.

TrueType fonts   A category of fonts that give you true WYSIWYG. Text prints exactly as it looks on the screen. TrueType fonts are also scalable to any size.

Undo   Edit menu command that reverses the last editing or formatting action.

Untitled   The filename given to every new document until you rename it.

Word wrap   As you type, this feature automatically moves your text cursor down to the beginning of the next line each time you reach the right margin.

5-1. This exercise will review the material presented in Lab 5-1. You'll start by typing several paragraphs of text, then proofread the text, save it, and, finally, print a copy of it. We'll pretend the document you are creating is a collection of the most memorable quotes from the writings of Norm.

    a. Start Windows and launch Write.
    b. Maximize Write.
    c. Type the paragraph below.

    "I always try to look at the bright side of things. After all, how much worse can it really get?" (SHARP INSIGHTS Norm:2)

    d. Insert one blank line and enter the following.

    "To win in today's business world, one must learn to stay a cut above the rest." (THOUGHTS ON BUSINESS Norm:8)

    "People waste too much time worrying about the moral problems in the world. If they would instead concentrate on my problems, I would be a much happier person." (PHILOSOPHY AND COMMON SENSE Norm:22)

    "My employees make this a great company. Without them I would be out of business. Oh sure, I could replace them with less costly robots who never get sick and work 24 hours a day. But machines can't take pride in their work, can they?" (ANNIVERSARY PARTY SPEECH Norm:4)

    e. Position your cursor at the top of the document and type the heading:

    Windows 3.1 Tutorial
    Chapter 5
    Exercise 5-1
    [Your Name]
    [Today's Date]

    f. Insert two blank lines between the heading and the first paragraph.

g. Save the document on your EXERCISES disk in the WPFILES subdirectory. Name the file 5-EXER.WRI

h. Print the file.

Your document should closely match the one portrayed in Figure 5–34. Don't be concerned if some of the lines wrap at different points. Slight variations will naturally occur when different fonts are used.

i. If you're stopping here, exit Write and quit Windows after checking to make sure the *Save Settings on Exit* command in the Options menu of Program Manager is toggled off.

5-2. To do this practice set, you must have completed Exercise 5-1. The document created in the earlier exercise will be used to practice the *Cut* and *Paste*

Figure 5–34. Famous quotes from Norm.

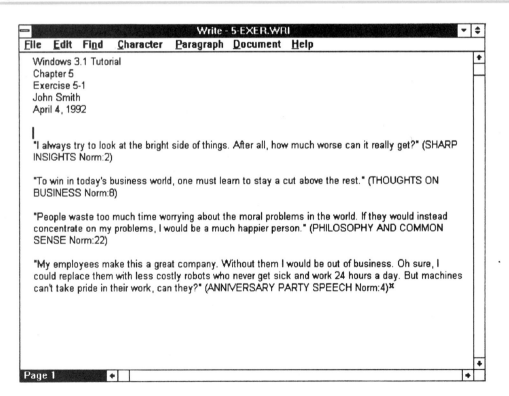

commands introduced in Lab 5-2. Once you've reorganized the file, you'll save and print a copy of it.

    a. If necessary start Windows, launch and maximize Write, and open the file 5-EXER.WRI.

After some consideration, you decide the PHILOSOPHY AND COMMON SENSE quote is inappropriate for this collection of great sayings by Norm. So you elect to remove the passage.

    b. Select the third paragraph of text and delete it.

The organization of your document could benefit from some rearrangement. These changes will include moving the ANNIVERSARY PARTY SPEECH excerpt to the top, placing the quote from THOUGHTS ON BUSINESS next, and positioning the SHARP INSIGHTS statement last. Let's also move each citation above its respective quote.

    c. Select the paragraph containing the ANNIVERSARY PARTY SPEECH quote.
    d. Use the *Cut* and *Paste* commands from the Edit menu to reposition the paragraph two lines below your heading.
    e. Select the THOUGHTS ON BUSINESS statement and move it beneath the first quote, leaving two blank lines.
    f. The SHARP INSIGHTS quote should be at the bottom of the document.
    g. Now place each citation directly above its respective quote. Make the necessary adjustments to retain the previous spacing between paragraphs. Then change the heading to read: Exercise 5-2

Compare your document with the screen illustrated in Figure 5-35.

    h. Save the file to the WPFILES directory.
    i. Print the document.
    j. If you're stopping here, exit Write and quit Windows after checking to make sure the *Save Settings on Exit* command in the Options menu of Program Manager is toggled off.

5-3. The instructions below build upon the work done in the two preceding exercises. You'll use the formatting commands demonstrated in Lab 5-3 to format the

Figure 5–35. The Write document after some rearranging with the *Cut* and *Paste* commands.

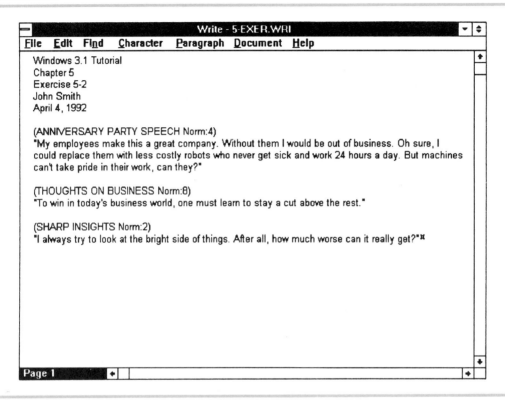

document created and refined in these earlier exercises. We'll conclude the practice session by saving and printing the file.

 a. If necessary start Windows, launch and maximize Write, and open the file 5-EXER.WRI.

We'll start with the formatting commands that affect individual words or phrases. In other words, the options found in the Character menu.

 b. To boldface your document heading, select the first five lines, and then choose the *Bold* command from the Character menu.

 c. Increase the size of your heading by a factor of 6 with the *Enlarge Font* option. Then change the heading to read: Exercise 5-3

 d. Underline all the citations.

 e. Change the font type of all the citations to Times New Roman.

To practice using the Paragraph menu, complete the following instructions.

> **f.** Right align your heading by selecting the first five lines of the document and issuing the *Right* command from the Paragraph menu.
>
> **g.** *Center* each of the citations.
>
> **h.** Block the entire document and adjust the line spacing to *1 1/2 Space*.

Compare your document with the one shown in Figure 5–36. If necessary, change it to match the figure as closely as possible. When you're satisfied, complete the directions below to gain experience with the formatting commands in the Document menu.

Figure 5–36. The Character menu options animate a document and help pull the reader's eye to important concepts and ideas. Alignment and spacing changes are controlled by the Paragraph menu.

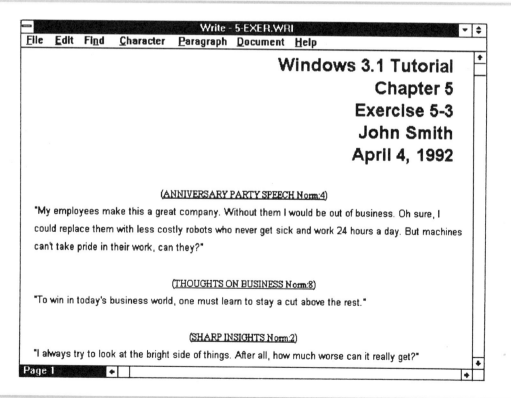

i. Choose the *Header...* command from the Document menu. Select the *Print on First Page* option.

j.   **Exercises for Chapter 5 by [Your Name]**

k. Tab twice, type Page, and press the Spacebar once.

l. To insert the page number code, click on the *Insert Page #* button and press the Spacebar once.

m. Position the header .5″ from the top of the page by typing *.5* in the *Distance from Top* text box.

n. Return to the document.

o. Issue the *Page Layout...* command and change the left and right margins to *2″*.

Your document should now resemble the one pictured in Figure 5-37.

p. Save the file.

Figure 5-37. Headers and margins are inserted or changed using the Document menu.

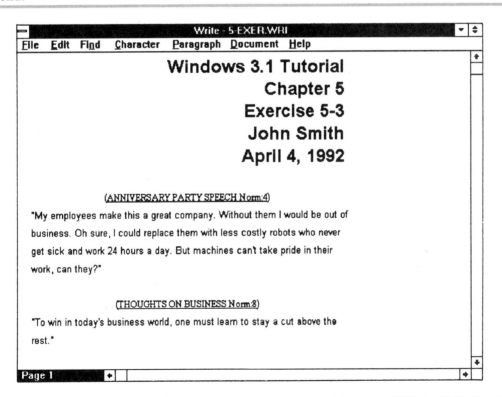

q. Print the document.

r. Exit Write and quit Windows after checking to make sure the *Save Settings on Exit* command in the Options menu of Program Manager is toggled off.

REVIEW QUESTIONS

True or False Questions

1. **T   F**   Word wrap allows you to type a stream of text without having to stop and press the Enter key.

2. **T   F**   Pagination is the process of assigning page breaks to a document.

3. **T   F**   The first time you save a document, the Page Setup dialog box appears.

4. **T   F**   When using a word processor, you should save your work approximately every 15 minutes.

5. **T   F**   Many of Write's formatting options are located in the Character, Paragraph, and Document menus.

6. **T   F**   A header is a line of descriptive text that typically appears at the top of every page of a document.

7. **T   F**   When blocking by a line, a paragraph, or a document, your mouse pointer must be located in the selection area.

8. **T   F**   Write allows you to print multiple copies of your documents.

9. **T   F**   Each time you press the Enter key you insert a Tab setting.

10. **T   F**   Your keyboard is layed out in a traditional WYSIWYG format.

Multiple Choice Questions

1. The mouse and what other key let you block a portion of your text?

   a. Enter key
   b. Print Screen key
   c. Escape key
   d. Shift key

2. Which one of the following menus contains the command to underline a block of text?

   a. Edit menu
   b. Find menu
   c. File menu
   d. Paragraph menu
   e. None of the above

3. Which menu formats the entire document?

   a. Document menu   c. Character menu
   b. Paragraph menu   d. Find menu

4. A font grows larger as the point size

   a. Decreases
   b. Increases
   c. None of the above

5. To insert text into a document, you would choose which command?

   a. *Undo*   c. *Open*
   b. *Cut*   d. *Paste*

6. When text appears ragged along the left margin and smooth along the right, it is

   a. Bottom aligned   d. Upper aligned
   b. Right aligned   e. None of the above
   c. Center aligned

7. When you launch Write, the blinking vertical line resting directly in front of the end-of-file marker is called the

   a. Header   c. Page break
   b. Insertion point   d. Paragraph marker

8. Blocks of text are easily deleted by selecting the text and pressing the

   a. Home key   c. Escape key
   b. Delete key   d. None of the above

9. Which menu formats individual words or phrases?

   a. Character menu   c. Document menu
   b. Paragraph menu   d. Word menu

10. When text is selected, it appears in

   a. Inverse video   c. Bold print
   b. Underlined   d. a and b

CHAPTER 6

Using Paintbrush

● *Objectives*

Upon completing this chapter, you'll be able to:

1. **Use a variety of graphic tools to create a drawing.**
2. **Save and retrieve a drawing.**
3. **Print a drawing.**
4. **Develop a drawing in an effective and systematic manner.**

OVERVIEW

Paintbrush is a graphics program that lets you produce a variety of drawings, such as greeting cards, newsletters, and letterheads for memos. These can be simple or complex. You don't have to be an artist to create useful and attractive artwork with Paintbrush.

If Paintbrush is your first experience with computer-aided drawing and graphics, fear not! Paintbrush is simple and intuitive to use and its icons are descriptive and easily understood. Lab 6–1 will introduce you to Paintbrush's general layout, including its flexible set of drawing tools. In the next lab, you'll create a floor plan to merge with the memo you developed in Chapter 5. The final lab will show you several advanced features for enhancing a Paintbrush drawing.

LAB 6–1   DRAWING BASICS

This lab will acquaint you with Paintbrush's basic features. You'll begin by activating the program and exploring the available drawing tools. Next, you'll experiment with the most useful of these tools and learn to save and print your drawings. The lab ends by showing you how to exit the program correctly.

Starting Paintbrush

Paintbrush's icon is located in the Accessories group window. It depicts a paintbrush and artist's palette. To invoke Paintbrush, select the Accessories group and double-click on the Paintbrush icon. When the Paintbrush window appears, be sure to maximize it because you'll want the largest space possible to work on your drawings.

1. Load Windows and open the Accessories group window.
2. Double-click on the Paintbrush icon.
3. Maximize the Paintbrush window.

The key areas of the Paintbrush window are labeled in Figure 6-1. Notice the **Toolbox** along the left border. It holds all your drawing tools. You can adjust the drawing size of many of these tools by using

Figure 6-1. The Paintbrush window includes a Toolbox, Linesize box, and Palette for creating custom drawings.

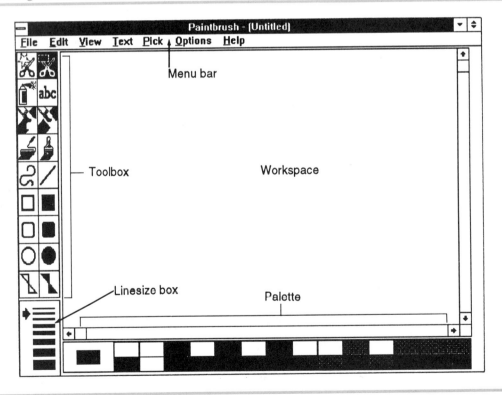

the **Linesize box** located in the lower left corner. The **Palette**, situated across the bottom of the window, offers an array of colors for enhancing and customizing your illustrations. Since Toolbox is the heart of Paintbrush, we'll concentrate on it and leave the Linesize box and Palette for the next lab.

Exploring the Toolbox

Toolbox contains Paintbrush's drawing tools. These tools can be divided into three categories: graphic, text, and editing. **Graphic tools** are used for drawing, the **text tool** for entering text, and **editing tools** for correcting and modifying the elements of your drawings.

Observe that each tool is represented by a descriptive icon. To select a tool, simply click on its icon. The icon will darken to indicate it is active. When you move the pointer into the workspace, its shape will change to reflect the abilities of the tool you selected.

Using Graphic Tools

The majority of the objects in the Toolbox are graphic tools. These utensils comprise the drawing capabilities of the program. Table 6-1 displays the name, icon, pointer shape, and a brief explanation of each graphic tool.

Table 6-1. Paintbrush's graphic tools.

Name	Icon	Pointer	Description
Airbrush			The Airbrush looks like a spray can. It produces a circular pattern of dots. It is a freeform utensil that can be dragged around the workspace.
Paint Roller			The Paint Roller fills in a bounded area with a color. For example, you can use the Paint Roller to fill a circle with the color of your choice.
Brush			The Brush is a freeform tool that paints a brush stroke as you drag it around the workspace.
Curve			The Curve utensil creates curved lines, double curved lines, and other complex shapes.

Name	Icon	Pointer	Description
Line	/	+	The Line tool draws straight lines. These lines may be drawn vertically, horizontally, or diagonally at any angle.
Box	☐	+	The Box utensil creates rectangles, squares, or lines. The Box tool draws just the frame of the box.
Filled Box	▨	+	The Filled Box utensil is the same as the plain Box tool except it fills the box with a color.
Rounded Box	☐	+	The Rounded Box tool forms boxes with rounded corners. You could, for example, use Rounded Box to draw the keys on a piano.
Filled Rounded Box	▮	+	The Filled Rounded Box fashions a box with rounded corners and fills it with a color.
Circle/Ellipse	○	+	The Circle/Ellipse utensil forms circles, ellipses, and ovals. Only the outline of the shape is drawn.
Filled Circle/Ellipse	●	+	The Filled Circle/Ellipse tool fashions circles, ellipses, and ovals that are filled with a color.
Polygon	◣	+	The Polygon drawing tool is different from the other shape-drawing utensils. It doesn't draw a predetermined shape, but instead lets you continue to add sides to a configuration until the starting point is reached.
Filled Polygon	◣	+	The Filled Polygon is essentially the same tool as the Polygon tool except that it fills the newly created polygon with a color.

To use a graphics tool, select it from the Toolbox, move the pointer into the workspace, and hold down the left mouse button at the point where you want to begin drawing. As you drag the pointer, the tool will draw a shape (e.g., line, circle, box, etc.). Releasing the button completes the figure. Using the Curve and Polygon utensils requires a few additional steps.

To practice using the graphic tools, follow these steps.

1. With the Brush tool selected, move the Brush pointer to the approximate center of the workspace.
2. To draw some freehand circles, hold down the left mouse button, and move the mouse using circular motions. When you are finished, release the button.
3. Try writing your name with the Brush tool. (The results might look something like Figure 6-2.)

You'll notice it takes only a moment of experimenting with a tool to clutter the entire workspace. Fortunately, Paintbrush provides a fast way to erase the figures you create with the active tool. Simply choose the *Undo* command from the Edit menu to eliminate all the work done since the last utensil was selected.

Figure 6-2. The Brush tool turns the mouse into a freehand drawing tool. You can use the Brush much like a pencil.

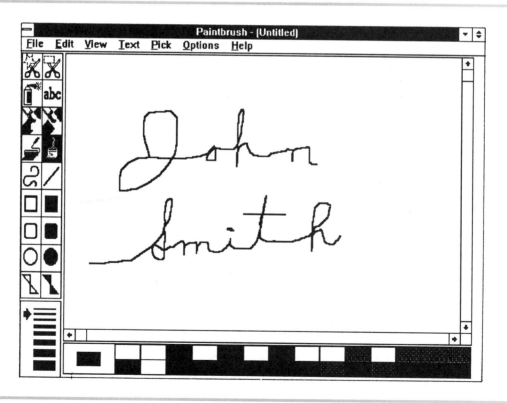

Print

4. Select the *Undo* command from the Edit menu to clear away the brush work instantly.
5. Let's change tools; click on the Line utensil.

Observe that the Brush icon lightens and the Line icon darkens, indicating it is now the active utensil.

6. Move the pointer to the center of the workspace.
7. Hold down the left mouse button, drag the utensil to the lower left corner of the workspace, and release the mouse button.

You should have just drawn a diagonal line stretching from the center of the screen down to its lower left corner. The Line utensil is one of the most useful drawing tools. You'll likely use it in every drawing you create.

8. Attempt to draw a perfectly straight vertical line from the lower left corner to the upper left corner of the workspace.

Absolutely vertical or horizontal lines are difficult to draw because they require precise mouse movements. Paintbrush permits you to draw perfectly straight lines by first holding down the Shift key and then dragging the Line pointer. You can use this technique to draw vertical lines, horizontal lines, or 45° angles.

9. To draw an exact horizontal line, position the Line pointer in the upper left corner of your workspace, press and hold the Shift key, press and hold down the mouse button, drag the pointer to the upper right corner, and release the mouse button and then the Shift key.

When you release the mouse pointer, Paintbrush draws a horizontal line. Vertical and 45° lines are accomplished using the same procedure.

10. To draw a vertical line, position the Line pointer in the upper right corner, press and hold the Shift key, and drag the pointer to the lower right corner.
11. To draw a 45° angle, place the Line pointer in the lower right corner, press and hold the Shift key, and drag the pointer diagonally to the upper edge of the workspace.

Compare your series of lines with those shown in Figure 6-3.

Figure 6–3. The Line tool is one of the most useful drawing utensils. You can draw a perfectly straight line by holding down the Shift key and dragging the pointer.

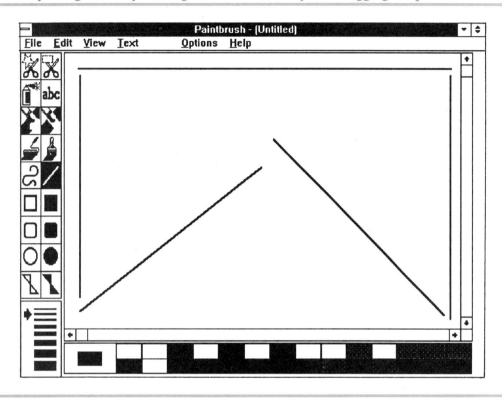

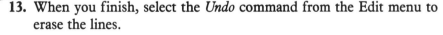

12. Feel free to experiment with the Line tool.
13. When you finish, select the *Undo* command from the Edit menu to erase the lines.

   To use Box or Rounded Box, select the utensil from Toolbox, click on the location in the workspace where you want to anchor a corner, drag the pointer to expand the box, and release the button when you are satisfied with the size and shape.
   Let's use this technique to draw a box that frames the workspace in Paintbrush.

14. Select the Box tool from the Toolbox. (It's directly below the Curve tool in the left column of the Toolbox.)
15. To create a rectangular box, place the pointer in the upper left corner of the workspace, drag it to the lower right corner, and release the mouse button to finalize the shape.

You should have seen the rectangle expanding as you moved the pointer down to the lower right corner. Pressing the Shift key while dragging the pointer lets you draw a proportionally perfect square (i.e., all four sides are the same length).

Print

16. To erase the rectangle, select the *Undo* command from the Edit menu.

17. You can form a square similar to the one shown in Figure 6–4 by positioning the pointer at the approximate center of the work-space, pressing and holding Shift, and dragging the pointer to the right.

18. Release the mouse button before you release the Shift key to complete the shape.

19. Draw a few more rectangles and squares to familiarize yourself with the way this tool works.

Figure 6–4. The Box tool draws rectangles and squares. To draw a perfect square, press the Shift key as you drag the mouse cursor.

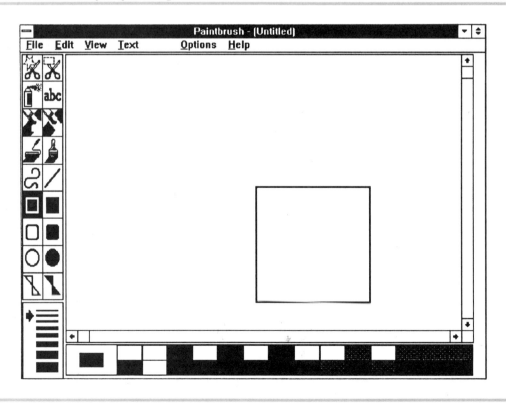

The Circle/Ellipse tools function much like the Box tools with one important exception. Since circles and ellipses don't have corners, you obviously can't begin fashioning the shape by anchoring a corner. You begin forming a circle or ellipse by clicking on the location you want to serve as one edge of the figure. Then, drag the cursor out away from this point to expand the shape and release the mouse button when you are satisfied with the size of the object.

Print

20. *Undo* the squares and rectangles you drew earlier.

21. Choose the Circle/Ellipse utensil from the Toolbox.

22. To draw a circle/ellipse, position the pointer near the middle of your workspace and drag it away from the center point in any direction.

As you move the mouse diagonally, the shape takes on circular characteristics. If you move the mouse in a more vertical or horizontal direction, the shape becomes more elliptical.

23. Release the mouse button to complete the shape.

You can use the Shift key to create a perfect circle. As before, Shift is pressed before the shape is created and held until after the mouse button is released.

Print

24. Choose the *Undo* command from the Edit menu to erase the circle.

25. To draw a perfect circle, position the pointer somewhere in your workspace, press Shift, drag the pointer in any direction to expand the circle, and release the mouse button followed by the Shift key to finalize the shape.

26. Experiment with this tool for a moment before moving on to the next section.

Print

27. When you finish, use *Undo* to erase the circular shapes.

Using the Text Tool

The Text tool is represented by the abc icon. Selecting this tool will change your pointer to an I-beam shape. To use the Text pointer, click the mouse in the workspace where you want the text to start and type the text. As you type, the characters will be displayed using the current settings for font, style, and size. In Lab 6–2, we'll show you how to change these settings. Use the Backspace or Delete key to erase any typing errors you make.

⊘ **HAZARD**_____

Once you have positioned the I-beam pointer and have begun typing, don't use the mouse to reposition the pointer until you finish entering text at that location. It is difficult, if not impossible, to return to the exact position at which you originally started typing.

1. Choose the Text utensil from the Toolbox.
2. Position the pointer approximately in the middle of your workspace and click the left mouse button.
3. Type the following information: Windows 3.1 Tutorial
4. Press the Enter key, and type: Chapter 6
5. Push Enter, and type: Lab 6-1
6. Press Enter, and type: [Your Name]

Check your screen against the one portrayed in Figure 6-5.

Figure 6-5. The Text tool is easy to use. Select the tool, position the cursor where you want to enter the text, and type.

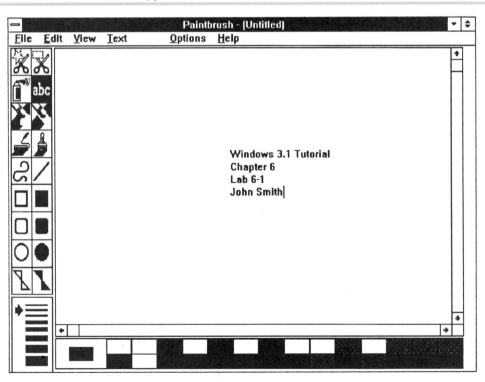

Using the Editing Tools

The editing tools let you change or manipulate portions of a drawing. Earlier, you employed the *Undo* command to erase work in progress. *Undo* is a bit like using a jackhammer to drill a tooth. It removes the problem, all right, but takes out everything else along with it. Normally, you won't want to Undo everything a tool has created. The editing tools are far more selective in what they obliterate. Table 6–2 lists the name, icon, pointer shape, and a brief description of each editing tool.

Table 6–2. Paintbrush's editing tools.

Name	Icon	Pointer	Description
Scissors		+	The Scissors tool selects an irregularly shaped portion of your drawing to be edited.
Pick		+	The Pick tool selects a rectangular area for editing.
Color Eraser		□	The Color Eraser is used to erase a specific color from your drawing. It functions like the Eraser utensil.
Eraser		□	The Eraser tool transforms your mouse pointer into an eraser. The Eraser deletes anything under the pointer when the mouse button is pressed.

The Scissors and Pick tools allow you to isolate a portion of a Paintbrush drawing and then manipulate just that selected area. Using Scissors and Pick, you can move, cut, copy, and paste an area of your drawing. The commands in the Pick menu offer additional ways to manipulate a selected area.

The eraser tools are straightforward and easy to use. The Eraser utensil erases anything in its path, while the Color Eraser removes only those items drawn or painted with a specific color. The editing tools most commonly used are the Pick and the Eraser utensils. Accordingly, these are the tools we'll be concentrating on.

1. To select or "pick" the text you typed a moment ago, click the Pick tool icon in the Toolbox.
2. Position the cursor just above and to the left of your text. Drag the cursor down and to the right until the dotted pick rectangle fully encloses the text. Make sure your screen matches the one shown in Figure 6–6 and then release the mouse button. If it doesn't, use *Undo* to cancel the Pick tool selection and try again.

Figure 6-6. The Pick tool isolates a portion of your drawing to manipulate.

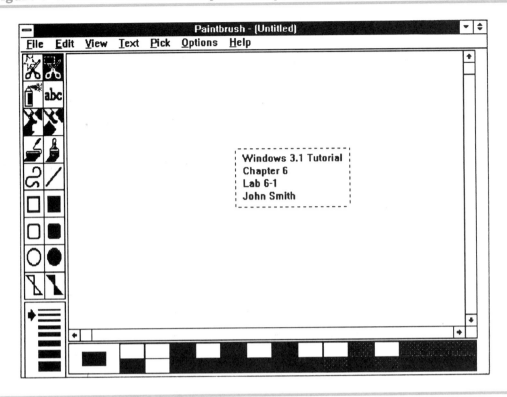

Once you have picked an area to work with, the pointer will change to an arrow shape whenever it's moved inside the dotted rectangle. The arrow configuration indicates that you can use the pointer to relocate the selected area. You do this by placing the pointer over any part of the selected area, dragging it to a new location, and releasing it.

3. To move your text to the lower right corner of the workspace, place the pointer inside the dotted rectangle.
4. Then, press the mouse button, drag the block to the lower right corner of the workspace, and release the mouse button.

Note that the area remains selected after the move. This allows you to continue editing the same block.

You use the Edit menu to copy or cut the selection. Simply select the part of your drawing you want to copy or cut (using the Scissors or Pick tool), and then issue the desired command from the Edit menu. Both the *Cut* and *Copy* commands place the selected block in Clipboard's temporary storage area. (Clipboard functions in Paintbrush just as it does in Write.)

5. To copy the text you picked earlier, choose the *Copy* command from the Edit menu.
6. To paste a duplicate of the selected area into your drawing, select the *Paste* command from the Edit menu.

When you select the *Paste* command, Paintbrush inserts a copy in the upper left corner of the workspace. The copy is automatically selected and the Pick tool becomes active. To place the copy in the desired location, move the pointer inside the paste block and drag it to the point you want the copy positioned.

7. Move the duplicated text to the upper right corner of the workspace by dragging it with your pointer and then releasing the mouse button.

You can choose the *Paste* command again to paste an additional copy of the text into your document. Remember, a block remains in Clipboard until it is replaced by another selection.

8. Paste another copy of the text and move it to the lower left corner of your workspace.
9. Paste a third copy in the upper left corner.

You should now have a copy of the text in each corner of your workspace, as illustrated in Figure 6–7. You can use the Eraser tool to selectively edit portions of these text copies. Dragging the Eraser cursor over the text will instantly delete it. As you follow the steps below, be sure to move carefully to avoid erasing the text you want retained.

10. Select the Eraser utensil from the Toolbox.
11. Position the Eraser box over the first row of text in the upper right corner of your workspace.
12. Erase this text by dragging the eraser back and forth over *Windows 3.1 Tutorial*.

If you accidentally erase something you want to keep, use the *Undo* command to bring back the erased area. You can do this as long as no other tool has been activated since the erasure occurred.

13. To return the text, select the *Undo* command from the Edit menu.

Figure 6–7. The *Paste* command in the Edit menu makes short work of repetitive duplications.

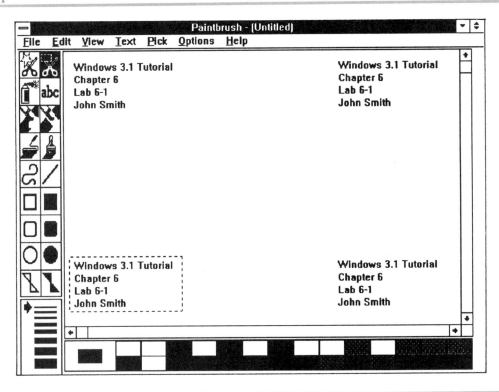

Saving Your Artwork

Figure 6–8.

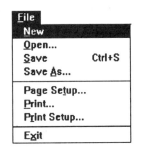

The File menu holds the commands for maintaining your Paintbrush files, as shown in Figure 6–8. These commands should look quite familiar because they are essentially the same as those used for working with Write files. You can save a new piece of artwork by issuing either the *Save* or *Save As...* command. This triggers the Save As dialog box shown in Figure 6–9.

You'll notice that this dialog box has a few additional features. The *Save File as Type* drop-down list box in the lower left section produces a list of the available file formats for saving your drawing, as pictured in Figure 6–10. The different formats are provided to maintain compatibility with other graphic

Figure 6-9.
The Save As
dialog box
appears the
first time you
save a new
drawing.

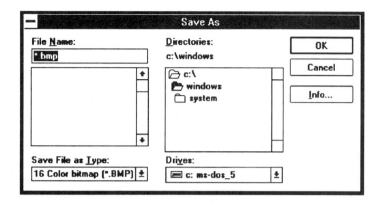

Figure 6-10.
The *Save File
as Type* drop-
down menu
reveals the
available file
formats and
extensions.

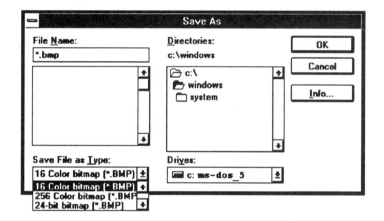

software as well as older versions of Paintbrush. Normally, Paintbrush
will save your drawing as a bitmap (BMP) file (either Monochrome or
Color). Bitmap is the default file format for Paintbrush. However, you
can also elect to save your artwork using a PCX format. If you do,
Paintbrush will automatically change the extension of your filename
from .BMP to the new format (e.g., if you choose the PCX format, the
file name will end with .PCX).

If a file has been saved before, you can use the *Info...* button,
positioned just below the *Cancel* button, to reveal specific information
about the image. The remaining options in the dialog box are identical
to those found in Write's Save As dialog box. The *File Name* text box
lets you name your drawing, the *Drives* drop-down list box shows the

available disk drives, and the *Directories* list box shows the directories for the current drive.

1. To save your image, choose the *Save* command from the File menu. Insert the EXERCISES diskette.
2. Select drive A by clicking the arrow in the *Drives* drop-down list box and clicking on the a: icon, and then choose the PBFILES directory from the *Directories* list box.
3. To name the image, type EX6-1A.BMP in the *File Name* text box, and click *OK* to save the file.

Once an image has been stored on disk, the *Save* command will no longer prompt you for a filename. Instead, it will save the current drawing using the name previously entered. If you want to assign a new name to your current image, use the *Save As...* command.

4. Issue the *Save* command from the File menu.

Observe that the image is immediately saved.

Printing Your Artwork

The commands for printing a drawing are also located in the File menu. The *Page Setup...* command brings up the dialog box pictured in Figure 6-11. You can use this dialog box to alter the margins of your drawing and add a header or a footer. The *Printer Setup...* command allows you to change the setting for the active printer or switch to another printer.

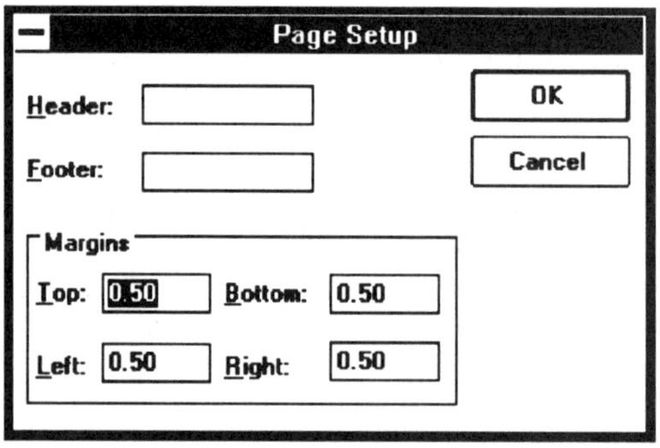

Figure 6-11.
The Page Setup dialog box lets you change margins and insert headers.

The *Print...* command opens the Print dialog box shown in Figure 6-12. This dialog box controls the print quality, the number of copies to print, the scaling or size of the printed area, and the area to be printed.

The Quality options determine both the appearance of the printed output and the speed of printing. Selecting the *Proof* button will yield the best print quality, but a file takes longer to print at *Proof* quality than at *Draft* quality. You should reserve *Proof* quality for your finished work and use *Draft* for the interim printouts.

The Window area of the Print dialog box specifies the amount of the drawing to be printed. You can elect to print the entire drawing or select just a portion. Clicking the *Partial* button will return you to your document with the same crosshairs pointer used by the Pick tool. Select the portion you want to print by using the same technique you employ to block an area for editing.

The last three Print dialog box options control the number of copies, size, and resolution of the image you want to print. The *Number of copies* text box allows you to designate the number of copies to be printed. You can use the *Scaling* text box to determine the size of the final printed drawing in relation to the drawing in Paintbrush. A document printed at the default setting of 100% prints the same size as the Paintbrush image. A document printed at 50% prints precisely one-half as large as the Paintbrush image. With the *Use Printer Resolution* check box toggled off (the default setting), Paintbrush automatically compensates for differences between printer and screen resolution so that your printout will match the dimensions of your screen image.

1. Choose the *Print...* command from the File menu.
2. To print as quickly as possible, select the *Draft* button in the Print dialog box.

Figure 6–12.
The Print
dialog box.

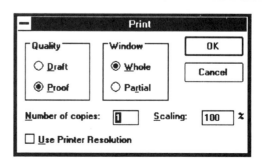

3. Make sure the *Whole* button is toggled to print your entire image.

4. Check to see that the *Number of copies* is set to 1 and the Scaling is at 100%.

5. Once you're certain the printer is on-line, click the *OK* button to print.

Exiting from Paintbrush

Leave Paintbrush by clicking on the *Exit* command from the File menu. Paintbrush will display a warning message if you attempt to quit without saving your work.

1. To quit Paintbrush, select the File menu.

2. Then click the *Exit* command.

You've come a long distance in a short time. You now are able to launch and exit Paintbrush, save and print a drawing, and use many of the important utensils in the Paintbrush Toolbox.

It's worth repeating how the similarities in Windows' graphical user interface reduce your learning time. Much of the knowledge you acquired in the preceding chapters can be put to use in working with Paintbrush. This is because Windows strives to provide consistency across all its applications. Perhaps you can now appreciate why programs as diverse as File Manager, Write, and Paintbrush share a uniform look and feel.

3. You may now exit Windows after verifying that the *Save Settings on Exit* command in the Options menu of Program Manager is switched off.

LAB 6–2   CREATING A DRAWING

In this lab, you'll use Paintbrush to draw a simple floor plan. Although this graphic image is fairly uncomplicated, the methodology you'll follow can readily be applied to projects of almost any scale. Just as with word processing, creating graphic art is best done by adhering to a specific sequence of steps. In other words, an orderly approach to constructing a graphic image will give you the best chance of a successful outcome.

Art can be defined as the organization of basic elements into pleasing combinations. The difference, then, between a good artist and a great one is the way in which he or she combines these elements. As William King put it, "Beauty from order springs."

The following nine points will help you use Paintbrush to create drawings in an orderly fashion. This methodology will afford you a high degree of efficiency without sacrificing your creativity.

- Set a realistic goal.
- Set a time limit.
- Prepare the canvas.
- Rough out the graphic.
- Start large and work in.
- Master when to save your work.
- Construct the components.
- Assemble the pieces.
- Know when to stop.

We'll now use these guidelines to construct a graphic image.

Setting a Realistic Goal

Every graphic project starts with an idea or purpose. The purpose of this project is to draw a floor plan that (in Chapter 7) will be inserted into the orientation memo you created in Chapter 5. Figure 6–13 provides an example of the floor plan. This map was developed using Paintbrush and the tools introduced in the first lab.

Your floor plan need not be as elaborate as the one shown. However, it must illustrate all the rooms in the company's headquarters, along with a label and a number for each area.

When evaluating a graphic for a project, ask yourself the following questions:

- Does the drawing add value to the project?
- Is Paintbrush the right program for the job?

A negative answer to either of the questions indicates you should rethink your objectives. Perhaps you could spend your time more wisely on some other facet of the overall enterprise, or maybe you should consider a drawing tool other than Paintbrush.

A graphic image adds value when it supports and reinforces the project's overall message. An inappropriate graphic, no matter how professional, dilutes the impact of the project. A graphic must be pertinent to be effective.

Figure 6-13. A sample floor plan created with Paintbrush.

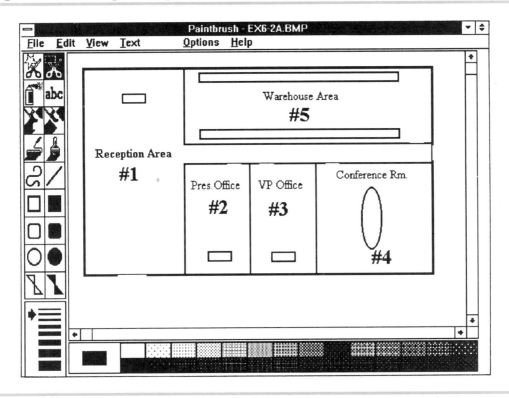

Paintbrush is an excellent entry-level drawing tool. It can be used with great success to create simple images. However, Paintbrush is not a desktop publishing program, nor does it offer the sophistication of a full-featured professional drawing package. Paintbrush, like Write, is intended as a quick and easy way to accomplish many commonly required tasks.

Set a modest goal for yourself. For example, appropriate Paintbrush goals might include developing custom letterheads, elementary illustrations, explanatory diagrams, and basic charts. Don't frustrate yourself by attempting drawings that are obviously too complex.

Setting a Time Limit

Assuming you have a minimum level of competency, you will need about one hour to complete a drawing like the example floor plan shown in Figure 6-13. More complex drawings can take days to finish.

Try to budget your time and keep in mind that drawings invariably take longer to complete than the initial estimate.

A good rule of thumb, when forecasting the length of a project, is to double your initial time estimate. Always remember that the computer should make you more, not less, productive. Drawing on a computer can quickly become a "black hole" where your time is literally sucked away. Don't let the drawing become the master.

Preparing the Canvas

Once you have set your goal and budgeted a suitable amount of time, you are ready to begin preparing your "canvas." In Paintbrush, the workspace becomes the "canvas" where your drawing will take form. Before starting a drawing, you must decide on the size of your graphic and whether it will include color. These decisions are communicated to Paintbrush via the *Image Attributes...* command in the Options menu. When this command is chosen, the Image Attributes dialog box shown in Figure 6–14 will appear.

The size of an image can be manipulated by changing the *Width* and *Height* text boxes. The size you enter, however, is limited to the amount of free memory available in your computer system. The default settings are usually large enough to accommodate most Paintbrush projects.

The *Units* options determine the standard of measurement used by Paintbrush. The *pels* option is an acronym for pixels. **Pixels** are the individual dots on the screen. A standard VGA display has a row and column array of pixels measuring 640 columns (wide) by 480 rows

Figure 6–14.
The Image Attributes dialog box lets you choose image size and color options.

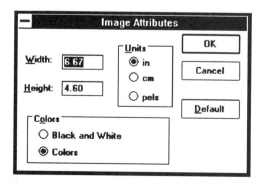

(tall). The total number of pixels is the product of 640 times 480. A screen with these dimensions has 307,200 individual dots or pixels. (A little later, you'll actually get a chance to manipulate these tiny dots!)

1. Start Windows and launch Paintbrush.
2. Maximize the Paintbrush window.
3. Select the *Image Attributes...* command from the Options menu.
4. To change the units of measure to pixels, click on the *pels* option.

The *Width* and *Height* text boxes will instantly change to reflect the new units of measure.

Another important consideration is the use of color. If you intend to print the completed image on a standard dot-matrix or laser printer, you should choose *Black and White* instead of color. These printers are capable of printing only in black and white. But if you just intend to display the drawing or you want to print it on a color printer, you should select the *Colors* radio button.

We'll assume you are using a standard printer to print your drawings. Thus, you'll need to select the *Black and White* option.

5. If necessary, toggle the *Black and White* radio button on.
6. Click *OK* to accept the modifications.

The canvas now has a monochrome Palette across the bottom of the screen. You'll learn more about the Palette in the next section.

Paintbrush provides a handy feature to guide your pointer or cursor. The *Cursor Position* option in the View menu lets you display the location of the pointer on the canvas. When you select this command, Paintbrush turns on a small window that appears on the right side of the menu bar. The current pointer location is displayed in column and row format using pixels as the units of measure.

For example, a reading of (0,0) indicates the pointer is currently residing in the upper left corner of the screen, while a reading of (640,480) places the pointer in the lower right corner. As you move the pointer about in the workspace, its position is constantly monitored and updated. Figure 6-15 shows a Paintbrush window with the *Cursor Position* option activated.

7. To track the pointer location, select *Cursor Position* from the View menu.

Figure 6-15. The *Cursor Position* option lets you track the position of the pointer or cursor.

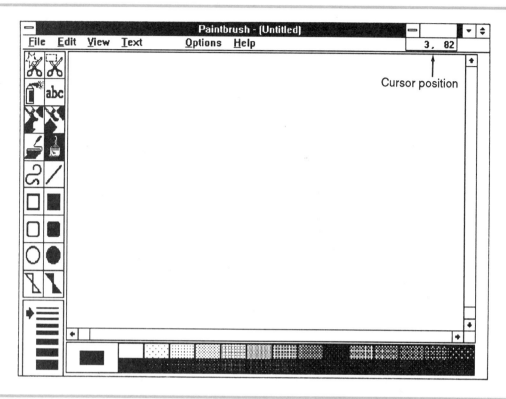

Cursor position

● **HINT**_____

The View menu also allows you to turn off the Toolbox, Linesize box, and Palette. Hiding these items will let you see more of the canvas (workspace) area at one time. This can make it much easier to select a portion of a drawing or move an object around.

Roughing out the Graphic

Artists commonly prepare several basic sketches to organize their thoughts and ideas. These sketches form the backbone of the completed work. Paintbrush simplifies sketching with its array of editing tools. Often you'll be able to work directly from your initial sketch.

We have done much of the sketching for you on this project. This way, we can give you precise instructions for positioning and tool choice. In the future, however, you'll need to sketch out your own ideas and visualizations.

Before actually putting brush to canvas, you need to select the thickness and color (pattern) of your drawing utensil from the Linesize box and Palette.

The Linesize box is a gauge that adjusts the thickness of the stroke used by the currently selected drawing tool. It is found below the Toolbox on the left side of the screen. The arrow indicator, on the left side of the gauge, points to the present line thickness. The default setting is the second line from the top. To choose a different thickness, simply click on the line size you want to use. The Linesize box setting affects all the graphics tools as well as the Eraser tools. The Erasers become larger or smaller depending on the size of the setting.

1. To select a slightly thicker stroke than the default setting, click on the third line from the top of the Linesize box.

The Palette contains two important elements: the Select Colors box and the color or pattern choices available for the current canvas, as shown in Figure 6-16. Your canvas displays only monochrome patterns since you chose the *Black and White* option in the Image Attributes dialog box.

The Palette controls the background and foreground colors. The **background color** is the color that appears when you select the *New* command. The default background color is white. The **foreground color** is the color or pattern used by the tools. You can change the foreground color or pattern by pointing at the Available Colors or Patterns section and clicking the left mouse button. You can change the background color or pattern by pointing at it and clicking the right mouse button.

To practice changing the foreground and background colors, we'll backtrack a bit. Let's prepare another canvas, but this time with colors visible.

2. To switch to a color palette, select the *Image Attributes...* command from the Options menu.
3. Select the *Colors* option and click *OK*.
4. To change the foreground color from black to red, point at the red color square in the Palette (the one located between the gray and yellow color squares), and click the left mouse button.
5. To change the background color from white to yellow, point at the yellow color square, and click the right mouse button.

Figure 6-16. The Palette is composed of the Select Colors box and the Available Colors or Patterns area.

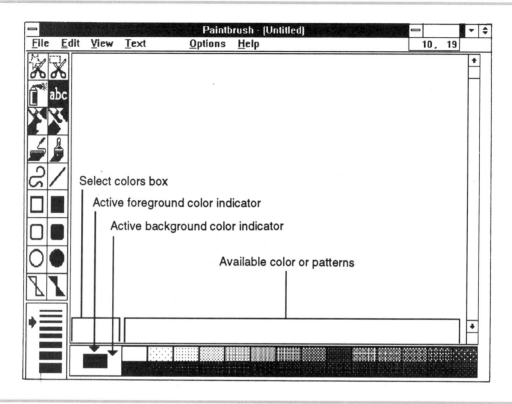

6. To prepare a fresh canvas with these new default colors, issue the *New* command from the File menu.

Your workspace will now display a yellow background and a red foreground color.

Now that you've gained some experience with colors, let's return to the settings for the floor plan.

7. To switch back to the black and white palette, select the *Image Attributes...* command from the Options menu.
8. Select the *Black and White* radio button and click *OK.*
9. Change the foreground color to black and the background to white.
10. To prepare the canvas, select the *New* command from the File menu.

Starting Large and Working In

Any design project necessarily starts with the largest components and works in from there. Be careful to avoid "bogging" yourself down with minute details until the larger picture is in perspective. With this in mind, we'll begin by constructing the largest objects in the floor plan and then work our way down to the smaller ones. The items you'll need to create are listed below.

- exterior walls
- interior walls
- doorways
- warehouse shelving
- furniture
- labels and orientation numbers

We'll employ two separate workspaces to construct your floor plan. The exterior frame, walls, and doorways will be fabricated on one canvas. The furniture will be drawn on another and then pasted into the original.

Mastering When to Save Your Work

Saving on a regular basis using descriptive names makes it possible to return to an earlier version of your drawing if an idea doesn't pan out. *Force yourself to save often.* The importance of this admonishment will become painfully clear the first time you make a disastrous mistake and have no recent backup.

Constructing the Components

The instructions below show you how to draw the exterior walls of the floor plan. These directions will constantly refer to the cursor position window as a means of sizing and locating objects on your canvas. So be sure you have the *Cursor Position* option activated before proceeding.

To form the exterior walls, follow these steps.

1. Broaden the brush stroke by clicking on the third line from the top of the Linesize box.
2. Select the Box tool, located beneath the Curve tool.
3. Position your crosshairs pointer at the coordinates (20,20).

● **HINT**_____

The mouse is difficult to maneuver into a specific column/row position. To make this process easier, use the mouse to position the pointer near the given coordinates and then use the arrow keys on your keyboard to locate the cursor exactly. Each time you tap an arrow key, the pointer location is incremented by one pixel in the direction of the arrow. Holding an arrow key down moves the cursor quickly in the direction of the arrow. This combination of mouse and arrow key movements will enable you to position the pointer precisely.

4. To complete the exterior walls, drag the mouse to coordinates (500,300) and release the mouse button.

You should now have a rectangle stretching from the upper left corner (20,20) to the lower right corner (500,300) of your canvas. Compare your drawing with the exterior walls shown in Figure 6–17. The lines forming this rectangle should be a linesize thickness of three.

Next, we'll construct the interior walls (see Figure 6–18). You'll use the Line tool to draw them. This will involve setting the Linesize gauge to a thickness of two, selecting the Line utensil from the Toolbox, and using the coordinates given to sketch in the walls.

5. To create narrower interior walls, pick the second line from the top of the Linesize box.
6. Select the Line tool.
7. To draw the upper boundary of the hallway, position the pointer at coordinates (160,125).
8. Hold down the Shift key, drag the cursor to (499,125), and release the mouse button.
9. To draw the lower boundary of the hallway, place the pointer at coordinates (160,150).
10. Hold down the Shift key, drag the cursor to (499,150), and release the mouse button.

With the exterior walls and hallway area completed, it's time to save your work.

11. To name and save your art, select the *Save* command from the File menu. Insert the EXERCISES diskette.
12. When the Save As dialog box appears, name the file FRAME.BMP and save it in the PBFILES directory on drive A.

Figure 6-17. A rectangle created using the Box tool and a linesize thickness of three.

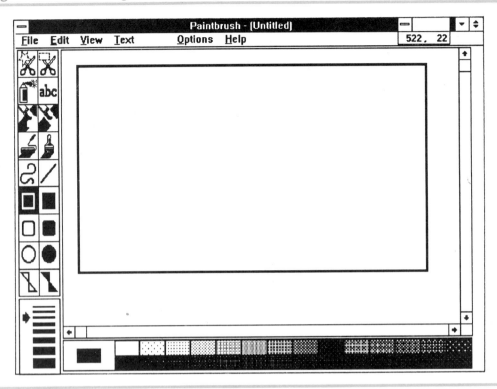

You can now draw the remaining interior walls without fear of accidentally ruining your entire drawing. Remember to hold down the Shift key when you draw a straight line.

13. To continue drawing the interior walls, position the pointer at (250,150).
14. Drag the pointer to (250,299) and release the mouse button.
15. Place the pointer at (340,150), drag it to (340,299), and release.
16. To draw the upper reception area wall, position the pointer at (160,20), drag it to (160,125), and release.
17. To complete the inside walls, position the pointer at (160,150), drag it to (160,299), and release.

Now that you've completed the frame and walls, check your floor plan against the one shown in Figure 6-18. You have constructed the largest component of the building map. It's prudent, at this point, to protect your work by saving it.

18. Issue the *Save* command.

Figure 6-18. Using just the Line and Box tools, the frame and walls of the floor plan have been constructed.

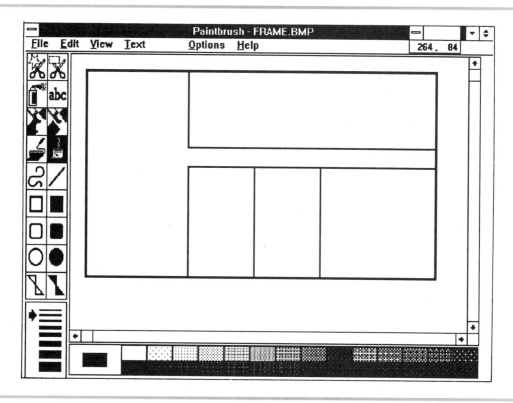

Zooming In and Out

Let's add some doorways to your building layout. Recall that you made the exterior walls three pixels thick and the interior walls two pixels thick. To show doorways, we'll thin the walls down to just one pixel width. This is easily accomplished utilizing Paintbrush's *Zoom In* command.

When you select this command from the View menu, a rectangular pointer appears in the upper left corner of the workspace. Simply drag this pointer box over the area you want to magnify and click the left mouse button. The selected area will be expanded into a grid of pixels as shown in Figure 6-19. (In this case, we are "zoomed in" on the hallway area of the floor plan.)

In addition to the pixel grid, a window showing the normal view of the magnified area (the surface covered by the pointer box) is displayed in the upper left corner of the workspace. As you modify the pixel grid,

Figure 6-19. You can perform pixel by pixel editing with the *Zoom In* command from the View menu.

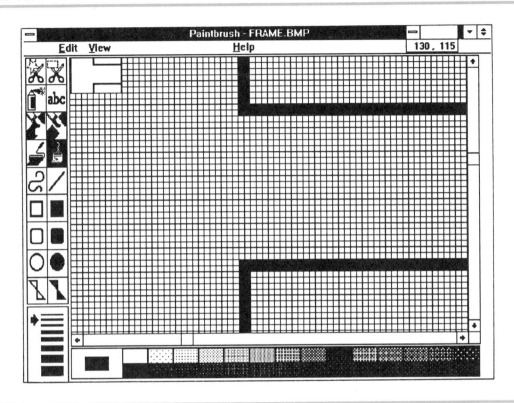

you can use this window to see what effect your changes are having on the drawing.

When you zoom in on an area, the Brush tool is automatically selected. The Brush and Paint Roller are the only two drawing utensils available to you while you're in the Zoom mode. You'll find that the Brush tool is best adapted for the fine detail work of coloring individual pixels.

Colors are still chosen in the same manner, but the Palette selection is limited to pure colors. Since the floor plan is a monochrome drawing, you'll be restricted to either black or white.

To change the color of a pixel in the pixel grid, simply move the pointer to it and click the left mouse button. The pixel will fill with the selected foreground color. Clicking the right mouse button fills it with the background color. Once you have finished editing, choose the *Zoom Out* command from the View menu to restore the normal workspace.

The next items to be created are the doorways. Their approximate locations are marked in Figure 6–20. The exterior doorway is 40 pixels long while all the other doors are 20 pixels long. These objects offer an excellent opportunity for you to practice the Zoom mode. The following steps will serve to guide you through their construction.

1. To create the exterior doorway, first select the *Zoom In* command from the View menu.
2. Position the box pointer over the exterior wall at the bottom of the reception area and click the left mouse button (approximately 50,275).
3. When the pixel grid appears, move the arrow pointer to the spot on the line where the exterior doorway is to be placed (approximately 13 pixels from the left on the bottom side of the line).
4. To change the black pixel in the wall to white, click the right mouse button.

Each time you point at a black pixel and click the right mouse button you are changing its color from black to white. You need to continue doing this until you have a doorway that is 1 pixel wide and 40 pixels long.

5. Move the pointer one pixel to the right and click the right mouse button again. Continue this action until you have replaced 40 black pixels with white ones.

Figure 6–20.
Location of
doorways.

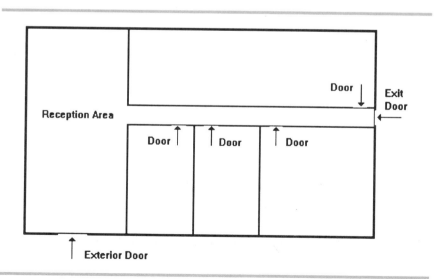

6. Repeat this process to remove the row of black pixels immediately above the space you just cleared.

Check your doorway against the one pictured in Figure 6–21.

You can use the horizontal and vertical scroll bars to move about the drawing when you're in the Zoom mode. We'll use the horizontal and vertical scroll bars to reposition the pixel grid over the area where we want to carve out the office doors. You should be able to position the pixel grid so that you can work on both doors. Refer back to Figure 6–20 for the approximate locations of these two doorways.

7. Select the *Zoom Out* command to resume the normal view mode.
8. Choose the *Zoom In* command and move the pixel grid over the area where an office door is to be located (see Figure 6–20).

Figure 6–21. The Zoom mode allows you to do detailed editing.

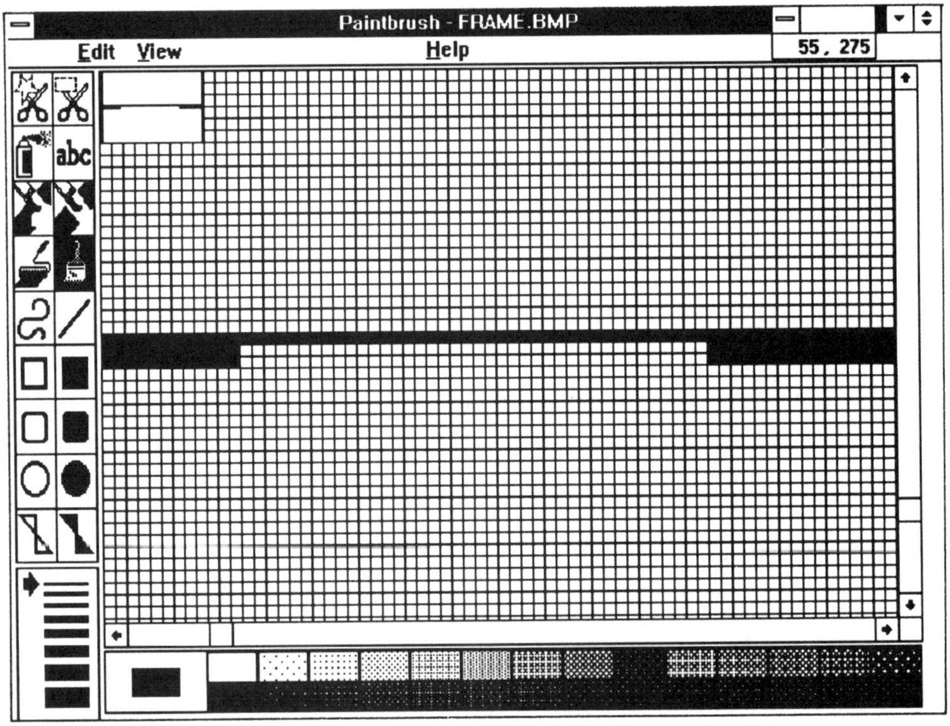

9. To draw a 1 by 20 pixel opening, use the pointer and the right mouse button as you did in the exterior doorway.

If you accidentally paint a pixel white, you can make it black again by clicking on it with the left mouse button.

10. Repeat steps 6–8 to create all the office doors shown in Figure 6–20.
11. Select Zoom Out to resume the normal view mode.
12. Save your work.

● **HINT**_____

The *Zoom Out* command also permits you to display a drawing larger than the workspace. All you have to do is choose the *Zoom Out* command from the View menu while in the normal view mode. This will turn the entire desktop into your canvas. If the graphics image is considerably larger than your screen, some of the detail will be lost when it expands. However, the picture will retain all its finer points and will again display them when you return to the normal view mode by choosing the *Zoom In* command.

Creating an Image Library

When working on a detailed drawing, you might consider creating a library of image components. Each item from the library can then be pasted into the drawing. The advantages of separate images are twofold. First, if you're developing several similar drawings, your library can contain the most commonly used elements. This way, you save time by drawing the objects only once and then pasting them where you want. Second, an image library lets you experiment with different images and be more creative. You can paste and undo endlessly without fear of ruining your drawing.

At this point, we're ready to add the smaller and more detailed objects to your floor plan. We can use an image library to eliminate the risk of damaging your drawing. The library will contain the shelving for the warehouse, the desks for the offices and reception area, and the table for the conference room. Once again, to simplify the tutorial, we'll give you the exact coordinates for creating each component.

1. Select *New* from the File menu.
2. To draw the shelving, select the Box utensil from the Toolbox and click on the second line from the top of the Linesize box.
3. Position the pointer at (151,162), drag the cursor to (425,176), and release the mouse button to complete the shelving rectangle.
4. To save the image, select the Pick tool from the Toolbox.
5. Surround the entire shelving rectangle with the Pick tool's dotted selection area, leaving a quarter of an inch of space around the shelf rectangle.
6. Select the *Copy To...* command from the Edit menu, and choose drive A and directory PBFILES.
7. Save the image as SHELF.BMP
8. To draw the desk image, choose the Box tool.
9. Position the pointer at (244,282), drag the pointer to (278,296), and release.
10. Use the Pick utensil and the *Copy To...* command to save the images as DESK.BMP to the PBFILES directory.
11. To draw the table, select the Circle/Ellipse tool.
12. Position the pointer at (66,41) and drag the pointer to (95,125).
13. Release the mouse button to complete the table ellipse.
14. Use the Pick tool and the *Copy To...* command to save the image as TABLE.BMP to the PBFILES directory.

You have all the components that comprise the small library of images you'll use to annotate your simple floor plan. We can now bring them together to form the final product.

Assembling the Pieces

The last stage of your graphic project consists of assembling all the pieces. The images you created just a moment ago will be combined with the frame and walls you built earlier. To do this, you'll use the *Paste From...* command found in the Edit menu.

1. Retrieve the completed frame by selecting the *Open...* command from the File menu.
2 When asked if you want to save the canvas used to create the image library, answer *No*.
3. Load FRAME.BMP from the PBFILES directory on the EXER-CISES disk.

We'll start by importing the shelf image. You'll use the *Paste From...* command to place it in the warehouse area of the floor plan, as shown in Figure 6–22. (If necessary, refer back to Figure 6-13.)

● HINT_____

Images selected with the Pick or Scissors tools or the *Paste* or *Paste From...* commands can be sized, flipped, inverted, and tilted by using the options in the Pick menu.

4. When the image appears, choose the *Paste From...* command in the Edit menu.
5. Select the SHELF.BMP image from the PBFILES directory.

The image will appear on the canvas in a pick box. To move it, place the pointer inside the dotted pick box, hold down the left mouse

Figure 6–22. The floor plan with the shelving, desks, and table pasted in.

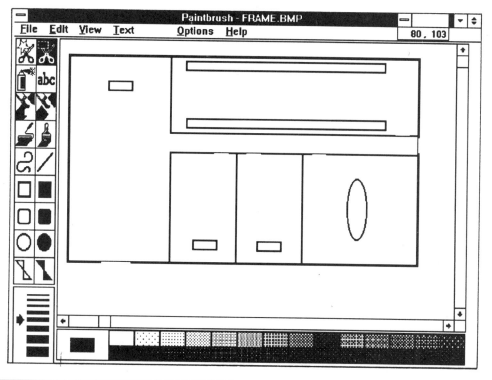

button, drag the box to the desired location, and release the button. Let's use this technique to position the shelf image inside the warehouse.

6. To move the image, place the pointer inside the pick box.
7. Drag the image into the warehouse area and release.

You need another copy of the shelves for the other side of the warehouse. You can use the *Paste From...* command again or use the Pick tool to copy the image you just pasted.

8. To paste another shelf into the drawing, choose the *Paste From...* command from the Edit menu once more, and load SHELF.BMP.
9. Move the shelf into the warehouse and position it against the wall opposite from the first shelving unit.

Next, we'll paste the desks and table into the floor plan.

10. Issue the *Paste From...* command from the Edit menu and retrieve DESK.BMP from the PBFILES directory.
11. Move the desk into the reception area and center it along the back wall.
12. Place desks in each of the two offices.
13. Retrieve TABLE.BMP and move it into the conference room.

You have only to add the room labels and numbers to complete the floor plan. But first save your drawing.

14. Choose the *Save* command from the File menu.

As you saw in the first lab, text is easily added to your drawings. You can customize the text you enter by choosing a different font, embellishment (such as bold or underline), or font size.

15. Choose the Text utensil from Toolbox.
16. Select the *Fonts...* command from the Text menu.

The Font dialog box will appear, as shown in Figure 6–23.

17. Find and click on the *Times New Roman* font in the *Font* list box.

Observe that the *Sample* box displays an example of the font. This lets you quickly view the various font types without actually applying one to your document.

Figure 6–23.
The Font
dialog box.

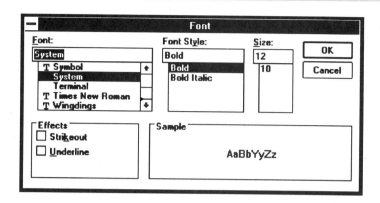

18. Choose *12* as the font size from the *Size* list box and click *OK*.
19. Position the text cursor by placing the pointer in the approximate center of the reception area and clicking the left mouse button (see Figure 6–24).
20. Type Reception Area and then click on the Text tool again.

By clicking on the Text tool a second time, you lock in the text with its font, style, and size. Next, you'll type the room number for the reception area. To highlight these numbers, you can use a slightly larger font and bold print.

21. Select *Bold* from the Text menu.
22. Open the Font dialog box by selecting the *Fonts...* command from the Text menu, select *20* from the *Size* list box, and click *OK*.
23. Place the text cursor below and toward the middle of the text line you typed a moment ago.
24. Type: #1

● **HINT**

You can use the Pick and Scissors tools to select text and then move or resize it. Paintbrush treats text as though it were just another graphic image.

25. Click on the Text utensil to freeze the text and styles you just entered.
26. Select *Regular* from the Text menu.

Figure 6-24. The floor plan with text labels.

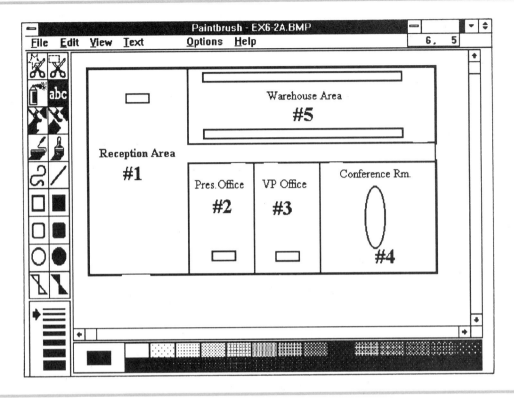

27. Select the *Fonts...* command from the Text menu, select *12* from the *Size* list box, and click *OK*.
28. Position the cursor in the first office, and type: Pres. Office
29. Type VP Office in the next office.
30. Type Conference Rm. in the conference area.
31. Type Warehouse Area in the storage room.
32. Click on the Text tool to lock in the above text entries.
33. Select *Bold* and a size of *20*.
34. Number the president's office as #2, the VP's office as #3, the conference room as #4, and the warehouse as #5.
35. Save your completed drawing as EX6-2A.BMP in the PBFILES directory of the EXERCISES diskette.
36. Print a copy of the floor plan.

Your map is complete. It should be very similar to the one portrayed in Figure 6-24.

Knowing When to Stop

You have created a fairly sophisticated drawing; however, much more detail could be added. For instance, you could construct furniture and other furnishings to adorn the floor plan further. But will such embellishments help you achieve your goal and do they actually improve the quality of the graphic? These are questions you should consider at every step of the drawing process.

Always bear in mind the purpose of a drawing and the people who will see the finished product. A presentation for a client or a supervisor probably warrants greater care and detail than a sketch for a friend or a colleague.

Also, cluttering a drawing with unnecessary objects makes it indecipherable. For example, your floor plan now displays all the elements germane to guiding new employees around the company headquarters. Further additions would simply detract from the relevant information conveyed by the current drawing. So we know it is time to stop.

1. Exit Paintbrush.
2. To increase the space available on your diskette, use File Manager to delete FRAME.BMP from the PBFILES directory.
3. End your Windows session after making certain the *Save Settings on Exit* command in the Options menu of Program Manager is toggled off.

COMING ATTRACTIONS . . .

This chapter has taken you on a brief tour of Paintbrush. The high points included launching Paintbrush, selecting tools, adjusting linesize, picking a color, drawing, saving, retrieving, and printing. Along the way, you even managed to create a pretty nifty drawing.

In Chapter 7, we'll introduce you to two exciting uses of Clipboard. First, you'll use Clipboard to paste the graphic developed in this chapter into the document created in Chapter 5. Next, we'll show you how to use Clipboard to capture a screen. This capability allows Clipboard to store a "snapshot" of anything on your desktop. You can bring a captured screen into Paintbrush or Write.

KEY TERMS

Airbrush   A freeform drawing utensil that simulates a paint sprayer. It produces a circular pattern of dots that can be sprayed around the workspace.

Art   The organization of basic elements into pleasing combinations.

Background color   The color that appears when you select the *New* command.

Box   A drawing tool for creating rectangles, squares, or lines.

Brush   A freeform drawing utensil that paints a brush stroke as you drag it around the workspace.

Circle/Ellipse   A drawing tool that forms circles, ellipses, and ovals.

Color Eraser   A tool used to erase a specific color from your drawing.

Curve   A drawing utensil that creates curved lines, double curved lines, and other complex shapes.

Editing tools   Utensils used for correcting and modifying the elements of your drawings.

Eraser   A utensil that transforms your mouse pointer into an eraser. The Eraser deletes anything it touches when the left mouse button is pressed.

Filled Rounded Box   A drawing tool that fashions a box with round corners and fills it with a color.

Filled Box   A drawing utensil that forms a box and fills it with a color.

Filled Circle/Ellipse   A drawing tool that creates a circle, ellipse, or oval and fills it with a color.

Filled Polygon   A drawing utensil that lets you continue to add sides to a figure until the start-

ing point is reached. The figure is then filled with the foreground color.

Foreground color   The color or pattern used by the tools.

Graphic tools   Drawing utensils found in the Toolbox.

Line   A drawing tool for creating a straight line. The line may be drawn vertically, horizontally, or diagonally at any angle.

Linesize box   The gauge for adjusting the thickness of the stroke used by the selected drawing tool. It is found below the Toolbox on the left side of the Paintbrush window.

Paint Roller   A drawing utensil that fills in a bounded area with a color. For example, you can use the Paint Roller to fill a circle with the color of your choice.

Palette   The Palette, located across the bottom of the Paintbrush window, lets you choose a color or pattern to work with.

Pick   A tool that selects a rectangular area for editing.

Pixels   The individual dots on the screen.

Polygon   A drawing utensil that lets you continue to add sides to a figure until the starting point is reached.

Rounded Box   A drawing tool that forms a box with rounded corners.

Scissors   A tool that selects an irregularly shaped portion of your drawing for editing.

Text tool   A utensil for entering text in your drawing.

Toolbox   The collection of icons representing the available drawing utensils in Paintbrush. The Toolbox is located along the left border of the Paintbrush window.

EXERCISES

6-1. This exercise gives you the opportunity to practice the concepts and techniques you explored in Lab 6-1. You'll get a chance to create the simple chart shown in Figure 6-25.

    a. Start Windows and launch Paintbrush.

Figure 6-25. A simple bar chart.

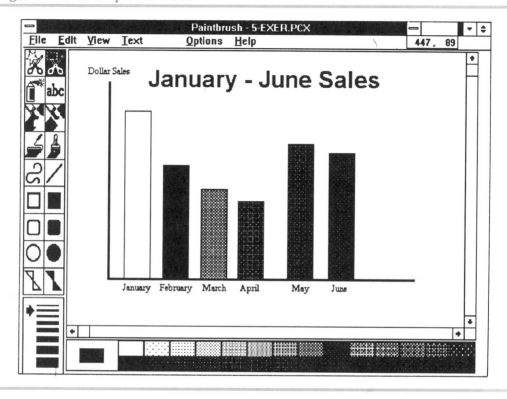

b. Maximize the Paintbrush window and prepare a canvas for a black and white drawing.

c. Select the Line tool.

d. Select the third thickness setting in the Linesize box.

e. Draw the horizontal and vertical lines that serve as the axes for the chart. (Remember that the Shift key is helpful for vertical and horizontal lines.)

f. Select the first thickness setting (the thinnest line) in the Linesize box.

g. Select the Box tool.

h. Draw the first bar (January's sales) for the chart.

Once you've drawn the first bar, you can use the *Copy* command to replicate it for each month. The height of each bar can be reduced by first drawing a new horizontal line at the lower height and then erasing the portion above the line. It's a good idea to copy from the tallest bar so you won't have to add height to any bar.

i. To replicate the tallest bar, choose the Pick tool, select the bar, and issue the *Copy* command followed by the *Paste* command.

j. Position the duplicate bar to the right of the first bar and even with the X-axis (see Figure 6–25).

k. Select *Paste* again and move the third bar to its position (again, see Figure 6–25). Continue this process until all six bars are in place.

l. Adjust the length of each bar by first drawing a horizontal line at the desired height. Then use the *Zoom In* command from the View menu to focus on the top of each bar and erase the extraneous lines. Use *Zoom Out* to return to the normal viewing mode.

m. Select the Paint Roller and fill the bars with the shades and patterns shown in Figure 6–25.

● HINT

If the shade or pattern flows out of the desired bar, then you have a leak in the bar. Use the *Undo* command to remove the paint spill and the *Zoom In* option to find the opening the paint leaked from. Patch the hole and fill the bar again.

n. Select black as your foreground color and then choose the Text tool. Select the *Arial* font, *Bold* style, and enter a size of *16* in the *Size* text box.

o. Position the text cursor above your chart and type the title shown in Figure 6–25.

p. Reselect the Text tool to finalize the font, style, and size of the title.

q. Select the *Times New Roman* font with a *Regular* style and enter a size of *8* in the *Size* text box.

r. Reposition the text cursor along the bottom of the X-axis and label each month. Label the Y-axis as shown in Figure 6–25.

s. Issue the *Save* command from the File menu and click the *Save File as Type* drop-down list box. To save space on your disk, choose the PCX file format.

t. Name the file 6-1EXER.PCX and save it to your EXERCISES disk in the subdirectory PBFILES. Print the file with the *Draft* quality setting toggled on.

u. Exit Paintbrush and then end your Windows session after confirming that the *Save Settings on Exit* command in the Options menu of Program Manager is toggled off.

6-2. This exercise is an opportunity for you to practice the drawing sequence introduced in Lab 6-2. You'll use the procedure to create the image illustrated in

Figure 6–26. Your drawing may appear somewhat different; however, it should have the same basic elements.

    a. Start Windows and launch Paintbrush. Maximize Paintbrush.

    b. Prepare a new canvas with a *Black and White* Palette.

    c. In keeping with the process discussed in the chapter, you'll start by creating the largest components of the drawing. Select the Circle tool.

    d. Draw the main shape of the balloon. (Notice that the balloon is not perfectly round.)

    e. Draw the basket with either the Box tool or the Polygon utensil.

    f. To draw the guide wires that suspend the basket from the balloon, use the Line tool with the Linesize gauge set at the thinnest setting.

    g. Use the Curve tool to draw the seams that divide the patterns on the balloon.

Figure 6–26. A more complex drawing.

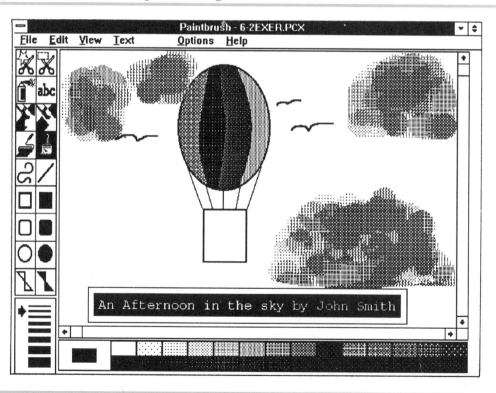

● **HINT**_____

The Curve tool works much like the Line tool, except it also lets you "bend" a line to form a curve. To use the Curve tool, click at the point where you want a line to begin and then click on the point where you want it to end. Next, to curve the line to the left, place the mouse pointer on the left side of the line, hold down the mouse button, drag the pointer left until the curve in the line is satisfactory, and release the mouse button. Click the left mouse button once more to "lock" or confirm the position of the new line. Repeat the same process to curve a line to the right except place the mouse pointer on the right side of the line and drag right.

---

   h. Use the Paint Roller to paint the balloon in the shades or patterns shown.
   i. To draw the clouds, select the Airbrush tool, the thickest line setting on the Linesize gauge, and a light pattern.
   j. Drag the Airbrush pointer in circular motions to create the cloud effect.

Use the *Undo* command to delete any mistakes you make with the currently selected tool. Use the erasers and the zoom commands to make other editing changes.

   k. To draw the birds, select the Brush tool and the second setting on the Linesize gauge.
   l. Drag the Brush pointer in the shape of the seagulls.
  m. To add the title, select the Text utensil with the *Courier New* font, *Regular* style, and enter a size of *16* in the *Size* text box.
   n. To display the title in inverse video, use the Pick tool to select the title. Select the *Inverse* command from the Pick menu.
   o. Frame the title with the Box utensil.
   p. Save the file using the PCX file format. Name the image 6-2EXER.PCX
   q. Print the drawing with the *Draft* quality setting toggled on.
   r. Exit Paintbrush and then end your Windows session after confirming that the *Save Settings on Exit* command in the Options menu of Program Manager is toggled off.

True or False Questions

1. **T   F**   The Palette is the heart of Paintbrush's drawing capabilities.

2. **T   F**   The Shift key is used with the Line tool to draw precise vertical, horizontal, and diagonal lines.

3. **T   F**   To use a graphics tool, you must first select it from the Edit menu.

4. **T   F**   The size of the Eraser utensil is determined by the Eraser size command in the Options menu.

5. **T   F**   The Paint Roller tool simulates an airbrush.

6. **T   F**   The Scaling option in the Print dialog box determines the size of the printed output in relation to the actual size of the drawing.

7. **T   F**   When creating a drawing, you should start with the smallest component and work outward.

8. **T   F**   The Undo command clears the work performed since the last tool selection was made.

9. **T   F**   Preparing a canvas requires the use of the *Image Attributes...* command on the Options menu.

10. **T   F**   The Brush is a freeform tool that paints a brush stroke as you drag it around the workspace.

Multiple Choice Questions

1. What tool fills in a bounded area with a color?

   a. Airbrush
   b. Paint Roller
   c. Box
   d. Filled Box
   e. None of the above

2. What command lets you save a portion of your canvas to disk?

   a. *Change*
   b. *Copy to...*
   c. *View Picture*
   d. *Page Setup*

3. What important component is located on the left side of the Paintbrush window?

   a. Scroll bars
   b. Menu bar
   c. Palette
   d. Toolbox
   e. None of the above

4. You can save a portion of a Paintbrush drawing by selecting the area of the graphic to be saved and then choosing

   a. *Save As...*   c. *Paste From...*
   b. *Paste To...*   d. *Copy To...*

5. The tool that allows you to control the number of sides a figure may have is the

   a. Rounded Box   c. Ellipse
   b. Circle   d. Polygon

6. The following is a useful feature for keeping track of the cursor in the workspace.

   a. Linesize box   c. Scroll bar arrows
   b. Cursor position   d. Pixel pointer

7. The tool that selects a rectangular area for editing is

   a. Pick   c. Eraser
   b. Shears   d. Color Eraser

8. Which text characteristics can be altered?

   a. Fonts   c. Size
   b. Style   d. All of the above

9. Whenever you issue the *Zoom In* command, this tool is automatically selected for you:

   a. Brush   c. Line
   b. Scissors   d. Eraser

10. Changing the background color in the Colors Select box requires that you point at the desired color or pattern and

    a. Click the left mouse button   c. Click the right mouse button
    b. Double-click the left mouse button   d. Press the Enter key

CHAPTER 7

Transferring Data Between Applications

- *Objectives*

Upon completing this chapter, you'll be able to:

1. **Transfer images from Paintbrush to Write using Clipboard.**
2. **Move and size a graphic image inside a Write document.**
3. **Save and open Clipboard files.**
4. **Capture windows and screens using Clipboard.**
5. **Edit the captured images using Paintbrush.**

OVERVIEW

This chapter explores Windows' ability to share text and graphics between different applications. Windows uses Clipboard to perform these transfers. You'll also see how some Windows applications take this process a step further by forming "links" between programs that make updating data both easy and convenient. Finally, you'll get a chance to use Clipboard to capture images directly from the screen.

In Lab 7–1, you'll complete the memorandum you began back in Chapter 5. You'll use Clipboard to bring the floor plan created in Chapter 6 into your memo. The simplicity of combining text and graphics is one of the true marvels of Windows. In the past, such integration was so time consuming and difficult that few users attempted it.

The second lab will acquaint you with Clipboard's ability to capture images directly from your monitor screen. Screen capture is an especially handy feature for sharing information with others. When a screen is "captured," its contents are copied into Clipboard and can be brought into Paintbrush for editing and printing. You can also save the captured screen to a file. This makes it easy to show others a "picture" of anything appearing on your desktop.

LAB 7-1   SHARING DATA BETWEEN APPLICATIONS WITH CLIPBOARD

We are going to use the Write memo you created in Chapter 5 and the Paintbrush floor plan you drew in Chapter 6 to produce an impressive and effective document. We'll do this by inserting a copy of the floor plan into the memo. Once the image has been placed in the document, you'll move and size it so it complements the surrounding text. You'll also learn how to update the image automatically.

In your previous encounters with Clipboard, you used it to cut, copy, and paste selections within an application. Here, you'll use it to transport information and form links between applications.

Cutting or Copying Data into Clipboard

In this lab, we'll refer to Paintbrush as the **source application** and Write as the **destination application**. Figure 7-1 illustrates the process for moving information from one program to another. It's important to note that this procedure will work equally well with applications other than Paintbrush and Write.

To move text or graphics between applications, first select the block to be transported using the techniques supported by the source application. Then use the *Cut* or *Copy* command from the source program to place the selection in Clipboard. Next, insert the contents of Clipboard into the destination program by issuing the *Paste* command from the destination application.

Figure 7-1. Clipboard serves as a temporary storage area for transferring information between different applications.

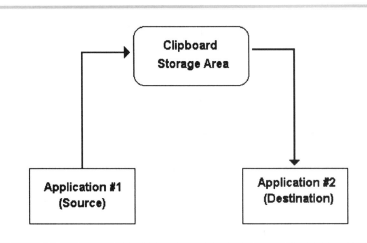

In our case, we'll begin by calling up Paintbrush and opening the file containing the floor plan. Next, we'll use the Pick tool to block the drawing and the *Copy* command to send a duplicate of it to Clipboard.

1. Start Windows and open the Accessories group window.
2. In anticipation of the final stages of the transfer process, prepare your desktop by launching Write and minimizing it to an icon.
3. Start Paintbrush and maximize it to provide the optimum amount of workspace.
4. Choose the *Open...* command from the File menu in Paintbrush.
5. Insert your EXERCISES disk. Select drive A and the directory PBFILES, then open EX6-2A.BMP.
6. When the image appears, select the Pick utensil from the Toolbox.
7. Position the crosshairs pointer above and slightly to the left of the drawing, drag it down beyond the lower right corner so that the entire map is enclosed, and release the mouse button.

All of the graphic image should now be inside the Pick rectangle, as pictured in Figure 7-2.

● **HINT**_____

If you don't have the entire image inside the Pick area, click on the Pick tool in the Toolbox to clear the current selection and then select the floor plan again.

_____

8. To send a duplicate of the image to Clipboard, issue the *Copy* command from the Edit menu.

Pasting Data from Clipboard

Once an image has been sent to Clipboard, you can minimize the source application and expand the destination application. This will provide the best possible view for completing the transfer operation. The next step is to open the destination file and position the cursor at the spot where you want to place the contents of Clipboard. To insert a copy of the selection, choose the *Paste* command from the Edit menu. (If you want to bring in another copy, simply reposition the cursor and issue the *Paste* command again.)

Figure 7-2. The first step in transferring the floor plan is to select it.

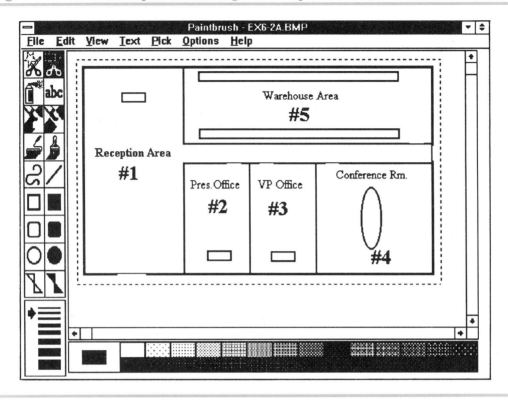

1. Minimize Paintbrush to an icon.
2. Expand Write by double-clicking on its icon at the bottom of your desktop.
3. Maximize Write.
4. Choose the *Open...* command from the File menu and select drive A.

Because the current subdirectory in drive A is PBFILES, you'll need to move back up to the root directory before you can select the WPFILES directory.

5. To select the WPFILES directory, double-click on the *a:* folder in the *Directories* list box. When the subdirectories on your EXER-CISES disk appear in the list box, double-click the WPFILES directory and open the file EX5-3A.WRI.

With the destination application maximized and the destination file open, we're ready to indicate where the insertion is to occur. Let's place the graphic between the third and fourth paragraphs of your memo. Before we bring in the floor plan, we'll insert an extra line between these two paragraphs to provide a border above and below the drawing. Figure 7–3 illustrates the location where the floor plan is to be inserted.

$SKIP$

6. First, to reduce the overuse of fonts, change the font type of the last three paragraphs to Times New Roman.
7. Now, to position the cursor, point at the blank line between the third and fourth paragraphs and click the left mouse button.
8. Press the Enter key to create a second blank line between the paragraphs.
9. To insert the floor plan, select *Paste* from the Edit menu.

Your document should now display the floor plan graphic, as pictured in Figure 7–4. Don't worry if some of the details are unclear. When you print the document, all the finer points will be visible.

Figure 7–3. The floor plan will be inserted between the third and fourth paragraphs.

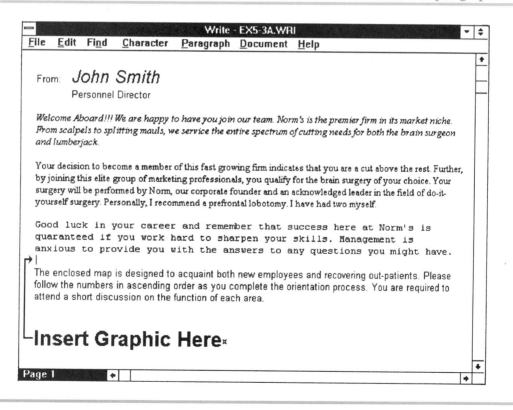

Figure 7-4. The floor plan pasted into the Write document.

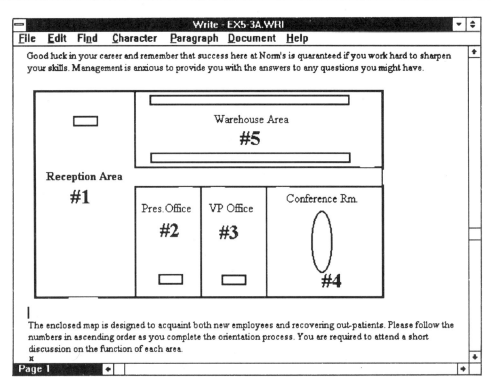

Moving and Resizing an Image in Write

To move or size a graphic in a Write document, use the *Move Picture* or *Size Picture* commands from the Edit menu. These commands perform exactly the actions their respective names imply.

The *Move Picture* command shifts an image horizontally. When the command is issued, a rectangular outline of the selected image will appear. You can drag the outline to a new horizontal location and release it.

● **HINT**

To move a graphic vertically, you must select the image and remove it using the *Cut* command. Position the cursor at the new location and reinsert it by issuing the *Paste* command.

The *Size Picture* command alters the dimensions of a graphic. Choosing this option will also produce a rectangular outline. You then move the pointer to the left, right, or lower border of the rectangle. This will give you control over the chosen border. Then, simply move the pointer in the direction you want the border to go. As you move the pointer, the rectangular outline will change to reflect the new dimensions. When you are satisfied, click the left mouse button to "lock in" the new dimensions.

1. Scroll the document so that all of the map is visible.
2. To select the map, click anywhere on it.
3. With the image highlighted, click the *Size Picture* command from the Edit menu.
4. To lengthen the map, first move the pointer so it rests halfway across the right edge of the rectangle.
5. Now slide the pointer to the right until the right border matches the width of the text. Click the left mouse button to complete the operation.

Your document should resemble the one shown in Figure 7–5. It's now ready to be printed. Before proceeding, it's a good idea to save your work to guard against an accident.

6. Issue the *Save As...* command from the File menu. Select drive A and the directory WPFILES, then save the file as EX7-1A.WRI

● **HINT**

You can center a graphic quickly and accurately by selecting it and then issuing the *Center* command from the Paragraph menu. You may also execute the *Left* or *Right* alignment commands.

Embedding and Linking Objects

Object Linking and Embedding or **OLE** is a Windows feature that lets different applications work together to create a seamless "compound" document. A **compound document** is a file that displays one or more data selections from other applications. When two applications support OLE, the simple act of copying data from one application and pasting it in the other forms a connection between the two programs. This connection makes it possible to edit and update the imported data both easily and quickly.

Figure 7–5. The *Move Picture* and *Size Picture* commands from the Edit menu in Write let you move and size a graphic.

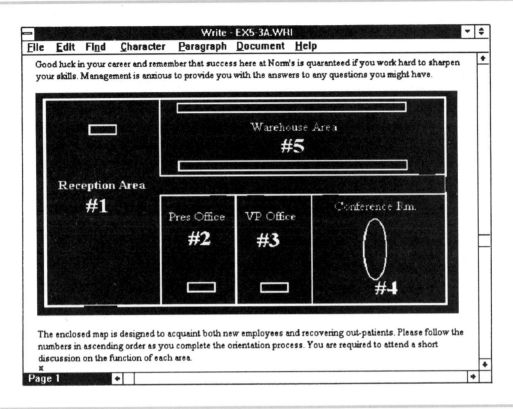

Before we can talk further of Object Linking and Embedding, it is necessary to define a few key terms. First, a data selection imported from another application (e.g., a block of text, a table of numbers, or a graphic) is called an **embedded object**. The word "embedded" signifies that the **object** (data selection) remains connected to its source application. Next, the destination application used to create a compound document is referred to as the **client application**. This term better describes the relationship between the source applications and the "client" program they service.

Finally, a **linked object** is a data selection that appears in a compound document but actually resides in its own file. The main difference between an embedded object and a linked object is that as changes occur in a linked object they are automatically reflected in a compound document regardless of whether or not the document and its client application are open. Since an embedded object is part of a compound document, both the client application and the document must be open in order for you to modify the object.

If this all seems a bit fuzzy, hold on. It will become much clearer as we step through creating and editing both an embedded and a linked object.

Working with Embedded Objects

To embed an object in a document, copy it from the source application and paste it into the client application. You can modify the object by double-clicking on one of its boundaries. This action will summon its source application with the object open and ready for editing. Once the modifications are complete, close the source application to make the changes part of the compound document.

Since both Write and Paintbrush support OLE, the floor plan you previously pasted into the Write document is an embedded object. Thus, we can call its source application (Paintbrush) by simply double-clicking on the floor plan.

1. Close Paintbrush.
2. Select the floor plan from the memo in Write.
3. If necessary, position the mouse pointer on the floor plan and double-click.

After you perform these actions, Paintbrush will appear with the floor plan loaded, as shown in Figure 7–6.

4. Use Paintbrush to relabel the Warehouse Area as the Storage Area
5. To make the change part of the compound document in Write, close Paintbrush.

The dialog box shown in Figure 7–7 will appear and ask if you want to update the embedded object with the change.

6. Confirm your intentions by clicking *Yes*.

The floor plan in the memo document will now display the new label.

7. Save the document as EX7-1A.WRI

Working with Linked Objects

To insert a link to an object in a document, save the object to a file, then copy it from the source application, position the pointer at the

Figure 7–6. OLE lets you directly edit the Paintbrush image embedded in your Write document.

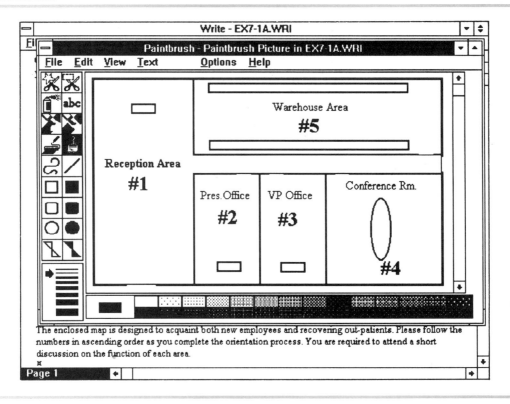

insertion point in the client application, and issue the **Paste Link** command from the Edit menu. Editing a linked object is easy. Just open the source application and make the modifications you want. Any changes to the object will automatically be reflected in the compound document the next time you view it.

Let's use this procedure to create and edit a linked object in our company memo.

1. Select the floor plan in the memo document.
2. Press the Delete key to remove the embedded object.

Since the floor plan is already saved as a file and stored in Clipboard, you can *Paste Link* it into your Write document.

3. Position the text cursor between the third and fourth paragraphs of the memo document.

Figure 7–7.
This dialog
box gives you
the option to
update the
embedded
object.

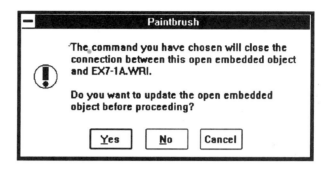

4. Choose the *Paste Link* command from the Edit menu in Write to insert a link to the object.

___NOTE_____

The Edit menu in Write also contains several other commands that pertain to embedding and linking objects. The **Paste Special...** command lets you choose a different format for data you plan to embed in or link to a document. The **Links...** command enables you to edit the linked data in a file. The **Object** command invokes the application used to create the currently selected data. **Insert Object...** presents a list of applications you can summon to embed information into your Write file. For more information on these options, consult Windows' *User's Guide* or the Help facility in Write.

Your memo will again display the floor plan. But this time the document contains only a link to the graphic file, not the actual drawing.

5. Save the compound document and close Write.
6. Open Paintbrush and the file EX6-2A.BMP. Add another shelf to the Warehouse Area so that your drawing matches Figure 7–8. (This may require moving or erasing and reentering some text.)
7. Save the floor plan.
8. Close Paintbrush, launch Write, and open the file EX7-1A.WRI.
9. When the dialog box appears, confirm that you want to update the document now by clicking the *Yes* button.

Figure 7–8. The floor plan with a new shelf in the "Warehouse Area."

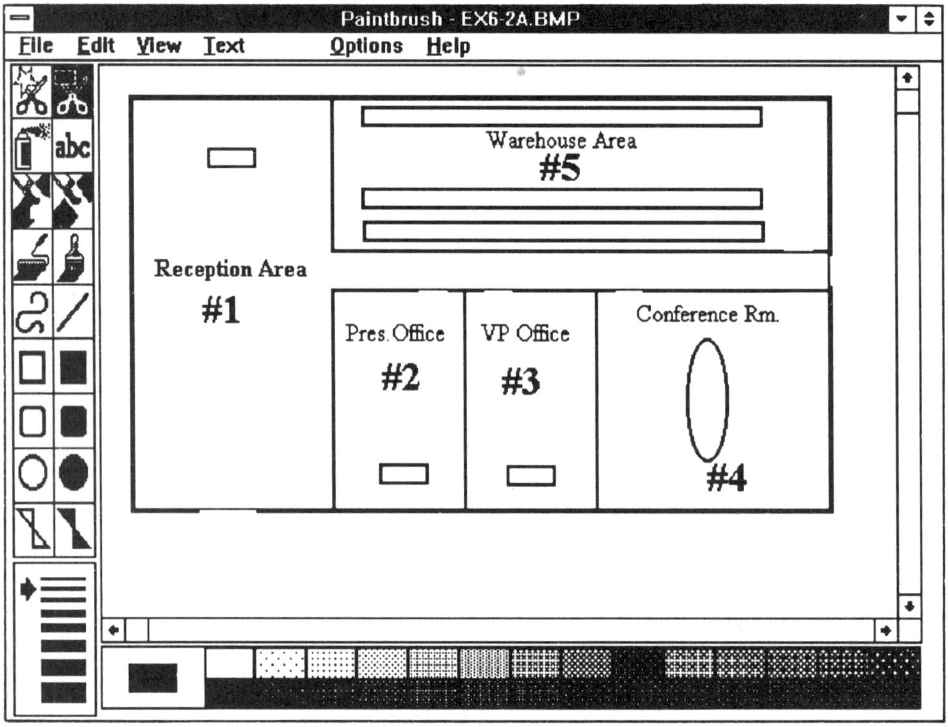

The change you made to the floor plan in Paintbrush will automatically appear in the company memo, as shown in Figure 7–9.

Before exiting, let's print a copy of this compound document.

10. Select the *Print...* command from the File menu.
11. Click the *OK* button to send the final copy of your memo to the printer.
12. Once the printing is complete, you may end your Windows session after confirming that the *Save Settings on Exit* command in the Options menu of Program Manager is turned off.

LAB 7–2   USING CLIPBOARD TO CAPTURE SCREENS

Although Clipboard's primary purpose is to move data within and between applications, it's also capable of "capturing" a window or even

Figure 7–9. The floor plan is automatically updated when the Write document is opened.

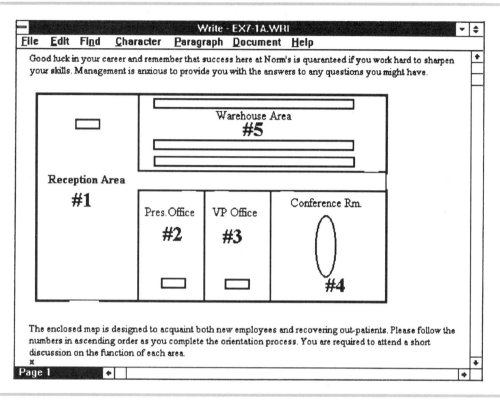

an entire screen. In this second lab, you'll learn to use this facility to take "pictures" of the various items on your desktop.

These captured images can be used for a variety of purposes. For instance, suppose you're constructing an Excel spreadsheet and run into a problem with a formula. By capturing the screen, you preserve the exact conditions under which the problem arose. You can then print a copy of the screen and take it to someone for help.

Captured screens are also commonly used in software training manuals (like this one). They provide clear and relevant examples of the features and functions of a program. In fact, many of the screens you see in this book were captured with Clipboard.

Capturing Screens and Windows

Clipboard lets you capture either the whole screen or just a window. A **captured screen** or window is simply the video image that was visible on your monitor when the capture took place. The image is not linked to the original application in any way. A Clipboard image is just a one-dimensional copy of the screen or window.

When capturing a screen, it's best to think of Clipboard as an instant camera. Just as a photo is taken by pressing the shutter release on a camera, you press Clipboard's capture keys to "snap" a picture of your desktop. The image is immediately sent to Clipboard, which acts as the "film" for storing the picture. Once a screen or window has been "photographed," it is available to view, save, or paste into a Windows application.

To capture all of your desktop (screen), simply press the **Print Screen** key. (This key is typically located in the upper right portion of your keyboard and may be labeled PrtScrn, PrintScrn, or PrtScr.) A copy of the current screen will be placed in Clipboard. To capture only the active window, hold down the Alt key and then tap the Print Screen key once. This will send a "picture" of the active window to Clipboard.

To give you some experience with screen captures, we'll start by having you capture a full screen and then use Clipboard Viewer to display it. Next, you'll capture a single window and save it as a Clipboard file.

1. Start Windows and open the Accessories group window.

At this point, your desktop should resemble the one shown in Figure 7–10. If not, arrange it to match the figure as closely as possible.

Figure 7–10. The full screens that you capture can be composed of any combination of application windows or document windows.

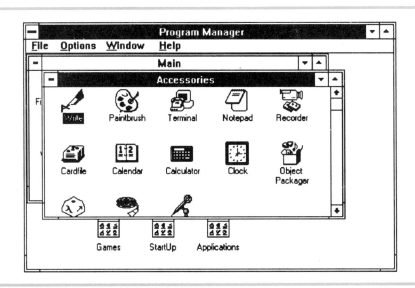

Program Manager should be visible with the Main group window partially hidden behind the Accessories group.

2. To capture the full screen, press the Print Screen key once.

Your mouse pointer will disappear until the screen capture is complete. This process can last anywhere from a couple of seconds to a full minute. The capture speed depends on the type of microprocessor and the amount of memory in your computer system. A faster processor and more memory increases the rate at which an image is copied to Clipboard.

Once a screen is in Clipboard, you can paste it into Paintbrush, Write, or any other Windows application that accepts a graphic image. You may also view the image by calling up Clipboard.

3. Minimize the Accessories group window to expose the Main group.
4. To open Clipboard Viewer, double-click on its icon in the Main group window.

Observe that the workspace in the Clipboard Viewer window displays a copy of your desktop. However, only a portion of the captured screen is visible. To see the entire image, simply maximize the Clipboard Viewer window.

5. For a better view of your captured screen, maximize the Clipboard Viewer window.

Check your Clipboard Viewer against the one pictured in Figure 7–11.

Saving the Image as a Clipboard File

Clipboard Viewer is also able to save a captured screen to a file. A Clipboard file is a convenient way to store commonly used images or text. For example, you could save a company logo and address in a Clipboard file and retrieve it whenever you want to incorporate these items into a document. When you open a Clipboard file, its contents are automatically placed in the workspace of Clipboard Viewer. To insert these contents in a Windows application, simply select the *Paste* command from the Edit menu.

Let's try capturing just one window and saving it as a Clipboard file.

Figure 7-11. You can display a captured screen or window by opening the Clipboard Viewer window.

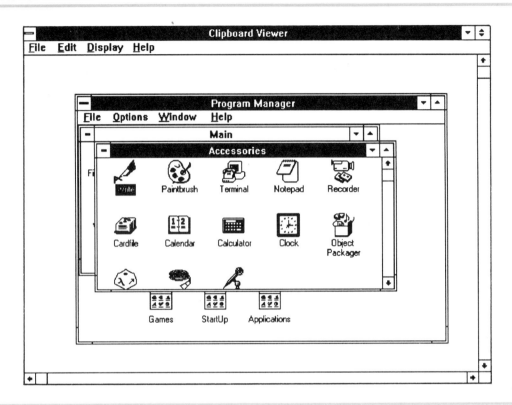

1. Minimize the Clipboard Viewer window.
2. Open the Control Panel by double-clicking its icon in the Main group window.

Your screen should match the one portrayed in Figure 7-12. Although the Main group and Program Manager are still visible, they will not be included when you capture the active Control Panel window.

3. To capture the Control Panel window, hold down the Alt key while you tap the Print Screen key once.

The cursor disappears to signal the capture has taken place. Clipboard Viewer now contains a copy of the Control Panel window. Because Clipboard can hold only one image at a time, the full screen image you captured earlier is lost.

Figure 7-12.
Since the
Control Panel
window is
active, it will
be the only
image
captured
when you
hold down
the Alt key
and press
Print Screen.

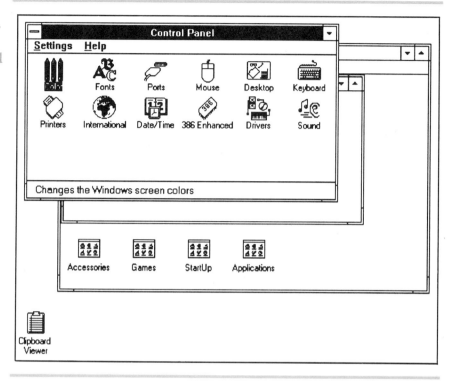

4. Close the Control Panel window by double-clicking on its control-menu box.
5. Double-click on the Clipboard Viewer icon at the bottom of your desktop. (If you closed Clipboard Viewer instead of minimizing it, double-click on its icon inside the Main group window.)

A copy of the Control Panel window will appear in the workspace of Clipboard Viewer, as pictured in Figure 7-13. To save this image, select the *Save As...* command from the File menu in Clipboard. Clipboard files use the extension CLP.

6. Choose the *Save As...* command from the File menu to save the contents of Clipboard.
7. Insert the EXERCISES diskette. Select drive A and the root directory, then save the file as EX7-2A.CLP

The file is now stored on your floppy disk and can be opened (placed in Clipboard's storage area) any time you need the data.

Figure 7-13. Clipboard can contain only one captured image at a time.

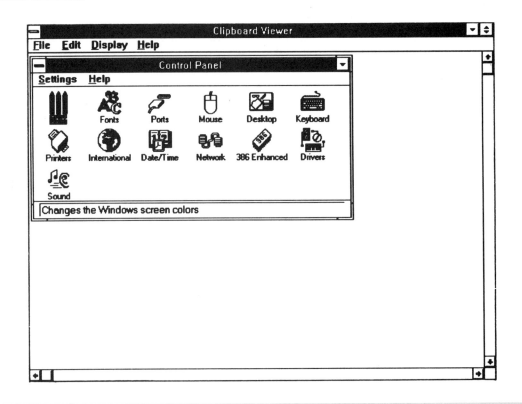

Clearing the Contents of Clipboard

To clear the contents of Clipboard, issue the **Delete** command from the Edit menu. Since an image stored in Clipboard depletes the amount of memory available for your other applications, it's a good idea to remove the image once you're done using it. This will free up the memory for other uses.

1. Select the *Delete* command from the Edit menu.
2. Confirm the operation by clicking the *Yes* button.

After you issue this command, Clipboard's workspace will be empty. The memory that was occupied by the Clipboard image has been returned to Windows for use elsewhere.

Opening a Clipboard File

You can retrieve a Clipboard file by choosing the *Open...* command from the File menu. When the Open dialog box appears, select the drive, directory, and filename you want to open. Clicking the *OK* button loads the file into Clipboard's workspace.

1. Choose the *Open...* command from the File menu in Clipboard Viewer.
2. Select drive A and open the file you saved a moment ago: EX7-2A.CLP.

The Control Panel image will again occupy the workspace in Clipboard Viewer. You're now ready to call up an application and paste the captured window into it.

Modifying an Image Using Paintbrush

You can use Paintbrush to edit and print the screens and windows you capture with Clipboard. All you have to do is select the *Paste* command from the Edit menu of Paintbrush to bring in a copy of the image. However, the image must fit within the size of the visible workspace of Paintbrush; otherwise, the portions extending beyond your view will be "cropped" off. Thus, you should always maximize Paintbrush to provide the largest possible workspace before bringing in a captured screen or window.

Once a captured image is placed in Paintbrush, you are free to use all the utensils in the Toolbox to modify it. Let's experiment with this capability by importing the Control Panel image presently stored in Clipboard.

1. Close the Clipboard Viewer window by double-clicking on its control-menu box.
2. Open the Accessories group window and launch Paintbrush.
3. Maximize Paintbrush.

When you are pasting a captured image into Paintbrush, you must set the program to display color or the image will appear in black and white. You can use the Image Attributes dialog box to set Paintbrush for color.

4. Choose the *Image Attributes...* command from the Options menu.

5. Check to be certain the *Colors* option is toggled on.
6. Click on *OK* to exit the dialog box.

The color Palette should be visible. When Paintbrush is set for color, the incoming image will retain all of its original colors.

7. To import the contents of Clipboard, choose the *Paste* command from the Edit menu.

When using a noncolor printer, you'll want to set Paintbrush for black and white to get the best printing results. You can set Paintbrush for a noncolor display by picking the *Black and White* option from the Image Attributes dialog box.

8. Select the *Image Attributes...* command from the Options menu.
9. Click the *Black and White* option.
10. Click *OK* to close the dialog box.
11. Respond *Yes* when asked if you wish to start a new session with the new image attributes.
12. Answer *No* when asked whether you want to save the current changes.
13. Once the black and white Palette appears, choose the *Paste* command from the Edit menu.

Compare your Paintbrush window with the one portrayed in Figure 7–14.

We can now use the commands and tools in Paintbrush to modify, save, and print the image. We'll start by adding some additional text to it. Next, you'll save it as a Paintbrush file, and you'll finish up by printing a copy of it.

14. Choose the Text tool.
15. Select the *Times New Roman* font from the Font menu.
16. Click on size *14* from the Size menu.
17. Type the following information below the captured window.

Windows 3.1 Tutorial
Chapter 7
Lab 7–2
[Today's date]
[Your name]

Figure 7–14. Setting Paintbrush for black and white causes some of the detail in a captured screen or window to be lost. However, it enables a graphic to be printed more clearly on a noncolor printer.

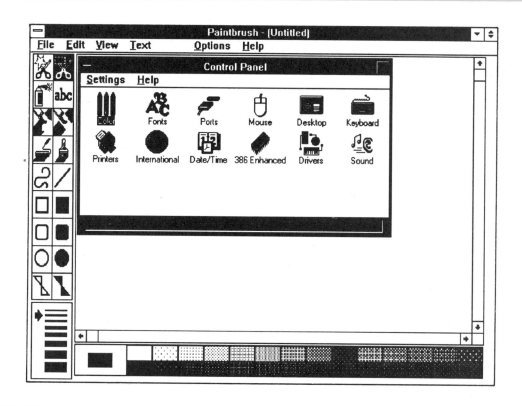

Your final product should closely match the screen pictured in Figure 7–15. Make any necessary corrections before proceeding.

18. To save the file, select *Save* from the File menu.
19. Select drive A, directory PBFILES, and save the file as EX7-2B.BMP
20. Choose *Print...* from the File menu.
21. Print the image using *Proof* quality.
22. Quit Paintbrush by selecting *Exit* from the File menu.
23. Quit Windows after confirming that the *Save Settings on Exit* command in the Options menu of Program Manager is toggled off.

Figure 7-15. Clipboard images can be edited and modified just like a Paintbrush drawing.

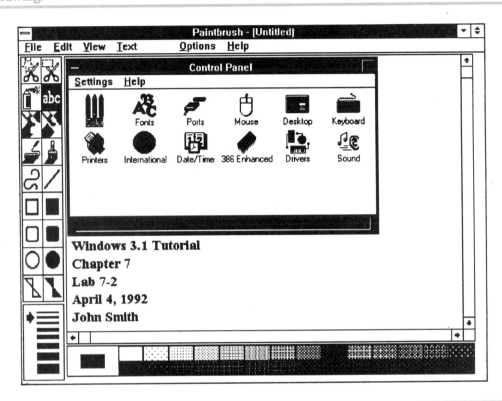

COMING ATTRACTIONS . . .

This chapter has further expanded your knowledge of Clipboard. You now know how to copy a graphic image from Paintbrush and paste it into a Write document. You can also adjust both the position and size of the imported image to complement the surrounding document.

In addition, you've become proficient at using Clipboard to capture images from your desktop. These captured screens can be pasted into Paintbrush where you can view, modify, save, and print them.

In the next chapter, we'll explore Print Manager. This Windows program controls the printing chores for all the other Windows applications. In the final chapter, we'll show you how to customize Windows to suit your individual needs and tastes.

KEY TERMS

Auto   Display menu command in Clipboard Viewer that displays the contents of Clipboard in their original format.

Bitmap   Display menu command in Clipboard Viewer that lets you change the format of the contents of Clipboard to a bitmap image.

Captured screen   A copy of a video image on your monitor.

Client application   A program used to create a compound document containing objects embedded or linked to other source applications.

Compound document   A document file that incorporates objects transparently connected to different applications.

Delete   Edit menu command in Clipboard Viewer that clears the workspace.

Destination application   The program you have elected to paste the contents of Clipboard into.

Embedded object   A data selection copied from a source application and pasted into a client application that remains connected to its source program. Both applications must support OLE.

Insert Object...   Edit menu command in Write that shows a list of applications you can summon to embed information into your Write file.

Linked object   A data selection that appears in a compound document but actually resides in a file. It is linked to the compound document so that automatic updating occurs when changes are made to it by the source application.

Links...   Edit menu command in Write that lets you modify the linked information in a file.

Object   Data such as text, numbers, or a graphic. Also an Edit menu command in Write that lets you invoke the application used to create the currently selected data.

Object Linking and Embedding (OLE)   A feature of Windows that lets you create a single document with objects embedded from and linked to different applications.

Paste Link   Edit menu command in Write that links the contents of Clipboard to the insertion point in a document.

Paste Special...   Edit menu command in Write that chooses the format data will be in when it is embedded in or linked to a document.

Print Screen   The key used to capture a copy of your entire Windows desktop (screen). (To capture just the active window, hold down the Alt key and press Print Screen.)

Source application   The program you have elected to cut or copy a selection from. The selection will be placed temporarily in Clipboard.

EXERCISES

7-1. The following directions review the concepts and procedures demonstrated in Lab 7-1. Until now, you've only pasted a single graphic image into a Write document. In this exercise, you'll be asked to insert multiple images.

    a. Start Windows. Launch Paintbrush and maximize it.

    b. Open the EX6-2A.BMP file in the PBFILES directory on your EXERCISES disk.

    c. Minimize Paintbrush and launch Write.

    d. Type the following text.

        Windows 3.1 Tutorial

        Chapter Seven

        Exercise 7-1

[Your Name]
[Today's Date]

e. Insert two blank lines below today's date by pressing the Enter key three times. Then type the following sentences, placing three blank lines after each.

The completed image I created using Paintbrush.
The desk shape from my image library.
The shelf shape from my image library.

f. Use Task List to switch back to Paintbrush.

g. Use the Pick tool to copy the floor plan into Clipboard and then switch back to Write.

h. Paste the Paintbrush image below today's date.

i. Switch to Paintbrush.

j. Open DESK.BMP and copy the shape into Clipboard.

k. Switch to Write and paste the desk into your Write document between the first and second sentences.

l. Retrieve and paste the shelf image between the second and last sentences in your document.

m. Center the images.

Your screen should now look like the one portrayed in Figure 7–16.

n. Close Paintbrush.

o. To change the shelf image, position the mouse pointer on the shelf and double-click.

Paintbrush will appear with the shelf image loaded.

p. Use the Paintbrush tools to reduce the length of the shelf by roughly half.

q. Close Paintbrush and confirm that you want to update the embedded object with the change.

r. Switch to Write.

Your document should resemble the one illustrated in Figure 7–17.

s. Save your file as 7-1EXER.WRI to the WPFILES directory.

t. Print the document.

u. Exit Write and then Windows after checking that the *Save Settings on Exit* command in the Options menu of Program Manager is switched off.

Figure 7-16. You can insert multiple images into Write.

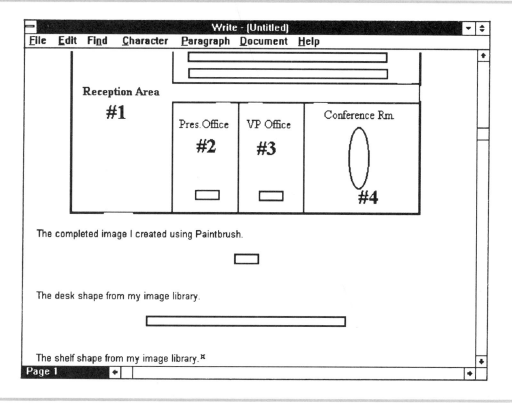

7-2. In this exercise, you'll review the screen capture techniques covered in Lab 7-2. We'll begin by having you capture the Directory Tree window in File Manager. Then you'll paste the window into a Write document. After typing a short description of the image, you'll save and print the document.

 a. Start Windows. Launch File Manager and maximize it.

 b. Insert your EXERCISES disk and then select drive A. (Make sure all the subdirectories are displayed in the Directory Tree.)

 c. Switch to Program Manager and launch Write.

 d. Type the following text.

  Windows 3.1 Tutorial
  Chapter Seven
  Exercise 7-2
  [Your Name]
  [Today's Date]

 e. Press Enter three times to place two blank lines below today's date.

Figure 7–17. Captured screens and windows can be easily pasted into a Write document.

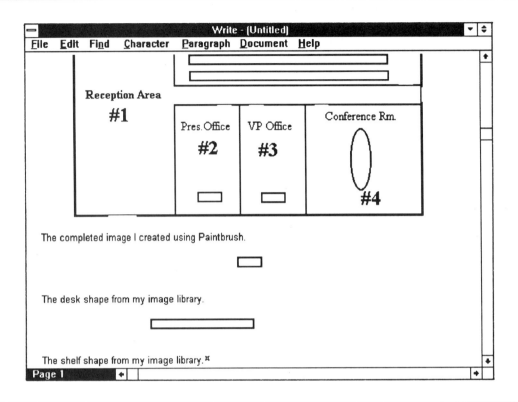

f. Switch to File Manager and capture just the File Manager window and its contents.

g. Switch back to Write. Paste the captured image two lines beneath the heading.

h. Center the image.

i. To place a description of the captured window below it, type:

This is the directory map of my EXERCISES disk. First, I formatted the disk to prepare it for use. Next, I created the subdirectories you see on the Directory Tree. Finally, I have saved my work from each chapter in the appropriate locations on the disk.

j. Save the file as 7-2EXER.WRI in the WPFILES directory on your EXERCISES disk.

k. Print the document.

Check your document against the one shown in Figure 7-18.

1. Exit Write and then Windows after checking that the *Save Settings on Exit* command in the Options menu of Program Manager is switched off.

Figure 7-18. The File Manager windows pasted into your Write document.

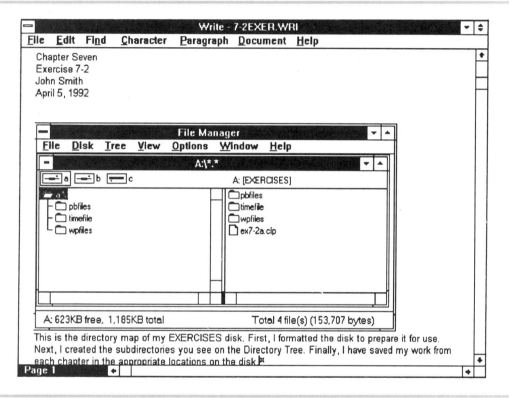

REVIEW QUESTIONS

True or False Questions

1. **T** **F** Both Write and Paintbrush support OLE.

2. **T** **F** An object must be saved before it can be embedded in an application.

3. **T** **F** After selecting a block of text or a graphic, you can transport it to another application by issuing the *Transport* command from the Edit menu.

4. **T** **F** All Clipboard images can be saved as CLP files.

5. **T   F**   Clipboard Viewer must be activated before it can receive text or graphics.

6. **T   F**   Once a graphic has been inserted into Write, you can move and size it.

7. **T   F**   Pressing the Print Screen key captures a selected block of text.

8. **T   F**   A destination application is where you copy from, while a source application is where you copy to.

9. **T   F**   The contents of Clipboard may be viewed by double-clicking on the Clipboard Viewer icon found in the Main group window.

10. **T   F**   Clipboard enables you to capture a window or an entire screen.

Multiple Choice Questions

1. To move a graphic in a vertical direction within Write, you would begin by selecting the image and issuing the command

    a. *Move Picture*
    b. *Size Picture*

    c. *Cut*
    d. None of the above

2. To capture an entire screen, what key(s) must be pressed?

    a. No keys are necessary; the mouse can do it all.
    b. Print Screen

    c. Alt key and Print Screen
    d. Enter and Ctrl

3. Clearing the contents of Clipboard Viewer

    a. Lets you exit Windows
    b. Keeps Clipboard Viewer from continually beeping

    c. Releases memory for use by other applications
    d. a and c

4. To send information to Clipboard from within an application, you must use either *Copy* or

    a. *Cut*
    b. *Select*

    c. *Paste*
    d. *Save As...*

5. Captured windows and screens can be modified with

    a. Notepad
    b. Clipboard Editor
    c. Paintbrush

    d. File Manager
    e. b or c

6. Clipboard Viewer can contain how many images at once?

    a. One
    b. Two

    c. Sixteen
    d. An unlimited number

7. Clipboard makes the following possible:

a. Sharing data between applications

b. Capturing and saving screens and windows

c. a and b

d. None of the above

8. Clipboard images are saved in special files with the file extension

a. CLP

b. BMP

c. PCX

d. WRI

9. To save a Clipboard image, it must be

a. Highlighted

b. Selected

c. In an open Clipboard Viewer

window

d. None of the above

10. Object Linking and Embedding lets you

a. Create compound documents that allow separate applications to work together in a transparent and seamless manner

b. Build integrated documents that

combine different DOS applications

c. Construct seamless documents that automatically update information from captured screens

d. a or c

CHAPTER 8

Managing Printing

● *Objectives*

Upon completing this chapter, you'll be able to:

1. View the status of the files you are printing.
2. Pause and resume printing.
3. Rearrange the order in which files are printed.
4. Delete files waiting to be printed.
5. Start and exit Print Manager.
6. Change the printing speed.
7. Control the messages displayed from Print Manager.
8. Display the size of the files sent to Print Manager for printing and the time and date they were sent.

OVERVIEW

This chapter is devoted to Print Manager, a utility program that controls printing for all Windows applications. Print Manager runs unseen in the background and is always available to receive printing jobs. It frees your applications from the time-consuming task of printing files. In addition, it provides a number of conveniences for monitoring and managing the printing of these files.

We'll begin by looking at the facilities in Print Manager for viewing and controlling the printing of files. You'll then be introduced to some features for customizing the way Print Manager operates and the information it displays.

LAB 8-1   PRINTING FILES WITH PRINT MANAGER

When you print from a DOS application, you must wait until the printing is complete before you can resume working with the application. If the file is large and the printer is slow, this wastes a considerable amount of your time. Thankfully, printing with a Windows application is different. When you print from a Windows application, the file is sent to a background program called Print Manager. **Print Manager** handles the printing for all Windows applications. Thus, when you print from a Windows application, you can continue to work with it while Print Manager supervises the printing.

Print Manager can accept multiple print jobs from different applications. It uses a "queue" to line these files up. The **print queue**, or waiting line, routes the files to the printer in the order they were received.

In this lab, we'll show you how to open the Print Manager window, check the status of the files in the print queue, and reorder and delete these files. We'll also demonstrate the procedures for pausing and resuming printing and the proper way to exit Print Manager.

Printing a File

When you issue the *Print...* command from the File menu of any Windows application, Print Manager springs into action, gathering the file and placing it in the print queue. Print Manager will then take over the printing process, freeing you to work with your application. However, when you print a large file, it may take some time for the file to transfer completely to Print Manager. During this period, you'll be unable to use your application. Keep in mind that it requires much less time to transfer a file to Print Manager than to print it. So your wait is still lessened considerably by the presence of Print Manager.

When you print a file or files, Windows will display the Print Manager icon in the lower left corner of your desktop. It'll remain there until every file slated for printing has been successfully routed to the printer. If the lower portion of your desktop is obscured by a window, you won't be able to see the icon.

Let's print a file from Write and watch for the appearance of the Print Manager icon.

1. Start Windows and Write.
2. Position the windows on your desktop so the lower portion of the screen is visible.
3. Insert the EXERCISES disk and open the document EX5-1A.WRI in the WPFILES directory of drive A.
4. Print a copy of the file.

The Print Manager icon will appear in the lower left corner of your screen, as shown in Figure 8-1. It will vanish when the document finishes transferring to the memory in your printer. A printer has its own memory (sometimes called a **buffer**) to store portions of the file it is currently printing. This speeds up the printing process by allowing large "chunks" of a document to be sent to the printer at a time.

Opening and Closing Print Manager

Normally, Print Manager runs entirely in the background. It's automatically invoked by printing from any Windows application and closes when all the pending files have been transferred to your printer. As you've seen, Print Manager runs as a minimized icon on your desktop. You can expand the icon into a window the same way you expand any other icon, by double-clicking on it.

Figure 8-1. The Print Manager icon will remain visible until the last print job has been sent to the printer.

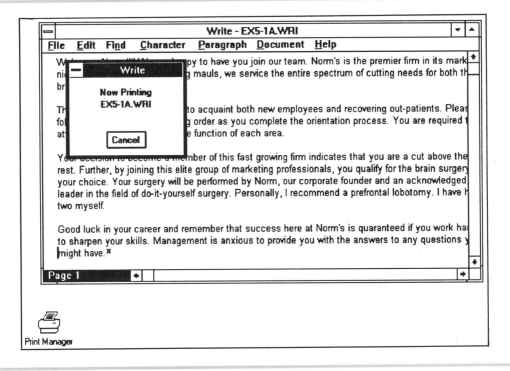

1. Use Write to print the file EX5-2A.WRI.
2. When the icon for Print Manager appears, expand it to a window by double-clicking it.

● **HINT**_____

If you're running an application maximized, you'll be unable to see the Print Manager icon to click on it. Remember, you can use Task List to switch to any Windows application. Switching to Print Manager will expand it from an icon to a window and make it active.

Your desktop will display a Print Manager window similar to the one shown in Figure 8–2. The window elements that are unique to this utility have been labeled. If you look below the menu bar, you'll see the *Pause, Resume,* and *Delete* buttons. These buttons enable you to suspend printing, recommence printing, and remove jobs from the print queue. The message box, immediately to the right of these buttons,

Figure 8–2. The Print Manager window shows the status of the print queue(s).

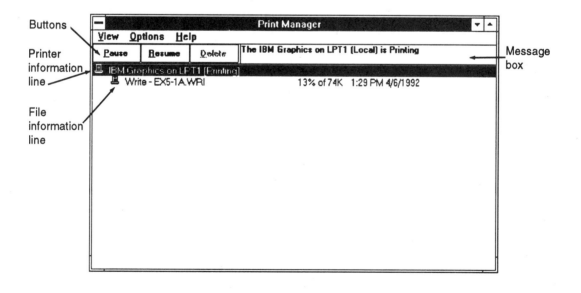

provides you with additional information about the item currently highlighted in the workspace below.

The workspace of the Print Manager window shows you the active printer(s), the file being printed, and any print jobs pending. If you're using more than one printer, you'll see a separate print queue for each active printer. The first line in a print queue is the **printer information line**. It lists the name of the printer (e.g., PCL/HP LaserJet), where the printer connects to your microcomputer (e.g., on LPT1), and the status of the current printer (e.g., [Printing]).

___ NOTE _____

You may recall from Chapter 4 that **LPT1** is a reserved DOS word. LPT1 is the name of the first parallel port located on the back of your computer. A port is used to connect to external devices such as printers. Most microcomputers also include a **COM1** serial port. A **parallel port** can transmit data faster than a serial port, so it's the preferred way to send data to a printer. However, a **serial port** can transmit data over greater distances than a parallel port. Thus, in situations where microcomputers and printers are separated by some space, you'll often find serial ports connecting these devices.

_____

Below the printer information line, you'll see the **file information line**. Each file you send to Print Manager will have a file information line in a print queue. This line consists of the position of the file in the queue, its title (i.e., the name of the application that generated it and the file's name), the size of the file in kilobytes, and the time and date Print Manager received it. When you click on a file information line, the message box will display a slightly more detailed account of the same information.

While a file is printing, the information line will display a print icon and the percentage of the document already sent to the printer. (If you are using a network printer, the percentage of the document sent to the printer may not appear.) When the print job has been transmitted, the file information line vanishes; however, Print Manager will remain visible. Print Manager, in the form of a window, will continue to run even after all the print jobs are completed. You can either click on its minimize box to reduce Print Manager to an icon or, to save memory, close it by choosing *Exit* from the View menu.

⊘ **HAZARD**_____

If you exit Print Manager before the queue is empty, the print jobs remaining will be lost. A warning message appears if you attempt to quit while files remain in the queue. To avoid aborting the print jobs, select the *Cancel* button from the message dialog box.

Pausing the Queue

One of Print Manager's more convenient features is its ability to halt printing temporarily. For example, if your printer jams or runs out of paper, you can suspend printing while you fix the problem. To interrupt printing, all you have to do is open the Print Manager window and click on the *Pause* button. The printer information line will then display the word [Paused] to show that printing is suspended. If you are using more than one printer, you'll need to select the correct printer information line before choosing the *Pause* button.

In order to demonstrate some of Print Manager's more interesting capabilities, we'll load up the print queue with several jobs. However, to avoid wasting paper while we're exploring these options, we'll first pause the print queue. Follow the instructions below and check your screen against Figure 8–3 when you finish.

1. Go to Print Manager and click on the *Pause* button to suspend printing.

Figure 8–3.
The *Pause* button lets you temporarily suspend printing of the jobs in the print queue.

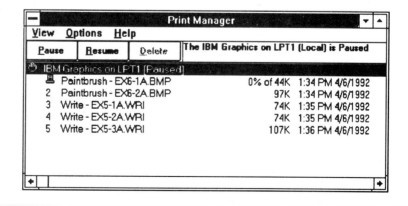

___NOTE_____

If you are currently using a network printer, the *Pause* button will
be unavailable (dimmed). You must have a local printer to complete the rest of this lab. You can use the *Print Setup...* command
in Write's File menu to select a local printer.

_____

2. Launch Paintbrush.
3. To reduce the clutter on your desktop, minimize the Program
   Manager window.
4. To organize your desktop, choose the *Tile* option from Task List.
5. Use Paintbrush to open and print the files EX6-1A.BMP and EX6-
   2A.BMP in the PBFILES directory.
6. Finally, open and print the Write files EX5-1A.WRI, EX5-2A.WRI,
   and EX5-3A.WRI in the WPFILES directory.
7. Maximize Print Manager.

Rearranging the Print Order

You can change the order of any file in a print queue, except the one
currently printing, by simply dragging it to a new location in the queue.
Moving a file higher in the queue causes it to print sooner, while a
lower position results in a later printing time. Every file awaiting
printing is assigned a number. The number indicates the order in which
files will be printed. When you rearrange the print jobs in a queue,
these numbers automatically change to reflect the new order.

Let's say you suddenly have an immediate need for a hard copy of
the file EX5-3A.WRI. We'll also assume you're now unsure about
printing the Paintbrush drawing EX6-2A.BMP. As a result, you've
decided to rearrange the queue so that EX5-3A.WRI becomes the next
file to print and EX6-2A.BMP the last. Follow the steps below to make
the necessary changes and then compare your queue with the one
pictured in Figure 8–4.

1. Point at the file information line for EX5-3A.WRI, press and hold
   down the mouse button, and drag the selection just below the top
   file in the print queue.
2. Position the pointer on EX6-2A.BMP and drag it to the bottom of
   the queue.

Figure 8–4.
You can change the order in which a file is printed by dragging its file information line up or down the print queue.

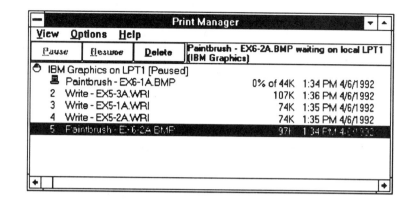

Deleting a File from the Queue

If you change your mind about printing a file, you don't have to waste paper or time printing it. All you have to do is delete the file from the print queue. You can delete any file in a print queue, even the one currently printing. To remove a print job from the queue, you select it and click the *Delete* button. Print Manager will prompt you to confirm the action. If you respond *OK*, the file will be erased from the queue.

Let's imagine that circumstances have changed and you want to remove every print job from your queue except EX6-2A.BMP.

1. To delete the file EX5-2A.WRI from the print queue, click on it and then choose the *Delete* button.

The Print Manager dialog box shown in Figure 8–5 will appear requesting you to verify your intention to delete the item.

Figure 8–5.
The Print Manager dialog box.

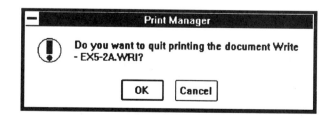

2. To confirm the deletion, click the *OK* button in the dialog box.
3. Next, delete the print jobs EX5-3A.WRI, EX5-1A.WRI, and EX6-1A.BMP.

   Your print queue should now match the one portrayed in Figure 8–6. Only the file EX6-2A.BMP remains in the queue.

⊘ HAZARD

If you delete a document that is currently printing, especially if it contains graphics, you may have to reset your printer before using it again. This simply involves turning the printer off and then on again. Resetting ensures that the buffer (memory) of the printer is clear and ready to accept a new file for printing.

Resuming Printing

To restart a paused printer, select the printer information line of the desired print queue and click the *Resume* button.

1. Click on the printer information line for your printer and choose the *Resume* button to proceed with printing.
2. Once printing is complete, use the *Exit* command from the View menu to close Print Manager.
3. Exit all the open applications.
4. You may now end your Windows session after verifying that the *Save Settings on Exit* command in the Options menu of Program Manager is toggled off.

Figure 8–6.
You can delete any file in a print queue to prevent it from printing.

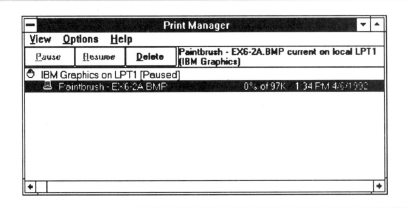

LAB 8–2   USING OTHER PRINT MANAGER FEATURES

Lab 8–2 covers Print Manager's other special features. You'll learn to start Program Manager manually and change the priority it receives in comparison with your other applications. Increasing the priority of Print Manager can improve printing speed. You'll also see how to control the amount and type of messages you receive from Print Manager while working with other applications. Finally, we'll show you the commands to suppress the time, date, and file size information that ordinarily displays in the file information line.

Starting Print Manager

If you want to open Print Manager, and it's not already on your desktop, select the Main group window from Program Manager and double-click its program item icon.

1. If necessary, start Windows.
2. Select the Main group window from Program Manager.
3. To launch Print Manager, double-click its icon.

Changing the Printer Speed

Because Print Manager prints in the background, you can continue to work in the foreground with your applications. Whenever two or more applications are running, Windows must allocate the processing power of your microcomputer among these applications. Normally, the programs running in the foreground receive the majority of the available computer resources. However, Print Manager gives you the option of changing its priority.

Figure 8–7.

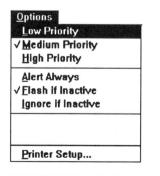

To adjust the priority printing will receive, choose one of the three commands from the Options menu shown in Figure 8–7. If you select **Low Priority**, more processing time goes to your foreground applications, making them run faster, while printing becomes slower. **Medium Priority** (the default) shares your computer's resources equally between Print Manager and your other application(s). **High Priority** provides for the fastest printing possible, but at the expense of performance in your foreground applications. Print Manager will get a larger share of your computer's processing power while foreground applications receive less. Your selection will stay in effect until you alter it.

1. Choose the Options menu in Print Manager.
2. To maximize print speed, click on *High Priority*.

____NOTE_____

Consult Windows' Help facility for information on the network-related commands shown in both the Options and View menus of Print Manager.

Displaying Print Manager Alerts

Although Print Manager normally runs in the background unnoticed, occasionally it will need to display a message. For example, if your printer jams, runs out of paper, or gets turned off, Print Manager will beep and flash to let you know it is waiting with a message. You can change the way Print Manager alerts you to the existence of a message. The Options menu contains three commands for this purpose: **Alert Always, Flash if Inactive,** and **Ignore if Inactive**.

If you choose the *Alert Always* option, Print Manager will immediately display a message when a condition occurs that requires your attention. The dialog box in Figure 8-8 is an example of a message from Print Manager warning that there may be a printer problem.

The *Flash if Inactive* option is the default setting. It causes your computer to beep and flash the Print Manager icon. If Print Manager is

Figure 8-8.
A message
from Print
Manager
warning of a
potential
printer
problem.

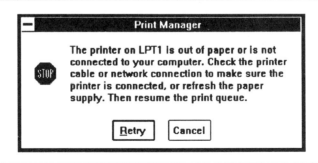

displayed as an inactive window, its title bar will flash. This signals that a message is awaiting you in Print Manager. To see it, you either expand Print Manager to a window or, if it's already in window form, simply activate it. A message will then appear.

When you don't want to be bothered with possible printer problems, choose the *Ignore if Inactive* setting from the Options menu. This mode prevents Print Manager from alerting you unless it is active.

The option you select will stay in effect until you change it. No matter which setting you choose, you'll still be alerted by system messages, such as a notice that your printer is off-line (unavailable).

1. Choose the Options menu in Print Manager.
2. To receive news immediately about your printer, click on the *Alert Always* command.

Displaying Print Time, Date, and File Size

The print queue normally displays the time and date a file was sent to it and the file's size. You can use the options in the View menu to suppress these items from displaying, as shown in Figure 8–9. By default, the **Time/Date Sent** and **Print File Size** commands have check marks in front of them indicating they are toggled on. To conceal either option, just click it to remove the check mark. You can reinstate the option by clicking it again.

Figure 8–9. The View menu lets you conceal the display of the time and date a file was sent to Print Manager and the file's size.

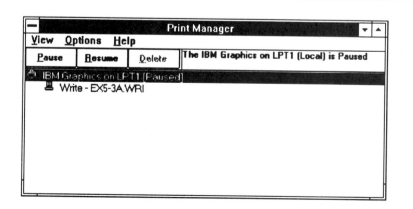

1. Toggle off the *Time/Date Sent* command in the View menu to prevent Print Manager from displaying this information.
2. Switch off the *Print File Size* option in the View menu to keep this information from being shown.
3. Start the accessory Write, open the document EX5-3A.WRI in the WPFILES directory, and print it.
4. Activate the Print Manager window.

Compare your print queue with the one pictured in Figure 8–9. The file information line for the print job EX5-3A.WRI will not include the time and date the file was sent or the file's size.

To restore Print Manager to its default settings, follow these steps.

5. Select the *Medium Priority* mode from the Options menu.
6. Choose the *Flash if Inactive* command from the Options menu.
7. Select the *Time/Date Sent* command from the View menu.
8. Choose the *Print File Size* command from the View menu.
9. Reduce Print Manager to an icon.
10. Exit the Write application.
11. When your document finishes printing, end your Windows session after checking to make sure the *Save Settings on Exit* command in the Options menu of Program Manager is switched off.

COMING ATTRACTIONS . . .

In this chapter, you peeked behind the scenes and took a look at Print Manager. Although this utility typically runs in the background completely unnoticed, you learned how to summon it and make changes to the way printing occurs in Windows. As a consequence, you're now able to control the order and the speed files are sent to the printer.

What lies ahead is the final saga in your journey through the land of Windows 3.1. In Chapter 9, we'll take you on a tour of Control Panel, a utility that lets you customize Windows' appearance and operations. You'll learn to change such things as the color and background patterns of your desktop.

KEY TERMS

Alert Always   Options menu command in Print Manager that immediately displays a message when a condition occurs that requires your attention.

Buffer   The temporary memory in a printer used to store portions of the file it's currently printing. A buffer speeds up the printing process by allowing large "chunks" of a document to be sent to the printer at one time.

COM1   The name of the first serial port on the back of a microcomputer.

File information line   Row(s) below the printer information line that displays information about the current print job(s). The file information line shows the position of the file in the queue, its title (i.e., the name of the application that generated it and the file's name), the size of the file in kilobytes, and the time and date Print Manager received it.

Flash if Inactive   Options menu command in Print Manager that causes your computer to beep and flash the Print Manager icon when a printer problem arises.

High Priority   Options menu command in Print Manager that provides for the fastest printing possible, but at the expense of performance in your foreground applications.

Ignore if Inactive   Options menu command in Print Manager that prevents Print Manager from alerting you to a printing problem unless Print Manager is the active window.

Low Priority   Options menu command in Print Manager that gives more processing time to your foreground applications, making them run faster, while printing becomes slower.

LPT1   The name of the first parallel port on the back of a computer.

Medium Priority   Options menu command that shares your computer's resources equally between Print Manager and your other application(s).

Parallel port   A connection for attaching external devices to your computer (e.g., a printer). A parallel port can transmit data faster than a serial port, so it's the preferred way to send data to a printer. However, a serial port can transmit data over greater distances than a parallel port.

Print File Size   View menu command in Print Manager that displays the size of waiting print jobs.

Print Manager   A utility program that handles the printing for all Windows applications. Print Manager lets you continue to work while it is printing and provides control over multiple print jobs.

Print queue   The waiting line in Print Manager for print jobs.

Printer information line   The first row in a print queue. The printer information line lists the name of the printer (e.g., PCL/HP LaserJet), where the printer connects to the microcomputer (e.g., on LPT1), and the status of the printer (e.g., [Printing]).

Refresh   View menu command in Print Manager that updates the display of information relating to print jobs.

Serial port   A connection for attaching external devices to your computer (e.g., a printer). A serial port can transmit data over great distances but lacks the speed of a parallel port.

Time/Date Sent   View menu command in Print Manager that displays the time and date a file is sent to Print Manager.

EXERCISES

8-1. This exercise will review the ideas and commands presented in Lab 8-1. To start, you'll create a print queue and use Print Manager to rearrange it. Once you have changed the list of print jobs, you'll use Clipboard to capture a picture of Print Manager. The image will then be exported to Paintbrush for printing.

    a. Launch Windows, Write, and Paintbrush. Minimize Write and Paintbrush. With Program Manager and the Main group window visible, open Print Manager.

    b. Select the *Pause* button to prevent print jobs from being sent to the printer.

    c. Minimize Print Manager and maximize Paintbrush.

   d. Open EX6-2A.BMP and print it.
   e. Open and print the Paintbrush files DESK.BMP, SHELF.BMP, and TABLE.BMP.
   f. Reduce Paintbrush to an icon and maximize Write.
   g. Open EX7-1A.WRI and print it.
   h. Minimize Write and open Print Manager.

At this point, your print queue should match the one portrayed in Figure 8–10. Because the queue is paused, the files are not being printed.

Figure 8–10.
The Print
Manager
window
shows the
print queue
paused and
five files
awaiting
printing.

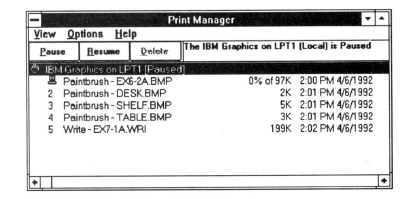

   i. Move the Write document to the top of the queue (just below EX6-2A.BMP).
   j. Move TABLE.BMP to below the Write file.
   k. Move DESK.BMP to the bottom of the queue.
   l. Delete EX6-2A.BMP from the queue.

Compare your queue with the one pictured in Figure 8–11.

   m. Capture the Print Manager window using Clipboard.
   n. Delete all the files in the Print Manager queue.
   o. Reactivate the printer with the *Resume* button and then minimize Print Manager.
   p. Maximize Paintbrush.
   q. Select the *New* command from the File menu.
   r. Paste the captured image of the Print Manager window into Paintbrush.
   s. Print the image and exit Paintbrush without saving.

Figure 8–11.
The print
queue now
displays four
rearranged
file informa-
tion lines.

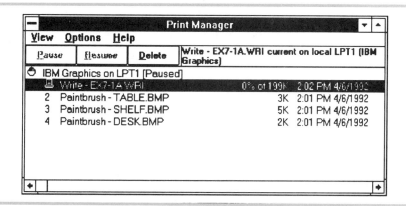

⊘ **HAZARD**_____

Your printout will be cropped if the image you paste into Paintbrush is too large for the workspace.

_____

t. Close all applications.
u. Exit Windows after checking to make sure the *Save Settings on Exit*
command in the Options menu of Program Manager is switched off.

8–2. The following instructions will strengthen the skills you developed in Lab 8-2.
You'll begin by creating a print queue. You'll then adjust the printing speed and
the information displayed in the queue. Finally, you'll use Clipboard to capture
the results of your work.

a. Launch Windows and Paintbrush. Reduce Paintbrush to an icon.
Open the Print Manager window.
b. Pause the print queue.
c. Minimize Print Manager and maximize Paintbrush.
d. Open and print these Paintbrush files: DESK.BMP, SHELF.BMP,
and TABLE.BMP.
e. Minimize Paintbrush and open Print Manager.

Check your print queue against the one pictured in Figure 8–12.

f. To achieve the best possible printing speed, choose the *High Priority*
command from the Options menu.
g. Turn off the *Time/Date Sent* and *Print File Size* commands.
h. Send a copy of the Print Manager window to Clipboard.
i. Delete all the files in the print queue.

Figure 8–12.
The Print
Manager
window
displays a
paused queue
with three
files.

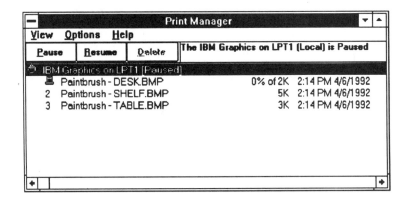

Figure 8–12.
The Print
Manager
window
displays a
paused queue
with three
files.

j. Reactivate the printer with the *Resume* button.

k. Return Print Manager to its default settings by toggling on the View commands you altered. Reset the print speed to *Medium Priority*. Close Print Manager.

l. Maximize Paintbrush.

m. Select the *New* command from the File menu.

n. Paste the image of the Print Manager window into Paintbrush.

o. Print the image and exit Paintbrush without saving.

⊘ HAZARD

Your printout will be cropped if the image you paste into Paintbrush is too large for the workspace.

p. Exit Windows after checking to make certain the *Save Settings on Exit* command in the Options menu of Program Manager is toggled off.

REVIEW QUESTIONS

True or False Questions

1. **T   F**   The first line in a print queue is the printer information line.

2. **T   F**   Quitting Print Manager with the *Exit* command cancels all pending print jobs.

3. **T   F**   Increasing the priority assigned to printing will often increase the speed at which your files print.

4. **T F** The *Pause* button cancels the current print job and removes it from the queue.

5. **T F** Print Manager runs in the background and is always available to receive printing jobs.

6. **T F** You can entirely suppress the display of files in a print queue.

7. **T F** A serial port can send information to a printer faster than a parallel port.

8. **T F** You can delete any file in a print queue, including the one currently printing.

9. **T F** Print Manager is activated whenever you select the *Open...* command from the File menu of any Windows application.

10. **T F** The print queue routes the files to the printer in the order they were received.

Multiple Choice Questions

1. The name of the most commonly used parallel port is

   a. COM1
   b. LPT1
   c. MAIN1

   d. IDKACCL
   e. None of the above

2. To print at the highest possible speed, Print Manager must be instructed to utilize the following priority setting.

   a. Low
   b. Medium
   c. High

   d. Complete
   e. c and d

3. The memory in a printer is referred to as a

   a. Print RAM
   b. Buffet
   c. Buffer

   d. Queue
   e. None of the above

4. Print Manager displays a print queue for

   a. Each active printer
   b. Only one printer at a time

   c. Each active and inactive printer
   d. All printers installed on the system

5. If your printer runs out of paper, this message will appear:

   a. Halted...
   b. Waiting...
   c. Feed me...

   d. Paused...
   e. None of the above

6. The file information line contains the following information:

   a. The position of the file in the queue
   b. The name of the application that generated the file
   c. The size of the file in kilobytes
   d. The date and time Print Manager received the file
   e. All of the above

7. The default Alert setting is which of the following?

   a. *Flash if Inactive*
   b. *Flash if Active*
   c. *Alert Always*
   d. *Ignore if Inactive*

8. Print Manager is a useful utility because

   a. Print quality is enhanced by using it
   b. Print Manager allows you to print while continuing to work with your applications
   c. Print Manager is not a useful utility
   d. None of the above

9. Print Manager handles the printing for

   a. Windows applications only
   b. All applications
   c. No applications
   d. None of the above

10. Printing that has been paused can be started again by selecting what button?

    a. *Restore*
    b. *Resume*
    c. *OK*
    d. *Confirm Begin*

CHAPTER 9

Customizing Windows

● *Objectives*

Upon completing this chapter, you'll be able to:

1. **Use a predefined color scheme to change the appearance of the elements on your desktop.**
2. **Create your own color layout for your desktop.**
3. **Decorate the background of your desktop with patterns or pictures.**
4. **Adjust the way windows and icons are aligned on your desktop.**

OVERVIEW

In this final chapter, we'll introduce you to Control Panel, a program that lets you tailor Windows to match your needs and preferences. Control Panel lets you customize the appearance of Windows by choosing from a wide variety of decorating alternatives. These options include color schemes, patterns, and layouts for the various objects on your desktop.

You can also use Control Panel to change such things as the way your keyboard and mouse respond, the devices connected to your computer, and the resources allocated among your applications. However, these features fundamentally alter the operations of Windows and are beyond the scope of this text. If you need information on one of these advanced options, either consult the Help facility or the documentation that accompanies Windows.

Although the coverage of Control Panel will be limited to the tools used to change the look of Windows, Lab 9–1 will briefly describe all the utilities available in Control Panel. In Lab 9–2, you'll get a chance to experiment with a range of different color schemes to enhance your desktop display. Lab 9–3 will demonstrate the techniques for embellishing Windows' background with patterns and wallpaper designs.

LAB 9–1   WORKING WITH CONTROL PANEL

In this lab, you'll learn to start Control Panel, to become familiar with its options, and to exit it properly. We'll take a quick tour of all the tools available in Control Panel; however, the remaining labs will focus only on those that change the appearance of Windows.

Starting Control Panel

Control Panel is an application that lets you customize Windows by changing its default settings. To launch Control Panel, you simply select the Main group window from Program Manager and double-click the Control Panel icon.

1. Load Windows and call up the Main group window.
2. Double-click the Control Panel icon.

The Control Panel window, as portrayed in Figure 9–1, will materialize. The tools for altering Windows' default settings are represented by the icons pictured there. Don't worry if your screen displays an extra icon or is missing one. The 386 Enhanced icon will only appear if you're running in the 386 enhanced mode; and if you're connected to a network, you'll see a Network icon on the far left of the Control Panel window.

Recognizing the Icons in the Control Panel Window

To activate an icon in the Control Panel window, all you have to do is double-click it. These icons invoke a varied set of tools that let you

Figure 9–1.
These icons
symbolize the
different tools
available for
customizing
Windows.

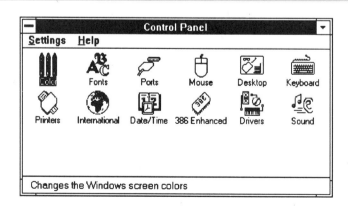

modify many of the original settings in Windows. The list below summarizes these options.

● **Color** lets you change the colors on your desktop.

● **Fonts** provides the means to add or remove True-Type and screen fonts.

● **Ports** makes it possible for you to define how printers and other devices are attached to your computer.

● **Mouse** allows you to adjust the responsiveness of your pointer and the speed at which you double-click to select an item, and switches the functions of the left and right mouse buttons.

● **Desktop** lets you change the pattern or pictures used to decorate the background of the desktop, determine how both windows and icons are aligned on your desktop, and display a "screen saver" after a certain length of inactivity.

● **Keyboard** lets you calibrate the rate at which characters are repeated on your screen when a key is held down and the speed at which keys respond when pressed.

● **Printers** is used for adding, configuring, and removing printers. It offers a host of settings to specify how printers are used.

● **International** allows you to change the language, keyboard, date, time, and currency format.

● **Date/Time** enables you to correct the date and time displayed by the Clock and Calendar applications and the date and time your files are stamped with when saved.

● **386 Enhanced** makes it possible for you to specify how your computer resources are allocated among your applications. This icon will only appear when Windows is running in the 386 enhanced mode.

● **Drivers** installs, removes, and configures programs to control devices you can add to your computer, such as sound boards and CD-ROM players.

Sound

● **Sound** assigns sounds to computer system and application events and switches off and on the warning beep you hear whenever a problem occurs.

Network

● **Network** controls your interaction with the network. The operations and commands will vary from one network type to another. Typically, they enable you to log on and off certain networks.

Closing Control Panel

You can quit Control Panel by either double-clicking on the control-menu box or choosing the *Exit* command from the Settings menu.

1. Point at the control-menu box in the upper left corner of the Control Panel window.
2. Double-click to close Control Panel.

LAB 9–2   CHANGING DESKTOP COLORS

When Windows is first installed, it uses the Windows Default color scheme to paint your desktop. However, Windows also comes with several other color schemes, ranging from the calming *Ocean* scheme to the eye opening *Fluorescent* scheme. You are free to choose from one of these predesigned alternatives or create your own. When designing a custom color scheme, you can assign colors to window frames, title bars, workspaces, and practically every other element of a window.

You can invent and save as many custom color schemes as you like. In this lab, you'll discover how to change your present color layout by picking a predefined color scheme or by concocting one of your own, complete with colors of your own creation.

Picking a Predefined Color Scheme

Windows comes with a list of preformatted color schemes. To select a color layout from this list, follow these steps.

1. Open the Control Panel window and double-click on the Color icon.

The Color dialog box exhibited in Figure 9–2 will appear. The top portion of this box contains the *Color Schemes* drop-down list box. It shows the name of the current color scheme and provides a drop-down list of the other color layouts available. The lower part of the dialog box displays a sample window for you to preview your color selections.

2. To see a list of the available color schemes, click the arrow button on the right of the *Color Schemes* list box.

A list similar to the one illustrated in Figure 9-3 will unfold, revealing the names of the first five predefined color layouts. When you click on one of these layouts, your sample window will change to reflect the new scheme.

3. Click on the *Arizona* color scheme and watch the sample window.

Figure 9-2.
The Color dialog box enables you to alter screen colors.

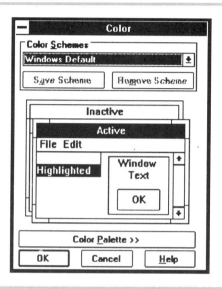

Figure 9-3.
The drop-down *Color Schemes* list box lets you change Windows' default colors by picking a different scheme.

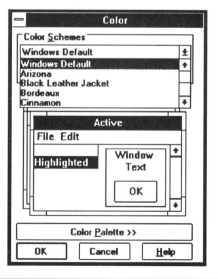

4. Use the scroll bar and select several other color layouts. When you are done experimenting, select the *Ocean* scheme.
5. Choose the *OK* button to make *Ocean* the new standard color scheme.

Creating Your Own Color Scheme

You can change the color of any element on your desktop. This enables you to create a custom color scheme to fit your particular needs and tastes. To design your own color scheme, follow these steps.

1. Double-click on the Color icon in the Control Panel window.
2. Click the *Color Palette* >> button.

Choosing this button expands the Color dialog box, as shown in Figure 9–4. The extension includes a *Screen Element* drop-down list box, a *Basic Colors* palette, and a *Custom Colors* palette. To select the desktop element you want to make a different color, simply click on it in the sample window.

The name of the selected component will appear in the *Screen Element* drop-down list box. In addition, the item's present color will be highlighted in the *Basic Colors* palette by a black frame. You can pick another color by selecting it from the *Basic Colors* palette.

Let's practice changing the color of desktop elements by first assigning a different color to the Application Workspace of a window.

Figure 9–4. You can expand the Color dialog box to display a color palette for choosing your own colors.

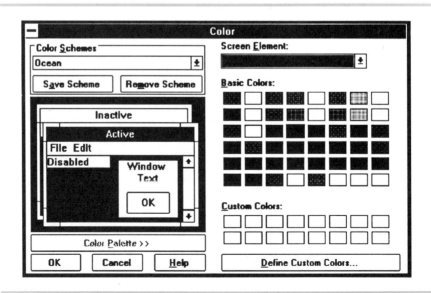

3. To choose the Application Workspace, click on the open area in the lower left corner of the sample window labeled "Active."

Look at your *Screen Element* drop-down list box and make sure the name "Application Workspace" appears there. If not, you can try clicking in the same general area again or read the hint box below. Once you've successfully chosen an item, you can go to the *Basic Colors* palette and click on the color you want to assign to it.

● **HINT**_____

Until you're more familiar with the elements of your desktop, you might prefer a slower but more exacting method for selecting items to color. Just click on the arrow button in the *Screen Element* drop-down list box and a list of every desktop element will unfold. You can then scroll to the item you want and click on it.

4. With Application Workspace selected, check the *Basic Colors* palette to see where the current color for this window element is located (it'll be the one surrounded by a black frame). Replace it by clicking on a light shade of green.

The sample window will instantly change to show the effect of your selection. You can alter the colors of other screen elements by repeating the above process.

5. Select several other screen elements and experiment with different color combinations.

Once you're satisfied with the color selections, you can save the scheme by clicking the *Save Scheme* button and then naming it. Choosing the *OK* button will activate the color scheme and make it the standard for Windows. If you select the *OK* button without saving your color selections, Windows will use the scheme until you make further changes or pick another format. At that time, your layout will be lost.

6. To display your new color scheme without saving it, click on the *OK* button.

_____ **NOTE**_____

If you want to get rid of a color scheme stored on disk, simply select it from the *Color Schemes* drop-down list box and click the *Remove Scheme* button. However, Windows won't allow you to delete the *Windows Default* color scheme.

Blending Your Own Colors

If the *Basic Colors* palette doesn't have the exact color you want, you can define your own by mixing the colors red, green, and blue. In fact, you can invent up to 16 custom colors and use them freely in your color schemes. To create a custom color, follow these steps.

1. Choose the Color icon from the Control Panel window.
2. Click the *Color Palette >>* button.
3. Click the *Define Custom Colors...* button from the expanded Color dialog box.

Your screen will display the Custom Color Selector pictured in Figure 9-5. We've labeled several items in this dialog box for easier recognition. Notice the Color refiner box (grid) and the Luminosity bar just to the left of it. The Color refiner box contains a cursor you can drag to any area of the grid. The Luminosity bar has an arrow indicator that can be dragged up or down the bar. These two control devices are used in concert to define a custom color.

Moving the Color refiner cursor and the luminosity indicator will cause the *Color/Solid* box to change constantly to display the color created by the different combinations of these two control devices.

Figure 9-5.
The Custom Color Selector enables you to blend your own colors.

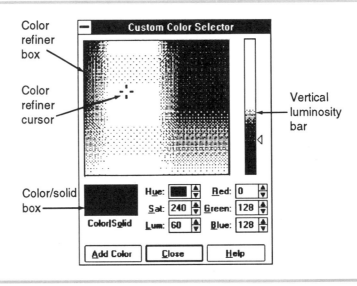

Every combination will produce a unique color, leading to literally thousands of colors to choose from! As you can imagine, this can make finding the exact color you want a bit difficult. Fortunately, these devices are governed by some simple rules that make locating the right color easy.

The Color refiner box works this way: When you drag the refiner cursor horizontally, it changes the **hue** (i.e., the position along the color spectrum), while moving it vertically alters the **saturation** or purity of the hue. In other words, if you drag the refiner cursor to the top of the Color refiner grid, you'll produce a pure color. The type of color depends upon where the cursor is located along the horizontal axis of the grid. As you drag the cursor downward, the color will become less vivid because it's being diluted with the color gray. When the cursor finally reaches the bottom of the grid, the color displayed in the *Color/ Solid* box will appear entirely gray.

The Luminosity bar is simpler yet: Dragging the arrow indicator up the bar will change the **luminosity** or brightness of the color from the extreme of black to the extreme of white.

Let's practice using these color control devices by creating the color shown in Figure 9-6. Although this illustration doesn't actually show a color, you can use the six readouts in the lower right corner of the Custom Color Selector to guide your actions.

Figure 9-6.
The Color refiner box and Luminosity bar let you define literally thousands of custom colors.

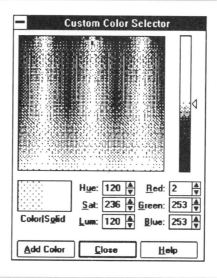

___NOTE_____

You can also use the arrow buttons on the six readouts in the Custom Color Selector to specify a color. Clicking an up arrow increases a readout, while clicking a down arrow decreases the readout.

_____

4. To produce a pure color, drag the Color refiner cursor to the very top and center of the Color refiner box, as shown in Figure 9–6.
5. To define a medium level of brightness for the color, drag the luminosity indicator to the center of the Luminosity bar (again check your screen against Figure 9–6).

When your readouts closely match those shown in Figure 9–6, you'll see a light shade of blue in the *Color/Solid* box. (If your computer system is not equipped with a VGA monitor and display card, you may get different results.) The right half of the *Color/Solid* box shows the solid version of the color, while the left side displays a nonsolid version produced by a pattern of dots. If you want to use the solid color, double-click on the right half of the box.

6. Double-click the right side of the *Color/Solid* box to produce a solid version of your chosen color.

Once you have found the right color, you can add it to the *Custom Colors* palette by selecting one of the palette's 16 boxes and clicking on the *Add Color* button. You can select either an empty box or one that already holds a color. If you select a box with an existing color, the new color will replace it.

7. To add a new color to the *Custom Colors* palette, click on one of its boxes and choose the *Add Color* button.

When you have defined all the colors you want to add to the palette, choose the *Close* button and you'll be returned to the Color dialog box. You can now add custom colors to your color scheme with the same technique you used to add colors from the *Basic Colors* palette.

8. Click on the *Close* button to exit the Custom Color Selector.
9. Use your new color to paint the Active Title Bar in the sample window.

10. Click the *OK* button to activate your color scheme.

The title bar of the Control Panel window should display your custom color. If you like, feel free to define other custom colors and add them to your color layout. However, to leave Windows as you found it, you'll need to "empty" the custom color boxes you created and set the color scheme back to the *Windows Default*.

11. Open the Color dialog box, select the *Color Palette >>* button, then the *Define Custom Colors...* button.

You can make the boxes in the *Custom Colors* palette appear empty by filling them with white. To add white to a box, drag the luminosity indicator to the top of the Luminosity bar, double-click the right side of the *Color/Solid* box, select the desired box in the *Custom Colors* palette, and click the *Add Color* button.

12. To produce a white box, drag the luminosity indicator to the top of the Luminosity bar.
13. Double-click the right side of the *Color/Solid* box and then select the box in the *Custom Colors* palette containing the first color you created. Click the *Add Color* button to "erase" it.
14. Repeat the process until the *Custom Colors* palette is "empty." Then close the Custom Colors Selector.
15. Click the down arrow button in the *Color Schemes* drop-down list box and select the *Windows Default* setting.

The Color dialog box should now match the one shown in Figure 9–7. Before you activate this color scheme, let's record the Color dialog box.

16. Hold down the Alt key and then press the PrtScr (Print Screen) key to send a picture of the Color dialog box to Clipboard.
17. Click the *OK* button to activate the *Windows Default* color format.
18. Close the Control Panel window, go to the Accessories group window, and launch Paintbrush.
19. Paste a copy of the Color dialog box into Paintbrush, print it, and close Paintbrush without saving.
20. You may now exit Windows after confirming that the *Save Settings on Exit* command in the Options menu of Program Manager is switched off.

Figure 9-7.
The *Color*
dialog box
now displays
the *Windows*
Default color
scheme and
the "empty"
Custom Colors
palette.

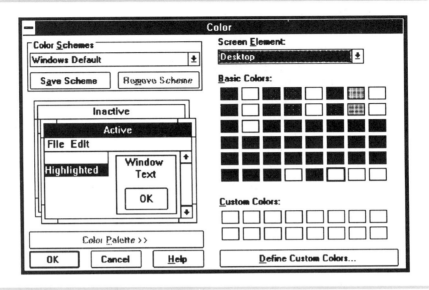

LAB 9-3   CHANGING THE DESKTOP ENVIRONMENT

The desktop environment is the background area or "wall" upon which all your windows and icons are positioned. In this lab, we'll show you how to decorate and change the behavior of this background wall. You can apply a predesigned or a custom pattern to the wall, cover it with a wallpaper, adjust the space between the icons appearing on it, and activate a "grid" to organize the position of objects on it. In addition, you'll learn to change the width of your window frames and the rate at which your cursor blinks.

Adding a Pattern

The Windows desktop will initially appear as a solid color. To add a pattern to your desktop, first select the Desktop icon from the Control Panel window. The Desktop dialog box portrayed in Figure 9-8 will materialize. Next, click the arrow button in the *Name* drop-down list box to unfold a list of patterns, select the one you want to display, and click *OK*.

1. If necessary, start Windows. Open Control Panel and choose the Desktop icon.

Figure 9–8.
The Desktop
dialog box
lets you
change the
appearance of
your desktop.

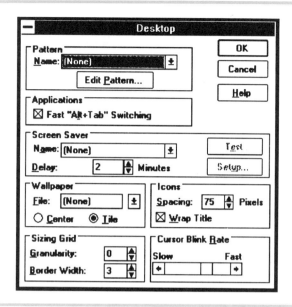

2. To produce a list of background motifs, click the arrow in the *Pattern Name* drop-down list box.

3. Select the *Diamonds* pattern by clicking on it.

If you want to preview a motif before covering your desktop with it, simply click the *Edit Pattern...* button.

4. Choose the *Edit Pattern...* button to see what your pattern looks like.

The Desktop - Edit Pattern dialog box shown in Figure 9–9 will appear. This dialog box lets you view a selected pattern, browse through other motifs, or create your own. The *Sample* box displays an example of the current pattern, while the cell immediately to the right reveals the design of the pattern. To view other motifs, click the arrow button in the *Name* drop-down list box, and select a pattern.

5. Choose the down arrow button in the *Name* list box, scroll to the *Weave* motif, and click it.

The *Sample* box and adjoining Design cell will instantly change to display the new pattern. You can repeat the same selection process to sample the other available patterns until you locate your favorite. Then

Figure 9–9.
The Desktop
- Edit Pattern
dialog box
enables you
to display and
edit available
patterns.

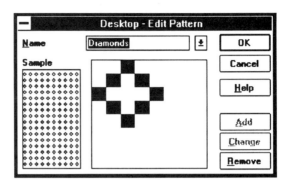

click the *OK* button to make it the default setting for your desktop. To quickly scan through all the patterns, simply continue to press either the down or up arrow key. This will cause the *Sample* box to display each pattern sequentially. Once you reach the end, you can switch arrow keys to review them again.

6. Select the *Diamonds* pattern and click *OK* to apply it to your desktop. Then click *OK* in the Desktop dialog box.

The exposed areas of your desktop will display a patchwork of tiny diamond shapes over the present background color. If you are not satisfied with this motif, you can create your own.

7. Open the Desktop dialog box from the Control Panel window and click the *Edit Pattern...* button.

To design a custom motif, you first select the pattern you want to edit from the Desktop - Edit Pattern dialog box and then rearrange the square dots in the Design cell to form the new motif. A dot pattern is rearranged by either adding or removing dots. To add a dot, click on any blank spot in the Design cell. To remove or delete a dot, just click on it. As you modify the dot design, the example motif shown in the *Sample* box will change to reflect these alterations. When you are satisfied with the design, type a name for the pattern in the *Name* box, and click the *Add* button to save it.

Let's fashion a new pattern by editing the *Diamonds* motif. We'll use the basic diamond shape to create a plus sign (+). Since the *Diamonds* background is already selected, you're all set to begin editing the pattern.

8. First, remove the four dots that connect the points of the diamond (see Figure 9–10) by clicking on them.

9. Next, add the five dots necessary to connect the points so they form a "plus sign," as illustrated in Figure 9–11. (Remember, to add a dot, you just click the spot where you want it to appear.)

10. To name your motif, click on the *Name* box, and type: Plus

The *Sample* box now provides an example of the motif, the Design cell shows a closeup of the pattern, and the *Name* list box displays the name, "Plus." Also, notice that the *Add* button is no longer dimmed but is now an available option. Whenever you enter a new name for a motif, Windows allows you to add it to the list of patterns. If the name already exits on the list, you can use the *Change* button to replace the previous motif with the new one.

Figure 9–10. The previously diamond-shaped pattern now displays only four points.

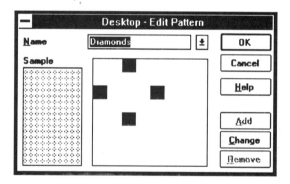

Figure 9–11. The Design cell and *Sample* box display the custom pattern *Plus*.

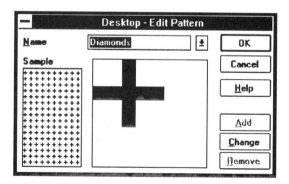

11. Click the *Add* button to save the custom pattern.
12. To activate it, click the arrow button in the *Name* drop-down list box, select *Plus* from the list, and choose *OK*. Click the *OK* button in the Desktop dialog box to close it.

Check your screen against the one shown in Figure 9–12. The exposed spaces of your desktop should be covered with miniature plus signs. When you become tired of a particular motif, you can drop it from your list of choices by calling up the Desktop - Edit Pattern dialog box, selecting the pattern you want to delete, and clicking the *Remove* button.

13. Click the Desktop icon in the Control Panel window to display the Desktop dialog box. Choose the *Edit Pattern...* button.
14. Before you delete the *Plus* motif, send a copy of the Desktop - Edit Pattern dialog box to Clipboard.

Figure 9–12. You use the Desktop - Edit Pattern dialog box to create a wide variety of custom patterns to decorate your desktop.

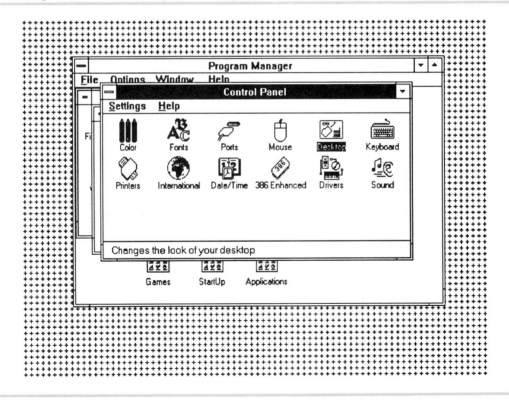

15. With the *Plus* pattern selected, click the *Remove* button to delete it from the list of available motifs. When the confirming dialog box appears, click *Yes.*
16. Close the Control Panel.
17. Now, go to Paintbrush and print the contents of Clipboard as proof of your work.

Activating a Screen Saver

You can elect to display a "screen saver" while you are not actively using Windows. A **screen saver** is a moving pattern or bitmap that covers your desktop after a specified period of time has elapsed since you last used your computer. A screen saver, as the name implies, minimizes wear on your monitor and also prevents others from viewing your work.

To activate a screen saver, double-click on the Desktop icon in Control Panel. When the Desktop dialog box appears, select a screen saver from the *Name* drop-down list box in the Screen Saver area, and click *OK.*

1. Open Control Panel and select the Desktop icon.
2. After the Desktop dialog box materializes, move to the Screen Saver area of the dialog box and click the arrow button in the *Name* drop-down list box.

A list will appear with the available screen savers, as shown in Figure 9–13.

3. Choose the screen saver *Starfield Simulation.*

The *Delay* text box, just below the *Name* drop-down list box, will display the default time of 2 minutes. If you don't use your computer during this period, the screen saver will automatically appear. You can increase or decrease the delay time by clicking the up and down arrows in the *Delay* text box.

To preview a screen saver, click the *Test* button, and the desktop will display the screen saver. When you are finished examining it, move the mouse or press any key on your keyboard and you'll be returned to the Desktop dialog box.

4. Select the *Test* button.

Figure 9–13.
The Screen
Saver area of
the Desktop
dialog box
enables you
to activate an
image to
cover your
desktop dur-
ing periods of
inactivity.

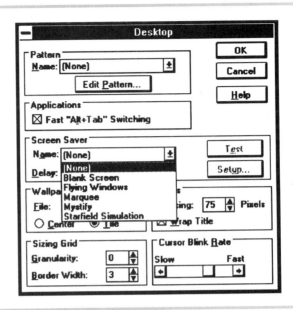

Figure 9–13.
The Screen Saver area of the Desktop dialog box enables you to activate an image to cover your desktop during periods of inactivity.

The desktop will suddenly change to a view of star-like objects. They appear to be moving past you as if you were in a starship cruising through the galaxy.

5. To end your galactic romp, move the mouse slightly or press any key.

6. Click the *OK* button in the Desktop dialog box to activate the screen saver.

Wait two minutes without touching your computer and the same starfield should appear. Go ahead and experiment with the other screen savers.

7. When you are done examining the screen savers, open the Desktop dialog box again, use the *Name* drop-down list box in the Screen Saver area to return to the original setting, and click *OK*.

NOTE

The *Setup* button in the Screen Saver area of the Desktop dialog box produces a Setup dialog box for customizing the current screen saver.

Picking a Wallpaper

If you prefer a more dramatic and lively background than a simple dot pattern, you'll love the Wallpaper option. It allows you to use a colorful picture or design as a backdrop for your applications. Windows comes with an impressive set of wallpaper images for decorating your desktop. However, you're not limited to these graphics. You can create your own with Paintbrush or any other application that generates .BMP files. You could, for example, design a background that features your company logo or use a scanner to digitize a picture of your family and use it as a backdrop.

To select one of the images included with Windows, open the Desktop dialog box, click on the *File* drop-down list box in the Wallpaper section, select a graphics file, and click *OK* to install it as your standard background.

1. Open the Control Panel window and choose the Desktop icon.
2. To view a list of wallpaper images, click the arrow button in the *File* drop-down list box located in the Wallpaper section.
3. Select the CARS.BMP file by clicking it.

The CARS.BMP picture is small and, thus, will not cover your entire desktop. The default *Center* option will position a smaller graphic in the middle of your desktop. In this situation, the uncovered edges will display the original background color or dot pattern. If you want a smaller image to cover all of your desktop, you must choose the *Tile* option. This will duplicate the graphic enough times to fill the background area completely.

Since the CARS.BMP image is too small to cover the whole desktop, we'll activate the *Tile* radio button. To finish and admire your wallpaper selection, follow these steps.

4. Select the *Tile* radio button.

Compare your dialog box with one pictured in Figure 9–14. The file CARS.BMP should be displayed in the *File* box and the *Tile* radio button should be switched on.

5. Click the *OK* button to "hang" your wallpaper image.
6. Close the Control Panel window and minimize the Program Manager so you can see the full effect of your new wallpaper.

Figure 9–14.
The Wall-
paper portion
of the Desk-
top dialog
box lets you
select and
position a
colorful and
lively image
to decorate
your desktop.

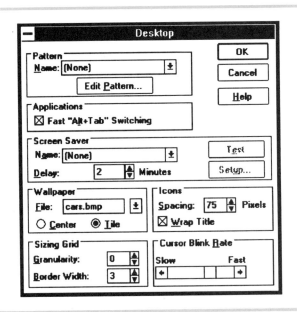

Your screen should match the one illustrated in Figure 9–15.

○ **HAZARD**

Displaying a wallpaper image requires more memory than a color
or dot pattern. Depending on the configuration of your computer
system, you may run out of memory when using larger applications. If this happens, you'll need to remove the wallpapering.

Adjusting the Spacing Between Icons

If your applications or program item icons are grouped so tightly
together that their titles overlap, you may want to increase the distance
between them. To expand icon spacing, open the Desktop dialog box,
click on the up arrow button in the *Icon Spacing* text box, and choose
OK.

To practice this procedure, follow these steps.

1. Choose the Desktop icon from the Control Panel window to display
   the Desktop dialog box.

The value in the *Icon Spacing* text box represents the number of
pixels separating the icons. A **pixel** is the smallest unit of measurement
on your video screen. As a result, you'll need to use increments of 10 or

Figure 9-15. The cars wallpaper image covers your entire desktop.

more to make a noticeable difference in the width between icons. The default setting for spacing is 75 pixels (a bit over an inch).

2. Click the up arrow in the *Icon Spacing* text box until the box displays 115. (You can also type a number in the box.)
3. Click *OK* to activate the new standard for icon spacing.
4. To observe how this change in spacing affects the alignment of your icons, close the Control Panel window, select the Main group window, issue the *Arrange Icons* command from the Window menu, and watch the program icons shift position.

___NOTE___

The *Wrap Title* check box in the Icons section of the Desktop dialog box causes icon titles to wrap around. Instead of stretching out on a single line, a title will occupy several lines below the icon graphic. Since the width of your icon title is reduced, the distance between icons is also reduced, thus saving space on your desktop.

Using a Grid to Organize Your Desktop

You can align the objects on your desktop more easily by turning on an invisible grid of lines. With the grid activated, you can move and release an application icon or a window and it will automatically "snap to" the nearest grid line. To switch the grid on, open the Desktop dialog box from the Control Panel window, click the up arrow button in the *Granularity* text box, and choose *OK*.

1. Open the Desktop dialog box from the Control Panel window.

   When the *Granularity* text box reads zero (0), the grid is off. This text box will accept values of 1 to 49. The higher the number, the greater the space between the grid lines. Each increment of 1 expands the grid lines by 8 pixels. The default granularity setting is off or zero.

2. Click the up arrow button in the *Granularity* text box once so that it displays a value of 1.
3. Choose *OK* to activate the invisible grid.
4. Experiment with the grid by moving and releasing the Program Manager window and the application icons.

Changing the Width of Window Borders

You can enlarge or reduce the width of the borders that surround every window, except those with a set or a fixed size (e.g., Control Panel). This can be a handy feature for making windows easier to size. However, thicker borders take up more room on your desktop. To adjust border width, open the Desktop dialog box from Control Panel, click on the up or down increment arrows in the *Border Width* text box, and select the *OK* button.

1. Activate the Desktop dialog box from the Control Panel window.

   The values in the *Border Width* text box can range from 1 to 49, with a default of 3. Let's fatten up your window borders by changing the setting to 5.

2. Click twice on the up arrow button in the *Border Width* text box to display the value of 5.
3. Select *OK* to make this window width the new standard.

Setting the Cursor Blink Rate

The final option in the Desktop dialog box lets you adjust the rate at which the cursor blinks. The Cursor Blink Rate portion of the Desktop dialog box contains a horizontal scroll bar. Dragging the slider to the left or right will slow or speed up the blink rate, respectively. You can use the blinking cursor beside the scroll bar to judge the impact of your adjustments.

1. Open the Desktop dialog box from the Control Panel window.
2. Move to the Cursor Blink Rate section of the dialog box.
3. Drag the slider in the horizontal scroll bar to match the position shown in Figure 9–16.

     Notice that the blinking cursor beside the scroll bar slows to reflect the change.

4. Send a copy of your Desktop dialog box to Clipboard, paste it into Paintbrush, and print it.
5. Return to the Desktop dialog box and restore the former default settings to the Wallpaper, Icons, Sizing Grid, and Cursor Blink Rate sections. For your convenience, the settings are listed below.

Figure 9–16. The Desktop dialog box now displays all the changes made to your default settings.

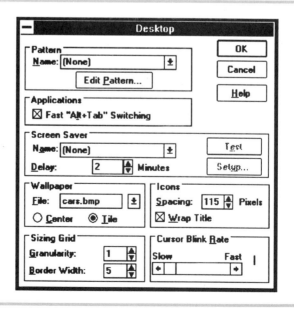

Wallpaper	=	(None)
Icon Spacing	=	75
Granularity	=	0
Border Width	=	3
Cursor Blink Rate	=	adjust the slider to match the rate shown in Figure 9–14

6. After you restore all the settings, send another copy of the dialog box to Clipboard, paste it into Paintbrush, print it, and close Paintbrush without saving.

7. End your Windows session after confirming that the *Save Settings on Exit* command in the Options menu of Program Manager is switched off.

This completes our odyssey into the world of Microsoft Windows 3.1. We hope it has been an interesting and productive journey. We encourage you to explore the many other fascinating and useful applications that exist for Windows.

KEY TERMS

386 Enhanced The Control Panel option that specifies how computer resources are allocated among your applications. This feature is only available when Windows is running in the 386 enhanced mode.

Color The Control Panel item that allows you to change the colors on your desktop.

Date/Time The Control Panel element that enables you to correct the date and time displayed by the Clock and Calendar applications. This option also affects the date and time used to record when a file is saved.

Desktop The Control Panel feature that lets you change the pattern or pictures used to decorate the background of your desktop. This item also determines the icon spacing.

Drivers The Control Panel option that installs, removes, and configures programs to control devices such as sound boards and CD-ROM players.

Fonts The Control Panel option that provides the means to add or remove printer and screen fonts.

Hue A position along the color spectrum.

International The Control Panel element for changing the language, keyboard, date, time, and currency format of Windows.

Keyboard The Control Panel item that lets you calibrate the rate at which characters are repeated on your screen when a key is held down.

Luminosity The brightness of the color from the extreme of black to the extreme of white.

Mouse The Control Panel option for adjusting the responsiveness of your pointer, the speed at which you double-click to select an item, and the functions of the left and right mouse buttons.

Network The Control Panel feature used to interact with a computer network.

Pixel Individual dots that comprise the screen image on your monitor. A pixel is the smallest unit of measurement on your video screen.

Ports The Control Panel option that makes it possible for you to define how printers and other devices are attached to your computer.

Printers The Control Panel option for adding,

configuring, and removing printers. It offers a host of settings to specify how printers are used.

Saturation The amount of gray used to dilute a pure color.

Screen Saver A moving pattern or bitmap that covers your desktop after a specified period of time has elapsed since you last used your computer.

Sound The Control Panel item for switching off and on the warning beep you hear whenever a problem occurs.

EXERCISES

9–1. Control Panel contains many settings and adjustments that let you tailor the Windows environment to suit your own preferences. Many of these settings will be rarely, if ever, altered. However, adjusting Windows' visual appearance is perhaps the one area where you'll find yourself continually tinkering.

In this final exercise, you'll create a unique Windows environment replete with custom colors and patterns. This will involve wallpapering your desktop, decorating it with a new color scheme, and choosing a background pattern. Then, you'll use Clipboard to capture a "picture" of the new desktop. We'll end by having you return Windows to its default status.

a. Start Windows, launch Paintbrush and minimize it, and open Control Panel.

b. Select the Color option from the Control Panel window and change the color scheme to *Arizona*.

c. Next, activate the Desktop option and set the pattern to *50% Gray* and the wallpaper pattern to WINLOGO.BMP.

d. Now use the *Tile* radio button to display the wallpaper pattern in a four-pattern format that covers your desktop.

e. Set the *Icon Spacing* to 200.

f. Set the *Border Width* to 10.

g. Close the desktop and minimize Program Manager.

Check your screen with the one illustrated in Figure 9–17.

h. Capture the entire screen using Clipboard.

i. Maximize Paintbrush.

j. To maximize the size of the canvas, use commands from the View menu to hide the Palette and Toolbox.

k. Paste the captured screen into Paintbrush.

l. Print the image and exit Paintbrush without saving.

m. Use the following list to set your desktop back to its original default settings and close it.

Figure 9-17. The Windows desktop with a wallpaper background.

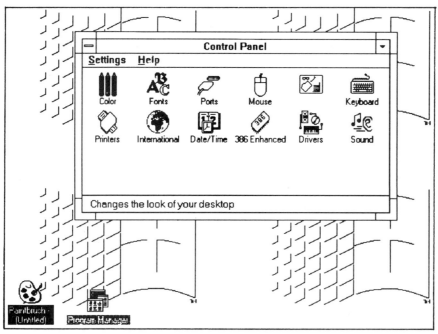

Color Scheme	=	Windows Default
Pattern	=	(None)
Wallpaper	=	(None)
Icon Spacing	=	75
Border Width	=	3

n. You may now exit Windows after confirming that the *Save Settings on Exit* command in the Options menu of Program Manager is toggled off.

REVIEW QUESTIONS

True or False Questions

1. **T   F**   The desktop environment is the background area upon which all your windows and icons are displayed.

2. **T   F**   Options in the Control Panel let you customize the Windows environment.

3. **T**   **F**   Windows has several predefined color schemes to choose from.

4. **T**   **F**   You are limited to the wallpaper patterns provided by Windows.

5. **T**   **F**   The keyboard repeat rate adjusts the speed at which a character is duplicated when a key is pressed and held.

6. **T**   **F**   The luminosity of a color is a measure of its purity (i.e., how much gray is contained in the color).

7. **T**   **F**   The Control Panel icon is located in the Accessories group window.

8. **T**   **F**   Shrinking the borders of a window makes it easier to size.

9. **T**   **F**   The Color option lets you change the patterns or pictures used to decorate the background of your desktop.

10. **T**   **F**   Windows allows you to create up to 16 custom colors for use in a color scheme.

Multiple Choice Questions

1. What is the maximum number of custom color schemes?

    a. 1   c. 16
    b. 10   d. Practically unlimited

2. Which property of a color represents its brightness?

    a. Hue   d. Lightness
    b. Saturation   e. c and d
    c. Luminosity

3. Which Control Panel option lets you activate a screen saver?

    a. Color   d. Desktop
    b. Fonts   e. None of the above
    c. Ports

4. Which Control Panel option allows you to add or remove printers from your Windows configuration?

    a. Ports   c. Keyboard
    b. Printers   d. Desktop

5. To create a custom color, you would use the

    a. *Basic Colors* palette   c. *Coloring Tool*
    b. *Color Palette*   d. None of the above

6. Which Control Panel option allows you to change the background image displayed by Windows?

    a. Color   c. Fonts
    b. Keyboard   d. Desktop

7. To repeat a wallpaper design so it fully covers your desktop, choose the following option.

    a. *Granularity*   c. *Tile*
    b. *Key Repeat Rate*   d. *Center*

8. You can reorganize the elements on your desktop by activating what Control Panel option?

    a. Printers   d. Mouse
    b. Network   e. None of the above
    c. Ports

9. Which Control Panel option specifies how computer resources are allocated among your applications?

    a. Windows Setup   c. Ports
    b. Desktop   d. 386 Enhanced

10. To change the date and time, you should choose which option?

    a. Chronology   c. Clock
    b. Timer   d. None of the above

INDEX

345